Critical Latin American
and Latino Studies

CULTURAL STUDIES OF THE AMERICAS
Edited by George Yúdice, Jean Franco, and Juan Flores

Volume 12   *Critical Latin American and Latino Studies*
Juan Poblete, Editor

Volume 11   *Mexican Masculinities*
Robert McKee Irwin

Volume 10   *Captive Women: Oblivion and Memory in Argentina*
Susana Rotker

Volume 9   *Border Women: Writing from La Frontera*
Debra A. Castillo and María Socorro Tabuenca Córdoba

Volume 8   *Masking and Power: Carnival and Popular Culture
in the Caribbean*
Gerard Aching

Volume 7   *Scenes from Postmodern Life*
Beatriz Sarlo

Volume 6   *Consumers and Citizens: Globalization and
Multicultural Conflicts*
Néstor García Canclini

Volume 5   *Music in Cuba*
Alejo Carpentier

Volume 4   *Infertilities: Exploring Fictions of Barren Bodies*
Robin Truth Goodman

Volume 3   *Latin Americanism*
Román de la Campa

Volume 2   *Disidentifications: Queers of Color and
the Performance of Politics*
José Esteban Muñoz

Volume 1   *The Fence and the River: Culture and Politics at
the U.S.–Mexico Border*
Claire F. Fox

Critical Latin American and Latino Studies

Juan Poblete, Editor

CULTURAL STUDIES OF THE AMERICAS, VOLUME 12

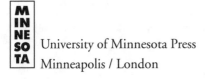

University of Minnesota Press

Minneapolis / London

Chapter 5 originally appeared in Kirsten Silva Gruesz, *Ambassadors of Culture: The Transamerican Origins of Latino Writing* (Princeton, N.J.: Princeton University Press, 2002), 1–19; copyright 2002 Princeton University Press; reprinted by permission of Princeton University Press. An earlier version of chapter 9 was published in *Harvard Educational Review* 67, no. 2 (summer 1997): 208–21; copyright 1997 by the President and Fellows of Harvard College; all rights reserved.

Published by the University of Minnesota Press
111 Third Avenue South, Suite 290
Minneapolis, MN 55401-2520
http://www.upress.umn.edu

Library of Congress Cataloging-in-Publication Data

Critical Latin American and Latino studies / Juan Poblete, editor.
    p.   cm. — (Cultural studies of the Americas v. 12)
Based on a conference held at University of California, Santa Cruz, February 26–27, 1999.
Includes bibliographical references.
ISBN 0-8166-4078-5 (alk. paper) — ISBN 0-8166-4079-3 (pbk. : alk. paper)
1. Hispanic Americans—Study and teaching (Higher)—Congresses.
2. Latin America—Study and teaching (Higher)—United States—Congresses.   I. Poblete, Juan.   II. Series.
E184.S75 C75 2003
305.868'0071'1—dc21

                                                                2002152214

Printed in the United States of America on acid-free paper

The University of Minnesota is an equal-opportunity educator and employer.

12 11 10 09 08 07 06 05 04 03   10 9 8 7 6 5 4 3 2 1

Contents

Acknowledgments / vii

Introduction / ix
Juan Poblete

Part I. On the History of Area and Ethnic Studies

1. Latino Cultural Studies / 3
Frances R. Aparicio (interviewed by Juan Zevallos Aguilar)

2. Capitalism and Geopolitics of Knowledge: Latin American Social Thought and Latino/a American Studies / 32
Walter D. Mignolo

3. Rethinking Area and Ethnic Studies in the Context of Economic and Political Restructuring / 76
George Yúdice

Part II. Different Knowledges and the Knowledge of Difference: Gender, Ethnicity, Race, and Language

4. Latina/o: Another Site of Struggle, Another Site of Accountability / 105
Angie Chabram-Dernersesian

5. The Occluded History of Transamerican Literature / 121
Kirsten Silva Gruesz

6. Indigenous Epistemologies in the Age of Globalization / 138
   Stefano Varese

7. Deconstruction, Cultural Studies, and Global Capitalism:
   Implications for Latin America / 154
   Román de la Campa

8. Linguistic Constraints, Programmatic Fit, and Political
   Correctness: The Case of Spanish in the United States / 171
   Giorgio Perissinotto

Part III. The Critique of the Future and the Future of Critique

9. Latino Studies: New Contexts, New Concepts / 191
   Juan Flores

10. At the Crossroads of Race: Latino/a Studies and Race Making
    in the United States / 206
    Tomás Almaguer

11. Multiculturalism and Hegemony / 223
    John Beverley

Contributors / 239

Acknowledgments

This book is the result of collective work even more than is usual in an edited volume. It originates in the confluence of previous and current efforts at my home institution, the University of California, Santa Cruz, where the Chicano/Latino Research Center, the Latin American and Latino Studies Department, and the Ford Foundation–funded Hemispheric Dialogues project provided the institutional and intellectual climate in which the questions pursued in this volume came to fruition. I would like to acknowledge first the impressive collective work of my colleagues at UCSC.

The volume's origins must also be traced to a conference, "Latino/ Latin American/Chicano Studies and the Rethinking of Area and Ethnic Studies," held at UCSC, February 26–27, 1999. The conference, which I co-organized, was the result of the collaboration of Cultures of the Americas and the Narratives of Globalization (an interdisciplinary project of the University of California Humanities Research Institute coordinated by Gwen Kirkpatrick) and what was then called the Hemispheric Dialogue on Social and Cultural Theory, a joint project of Latin American and Latino Studies and the Chicano/Latino Research Center at UCSC.

The early support and intellectual examples of Walter Mignolo, Alberto

Moreiras, George Yúdice, Sonia Alvarez, Manuel Pastor, and Norma Klahn have been fundamental for me. Thanks are also due to the Center for Cultural Studies and the Institute for Humanities Research at UCSC for financial support for the conference and the translations in this volume; to Jean Franco, Juan Flores, and George Yúdice, for accepting this volume in their series, Cultural Studies of the Americas; and to the staff at the University of Minnesota Press, for producing the book.

Richard Morrison and Pieter Martin have been patient and supportive editors throughout. Cheryl Van DeVeer of the Document Publishing and Editing Center at UCSC and Nancy Sauro of the University of Minnesota Press read the full manuscript and provided much-needed editorial assistance.

I would like to thank my colleagues and collaborators in this volume, who, at different speeds and rhythms, have made the long process worthwhile.

Finally, I dedicate this volume to my children, Miguel and Natalia, who are actually and beautifully living many of the ideas and concepts here developed.

Introduction

Juan Poblete

The end of the Cold War and the restructuring of U.S. and world economies, the demographic, economic, and cultural processes we now refer to as globalization and transnationalism, have all had and will continue to have a significant impact on area and ethnic studies (AES) generally and on those dealing with Chicano/a Latino/a Latin American studies (CLLAS) in particular. In the mainstream and popular press this has meant an unprecedented coverage of things Latino in the United States. At the university level, new budgetary and administrative pressures (such as elimination and/or consolidation of existing AES) along with new research agendas (such as new Americanism, hemispheric or inter-American studies, Latino studies, women of color feminism, and so on) and new conflicts and alliances (such as Chicano/a Latino/a Latin American studies) have also been produced by and have reacted to Latinas/os in a global dimension.

Despite the importance, possibilities, and stakes involved in this reshaping and/or questioning of CLLAS, there are to date few sources to which both academics and students can turn in order to organize and deepen a discussion taking place formally or informally on many U.S. campuses. *Critical Latin American and Latino Studies* is a collection

aimed at providing such a critical starting point. Thus one of the organizing principles of the book has been to offer a critical dialogical space
to scholars working in different AES traditions, i.e., Chicana/o, Puerto
Rican, Latino/a, and Latin American studies.[1]

Those new scenarios (pressures, research agendas, disputes, and coalitions) emerged or became stronger during the decade closing the last
century and continue today. What is the history of both AES and the
changes affecting them, how should they be analyzed, from whence are
their impulses coming, and where are they leading us? These are some of
the questions this volume has set out to explore.

RETHINKING AREA AND ETHNIC STUDIES: CHICANA/O, PUERTO RICAN, LATINO/A, LATIN AMERICAN SCENARIOS

Ethnic Studies

The emergence of ethnic studies in the 1960s can be seen as the victori-
ous result of the pressure of social movements or as the price that the
radical movements of the 1960s had to pay in order to be heard and legitimized at the institutional level. Whether you see them as crowning class
and racial protest and marking their triumph or as a governmentality-
induced change of focus from class struggle into cultural claims or as both
(J. Flores and Yúdice 1990, n.2), the fact is that ethnic studies marks, at
the very least, an important break both with the paradigm of the ethnic
immigrant perceived as an element in a constant and inexorable process
of socialization into a homogeneously conceived American society and
with the white American social imaginary itself.

Despite the mass nature of the immigration processes involved, the
operative unit of analysis of the assimilation paradigm had been the (im-
plicitly white) individual whose merits or demerits created a trajectory
of success or failure for a singular and transcendental actor with no (acknowledged) particular racial or ethnic marks. In the new ethnic model,
that unit became the community to which that individual belonged and
from which the model derived many of its cultural and identity marks.
A new group-based platform emerged from which to claim rights in a direct challenge to the traditional liberal focus on individual rights (J. Flores
and Yúdice 1990, 63).

This meant a relative displacement of the centrality of the sociological category of "immigration" by a political and political economy concept such as colonialism and, more specifically, internal colonialism. The

figure of the "immigrant assimilating" was displaced by the insurgent colonized in a struggle against cultural, political, racial, and economic domination. The ethnic studies moment[2] could then also be seen as the displacement of those narratives of white American national homogeneity by new ones that responded to a much more international imaginary (Third World anticolonialist struggles, socialist and anticapitalist movements) that stressed not American exceptionalism but the multiple connections linking its diverse ethnic populations with "foreign" national cultures. Somewhat paradoxically, nationalist movements fueled an international imaginary.

In this context, two sets of demands for real incorporation into a newly conceived multicultural American society were formulated. Ramón Gutiérrez (1994) has described them as partaking of two different natures: moral arguments whereby Chicano and Asian American activists "imagined themselves as internal colonies dominated by white America," and political arguments whereby educational institutions were forced to "address the educational needs of the entire citizenry" (159). This formulation reduces the actual nature of the claims,[3] but it captures the dual dynamics inscribed at the heart of ethnic studies: a tension between the emphasis on the internal link of nonwhite ethnicities with white America and the stress on their external connection with alternative national/ethnic imaginaries that provide them with their ethnic component, the "autonomous" nature of ethnic identity versus its relational and asymmetrical interdependence with mainstream American society.[4]

Christopher Newfield and Avery Gordon (1996), in studying different strands of American multiculturalism, link its most radical forms to the nationalist thought and activism of people of color in the United States in the 1960s and 1970s. In Newfield and Gordon's analysis, those nationalist discourses and practices provided the intellectual basis for a radical 1970s multiculturalism: "The multiculturalism that built on both pluralism and nationalism is the *only* meaningful form of cultural pluralism in existence, for it is the only form that is not a variant of assimilationism" (101). This type of multiculturalism does away with the idea of the single (white) core interacting with multiple (ethnic) cultures by replacing it with bicultural or multicultural lives where two or more equally important sides constitute the spaces within which the subjects operate and are constituted. Rather than the assimilationist motto of "e pluribus unum" common to both liberal and conservative versions of multiculturalism, the radical multiculturalism inspired by ethnic nationalisms offers the vision of a post-assimilationist America where a multicentered national culture, race consciousness, and anti-essentialist notions of identity form the cultural conditions of possibility of actual political and economic equality.[5]

Area Studies

In contrast to the social movement origins of ethnic studies, the standard story about area studies emphasizes its Cold War origins.[6] Latin American studies does and does not fit this standard history. It does because it is undeniable that what today we conceive of as characteristic of Latin American studies, namely, interdisciplinarity with a special social sciences predominance and an emphasis on socioeconomic and political issues, was the result of the renewed energies and resources that the Cold War made possible in U.S. academic history. Latin American studies, on the other hand, diverges from this story of its origins in at least two important respects. First, as Mark T. Berger (1995) has shown, before 1945 there was a sizable history of U.S.-based studies on Latin America.[7] Second, area studies practitioners were not always loyal to Cold War objectives and, in fact, oftentimes became highly critical of U.S. Cold War policies toward Latin America, especially in connection with Cuba and Chile.[8]

While it may not be appropriate to conclude from the Cold War origins of area studies the political valence of all the knowledge produced under its umbrella, the fact remains that because of World War II and after, in the Cold War scenario, new U.S.-centric, area-specific knowledges were generated.[9]

Area studies had from its inception as its organizing principle the centrality of the United States (and Western Europe) from which all the perspectives that constituted a certain sector of the world as a region emanated. As a nonregional center, knowledge of the United States (and Western Europe) was endowed with a particular epistemological claim that in many ways resembles the negative logic organizing ethnicity and ethnic studies: it was supposed to be the unmarked center that produced unmarked knowledge and cultural practices. While in the origins of ethnic studies whiteness was given the status of the nonethnic, that against which all ethnicities were defined and defined themselves, in the constitution of area studies, the United States functioned as the source of the nonregional around whose centrality all the regions orbited. It was not simply that the knowledge being produced in area studies was supposed to respond to U.S. national interests but that this American knowledge claimed for itself the space of universality against which all others were localized regional variations/deviations.[10]

One of the forms this claim to universality took was, of course, that of development theory. This ethnocentric and centralizing logic, as Immanuel Wallerstein (1997) suggests, was already the nineteenth-century organizing principle of the disciplines and their respective division of labor. While economics, political science, sociology, and history studied mostly the West (in a state-centric fashion, i.e., the United States, Germany, England, and France), anthropology and oriental studies focused mostly on the primitive and the high civilizations of the past in the non-Western world, respectively (80). It could also be argued that this disciplinary map was constituted by a fundamental denial of coevalness whereby the West produced knowledge about the present and the future, while the rest afforded an opportunity to know, via field trips, the past (Clifford 1986).

Developmentalism meant the full extension of the state as the often yet-to-be-consolidated sociopolitical unit of civilized existence in the modern world and as the naturalized analytic building block of social research. As a goal of the modernization process, the state and its concomitant processes of national homogeneity and bounded territoriality (based on Western models of industrialization) became a normative framework. Critical in this theoretical imaginary of development were the twin processes of mass migration from the countryside to the city, the urbanization of modern life, and the civilizing effects of mass media into the socialization of national modernity or development. The work of anthropologist and writer José María Arguedas dealt centrally with the cultural consequences of these processes of modernization in Peru. In his anthropological studies as well as in novels such as *Los ríos profundos* ([1958] 1997) and *El zorro de arriba y el zorro de abajo* ([1971] 1990), Arguedas explored what Antonio Cornejo Polar (1996) later termed the "non-dialectical heterogeneity of the migrant subject" who inhabits without dialectical resolution at least two cultural spaces from which she can or is condemned to talk. Not coincidentally, Arguedas's work has played a significant role in the discussion of Latin Americanism in both U.S. and Latin American cultural studies (Moreiras 1997; Sandoval and Boschetto-Sandoval 1998).

Assessing Area and Ethnic Studies

Chicano and African-American studies as fields have often seen a polarization of two contending factions. While the integrationists try to work within the system of liberal capitalism to eliminate discrimination and equalize the field of opportunities, the separatists insist on cultural and nationalistic autonomy. In our analysis they represent the two halves of the predicament of ethnic studies insofar as it is simultaneously a fight for relative inclusion and relative autonomy, further participating in sharing social resources and claims of cultural and political specificity.

Similarly, Puerto Rican studies has been criticized for reducing what in the foundational moment had been an "issue of class struggle to one of cultural sensitivity." In Antonio M. Stevens-Arroyo's (1987) words: "Alongside 'conflict' went 'mainstreaming,' the seductions of cultural pluralism made the successes of Puerto Rican studies temptations toward cooptation" (125).

Manning Marable (1993) has also referred to identity politics and "the dogmatic idea that 'race' alone explains virtually everything" as "symbolic representation" (117). Obscuring class stratification within the black community, "symbolic representation" provides an acceptable rationalization of the relatively privileged class position of the black middle class while preserving its elected cultural affinities.

Latin American studies has been charged with at least two problems: identifying itself with the national homogenizing developmental projects of the dependent bourgeois elites and being blind to issues of cultural diversity at the intranational and regional levels. From rational choice quarters it has also been seen as producing useless cultural observations with no predictive value that do not lend themselves to logical and epistemological generalizations.[11]

Ethnic and area studies have also meant, on the positive side, the ideological critique of university-based traditional disciplinary knowledge as biased against minorities in the United States and as incapable of perceiving cultural specificity abroad. The mainstream social sciences in particular were charged with promoting racist colonial stereotypes under the guise of scientific objectivity.

The disciplinary critique therefore included at least the following aspects: the need for reconnecting the production of knowledge with living communities and the need to go beyond the objective separation between the scholar and her object of study. Simplifying, we could say that while in area studies this meant a particular methodological emphasis beyond disciplinary borders and toward interdisciplinary approaches, in ethnic studies it meant a particular stress on community activism. These are two powerful and active legacies of area and ethnic studies that cannot be easily forgotten and become particularly important when we try to think of the ways of conceptualizing and politically articulating the new types of transnational communities emerging today in the Latino American world-region (see Flores, chapter 9 in this volume).

Latino Studies: The U.S. Scenario, Ethnic or Area Studies?

Latino/a studies seems to provide the institutional basis for an in-depth understanding of processes that have normally been resisted or have escaped the radar of nation-centered paradigms, be those ethnic or area studies–based. As a field in the borders of ethnic and area studies, Latino/a studies posits itself as the analytical space where borders themselves can be investigated and with them all kinds of transnational, translingual, and transcultural phenomena (see Mignolo, chapter 2 in this volume). Thus Latino/a studies can, in this view, perform the very healthy job of criticizing the nation-centered limitations of area and ethnic paradigms.

Problems arise when Latino/a studies becomes also the institutional interpellation of choice for university administrators in charge of "optimizing resources," "consolidating programs," and generally downsizing the human and the critical social sciences.[12] This desire to unify Latino populations is, nevertheless, politically ambivalent as it opens both dangers and possibilities. In the end, its value depends on its concrete and institutional political articulation. In this ambiguity it coincides with market-driven initiatives to create the "newness" of the Latino phenomenon and its own existence as an emergent market of "new" immigrants ready for capitalist attack or investment. The same market and institutional logic that constitutes and reduces Latinos/as as one homogenized new ethnic market niche among a plurality of other ethnicities in the supposedly democratic space of consumption is the one that continuously offers them social validation and, potentially, a popular or democratic subject position[13] and allows for broad coalitions among subalternized populations.[14]

Alongside the market, the state and the communities themselves—as well as their leaders—act as agents in the creation/promotion/imposition of ethnic identities. Michael Omi (1996) conceives of this process of racialized panethnicities as the result of a dynamic relationship whereby the state finds it useful to administer bloc demands—as opposed to a proliferation of more specific ones—while "the elites representing such groups find it advantageous to make political demands by using the numbers and resources panethnic formations can mobilize" (180). The question of agency in the labeling/constitution of ethnic identities has another important dimension. Linda Alcoff (2000), weighing the pros and cons of ethnic versus racial representations, concludes that David Theo Goldberg's category of "ethnorace" is useful insofar as it brings into play "the elements of both human agency and subjectivity involved in ethnicity . . . at the same time that it acknowledges the uncontrolled racializing aspects associated with the visible body" (42). That is to say, ethnorace is a useful category of analysis for Latino Americans to the extent that, on the one hand, it points to the voluntary forms in which people self-identify and to the multiracial composition of the Latino population, while on the other, it highlights processes of external identification of that community by other agents who actively racialize them on the basis not only of their cultural traits but also of perceived phenotypical differences. As a result of these (positive and negative) labeling dynamics, Latinos/as in the United States are constructed as totalities representing a social problem (welfare-ridden, AIDS-infected, school dropouts), a lucrative market of brand-loyal consumers, and an increasingly powerful voting bloc of citizens (Oboler 1995, 14).

Bilingualism is an important aspect in all three constructions of Hispanics in the United States. According to James Crawford (2000), there are three different approaches in this area: bilingualism as a problem (which emphasizes concepts such as *linguistic disability*), bilingualism as a right (focused on matters of access to/denial of basic rights), and bilingualism as resource (emphasizing concepts such as *language abilities*).[15] My claim is that instead of being limited to a "language as right" issue, which of course it is and importantly so, the bilingual question should be faced as a "language as resource" issue but not simply in the form of English Plus, that is to say, as an ability tuned only to the needs of capitalism in the twenty-first century.[16] From my viewpoint, bilingualism is a cultural practice engendering democratic results at the everyday level as well as creating demands and challenges for mainstream American politics. Language rights are collective rights that challenge American common law based on individual rights. Language as a community's right and as an expression of its cultural practice is always already politicized (J. Flores and Yúdice 1990, 60–61). Research on bilingual education shows, in fact, that truly bilingual programs work in enhancing performance in both languages, but only when they are part of an educational intervention that aims at challenging the low social status assigned to a linguistic-cultural community (Cummins 2000). Those cultural practices are thus always political in nature, and demand for their exercise shared ceremonies of participation and tolerance. They force the individual to engage his or her own social nature as well as the sociopolitical essence of the communities he or she inhabits, all of which at least potentially include the seeds of truly democratic political organizing.[17] In other words, the discussion around bilingual education eventually boils down to a political decision: who wants and who opposes the preservation of linguistic cultural communities that are bilingual in the United States? This is clearly a problem/decision that bilingual communities should not leave only to formal political structures but around which they must organize for political pressure. Although the institutionalization of bilingual education has meant clear progress over preexisting educational offerings, it has also involved a demobilization of the social movements that politically organized the demand and created the need for bilingual education in the first place (Crawford 2000, 117).[18]

It is in this context that we may ask with Sander L. Gilman (2000): why is it that bilingualism is good for the upper classes, who actively pay for its implementation, while it is socially and politically discouraged for the lower classes? Why is it that bilingual elites are an asset while bilingual Hispanic citizens seem to be a menace for the U.S. national polity? Perhaps we could posit that this is the way in which the dual, global and national, nature of U.S. society manifests itself most clearly. The American university system reflects this dual structure through its differential specialized functions: the Ivy Leagues and elite institutions in general prepare the new international or transnational elites for global domination. They provide them with the tools, including linguistic proficiencies, considered as cultural assets, to manage cultural diversity both nationally and internationally.[19] At the lower level, in an important sector of public primary, secondary, and tertiary education, those same active cultural assets are discouraged and stigmatized. Here, not always in theory but often in practice, cultural diversity is turned via assimilation and in particular via linguistic assimilation into a monocultural and monolingual U.S. national culture. Hispanic students (and other minority students, too) are, at these educational levels, actually deprived of their very few cultural capital advantages, their assets turned into cultural liabilities. Their expressions are policed into the strict borders of an English-only society. That the separation of elite/nonelite educational institutions is a function of the reproduction of the social status quo should come as no surprise. Less evident, however, is how this differential structure coincides today to an important degree with the separation between white and colored America.[20]

It is worth emphasizing that this negative and limiting cultural impact on minority subjects is present even in many liberal multiculturalisms where white tolerance for the other goes hand in hand with a limited multicultural and monolingual imaginary. The time seems ripe for exploring a multicultural, multilingual multiculturalism. Monolingual multiculturalism, on the contrary, seems to satisfy only at some superficial level the demands of subalternized internal multicultural populations in the United States. In actuality, it simultaneously defuses their most important political and cultural potential and their abilities to radically change the American polity.

Nevertheless, the "unmeltable new ethnics" (Nelson and Tienda 1985) have proved very resilient to the assimilationist attempts aimed at them. The reasons are historic, cultural, and economic.

Historically speaking, as Suzanne Oboler (1995) has carefully summarized, Latino/a Americans are different from older waves of ethnic immigrants. According to Oboler, there are three ways in which the experiences of Hispanic or Latino/a immigrants differ from previous European immigration to the United States: (a) the historical specificity of the Puerto Rican and Chicano/a populations within the Latino/a group: these populations have been colonized, discriminated against, and torn between a discourse of assimilation and citizenship and the realities of racial discrimination and endemic poverty; (b) geopolitical factors in the hemisphere: U.S. intervention in many Latin American countries has produced a certain degree of political resentment and resistance to assimilation and a link between economic and political immigration to the United States by those affected by U.S. interventions; (c) the particular historical and economic conjuncture during which each group entered the United States: a globalized economy has meant, in the current stage, a steady decline in industrial jobs historically linked to the European wave of immigrants in earlier moments. The increased demands of cultural capital in order to enter industrial employment have coincided with a growing political concern with the role of language

(English-only and antibilingual education campaigns) in what counts as American identity (Oboler 1995, 7–9; Nelson and Tienda 1985).

These three factors, incidentally, could be respectively linked to the traditional profiles of (a) Chicano/a and Puerto Rican studies, (b) Latin American studies, and (c) Latino studies and to the three historical stages their social origins could be said to exemplify: colonial, neo-colonial, and global. Their coexistence today, both at the social and disciplinary levels, is one of the most powerful reasons calling for dialogues (not substitutions) between these different traditions of study informed by a reciprocal understanding of their historical trajectories, critical concepts, and contributions.[21] These dialogues should not be modeled on the format of euphemistic consolidations and actual downsizing and/or elimination of currently existing programs and departments. Instead, they could follow one of the models suggested by the *Report of the Gulbenkian Commission on the Restructuring of the Social Sciences* (1996): one- to five-year interdisciplinary research groups and institutes that have "specific intellectual objectives and have funds for a limited period of time (say about five years)" (104–5).[22]

The resistance to assimilation has also manifested culturally and economically. It is in connection with these aspects that the framework of prevalent American social sciences models (and those of ethnic assimilation in particular) have proved more limiting. Joan Moore (1997), for example, has analyzed the reaction of Latino/a research to William Julius Wilson's theory of the urban underclass and the economic restructuring that produces it. According to Wilson, says Moore, "Two factors concentrated African-American poverty in Chicago: the loss of industrial jobs, and the opening up of non-ghetto housing" for middle-class blacks, which segregated the underclass from them. Aware that the latter factor "in part does not really pertain to Latina/os . . . Wilson suggests that the counterpart for Latino communities has been the recent influx of immigrants" (9). For Moore, the questions to be analyzed in this framework became, "Do immigrants concentrate poverty? And with what effect?" While this is partially true (they often do), "There is," says Moore, "a much more positive side to the story. . . . Immigrant concentration is not just a concentration of poverty: social and economic resources are concentrated as well. [Nestor] Rodriguez argues that the social isolation of immigrant communities is 'functional and apparently highly positive'" (9). Moore concludes that "the immigrant presence leads to cultural revitalization" when it connects older Chicano/a and

Hispanic immigrants with recent arrivals who bring new energies reconnecting Latinos/as to their ethnic/national roots (Moore 1997; Moore and Pinderhughes 1993; Bonilla 1998).

In another example of the lack of fit of certain dominant concepts for the analysis of Latino/a Americans, Moore (1997) refers to "two [traditionally invoked] so-called cultural 'deterrents to assimilation.' The first was the high degree of language loyalty, and the second was the cultural emphasis on family cohesiveness" (13). These factors were particularly highlighted in now admittedly old theories on the American social system and its relation to ethnic groups, but the cultural "explanations" of poverty have regularly found a way of resurfacing periodically in the way of "cultures of poverty" or "civilizational clashes."[23] Thus we see that at least some of the cultural factors that supposedly account for Latino/a poverty may in fact provide the basis for Latino/a communities' survival and further political organization under very unfavorable conditions.[24]

Because of the logics of institutionalization, the seemingly new phenomena located in the in-between that defines the specificity of the Latino/a field—Spanish-inflected English-based texts, code-switching bilingual and migrating communities, U.S. Latino/a popular culture—could come to occupy the only legitimate space while relegating the communities and the practices beyond these borders to a secondary status. In this specific version, but not in others, Latino/a studies may be thought of as an ideological mirage: it would offer the U.S. academy a chance to seemingly study globalizing processes of cultural hybridization while in actuality reframing that study under conventional nation-state–based narratives of minorities and assimilation. But we know that by their sheer numbers Latino/a, Chicano/a, and Latin American diasporic (and nondiasporic) demands may not be reducible to linear patterns of assimilation. It may be that those demands are positing what, following James Clifford (1997) and Edward Said (1984), we could call a contrapuntal dwelling in/of modernity, where the homeland is not simply left behind but enters into multidirectional processes and configurations. Here it would seem best to think of Latino/a Americans under globalization as inhabiting simultaneously and/or alternatively many cultural and political spaces of political and cultural articulation. This plurality of identification processes (as opposed to stable identities) moves back and forth between the national and the transnational, sometimes privileging panethnic forms such as Hispanics, Latinos/as, or people of color, and at other times emphasizing closer forms of national, regional, or more local identification. These processes are multiple and changing and depend on specific cultural and political contexts for their concrete articulation and political valence (S. Hall 1992).

It may now be crucial to ask, following the lead of Anna Tsing (2000) and James Clifford (1986), what kind of allegorical emplotment is communicated in the narrative of the supposed obsolescence of area and ethnic studies? How is that narrative linked to the globalizing one? To what extent are actually existing theories of globalism indebted to regional and disciplinary frameworks and assumptions such as the anthropological invention of static, overgrounded, and localized cultures versus dynamic cultures of flows, changes, and progress? May all this be the return of the repressed in globalization theory, the return of a U.S. national and disciplinary imaginary now gone global? While some of the limitations in ethnic studies had to do with the self-constraining nature of cultural nationalism, and while some of those in area studies derived from the centrality of the nation-state and national development as fundamental categories of analysis, could we not see in dominant discourses on globalization and some versions of Latino studies the presence of a homogenizing U.S. national imaginary?[25]

In this context, area and ethnic studies are again faced with their contradictory nature: while their studies can be seen as the needed cultural makeup for optimized local and global consumption of American and transnational corporations' market expansion plans (see Yúdice, chapter 3 in this volume), they can also be theorized as spaces whose intellectual traditions tend to the proper valorization and study of processes conceived along more positive lines as vernacularizations or hybridizations of globalization.

Anna Tsing (2000) states, "Since the globe is a region made large, the making of global scale brings forward questions of the various forms of region making that both facilitate and interrupt global claims." I would like to conceive the rethinking of Latino/a Chicano/a Latin American studies as the occasion for facilitating the reimagination of a cultural and political space of transamerican and transatlantic scale.[26] In it the colonized (in their multiple and contradictory forms) make themselves visible and/or return to the metropolis with their hopes, problems, cultures, and demands. I would also like to consider that rethinking as the interruption of monolingual and monocultural global imaginaries, the point of arrival of secular Latino American imaginaries (which must include Native American ones [see Varese, chapter 6 in this volume]), and the continuation and transformation of secular narrative memories, which are at least partially the result of the long process of enculturation of Latin American popular cultures into capitalism.[27]

But considering these secular narrative memories should not mean giving in to metaphysical forms of Hispanic essentialism, nor should it be the occasion for a form of analysis that is capable of seeing only continuities and stabilities but not discontinuities and breaks. My own idea of a Latino/a American world-regional imaginary and space attempts to circumscribe not ahistorical essences but grounded sociocultural processes and circuits well illustrated in their complexity by the development, for instance, of Latin(o) American television.[28] It is then necessary to understand that those forms of narratives and identifications were, are, and will always already be the result of cultural hybridizations between multiple, heterogeneous, and oftentimes conflicting agents further differentiated by race, class, and gender, not the expression of a single logic with homogeneous actors inscribed in a sacred and unchangeable cultural space. Clearly Latin American national identities today are not simply the result of subject formation processes orchestrated by the state with seemingly independent technologies of national range such as textbooks, national histories, stable cultural patrimonies, and monopolistic media control. When a very high percentage of the TV programs and videos Latin Americans watch as their preferred form of entertainment is produced predominantly in the United States, when so many hours of their daily life depend on such products, the distance between the real immigrant and the virtual one seems in some important respects, which include cultural consumption and everyday life forms of citizenship, less relevant than their multiple forms of connection (García Canclini 1995). How do the narratives of world folklore, such as the neutral forms of narrative spectacularization of films such as Steven Spielberg's, connect with the world-regional melodramatic imagination of Latin American soap operas (Ortiz 1994)? How are the national spaces and communities inhabited when the daily ceremonies are not only those of the national novel and newspaper but also those of the globalized and world-regional spheres of cable and satellite TV, Internet, video, and film?

Forms of globalizations happened a long time ago for Latino/a Americans via successive imperial and colonial projects by European powers and the United States. In its latest avatar, qualitatively and quantitatively different, globalization is, for our purposes here, a culturally specific Latino/a American circuit whose texts and practices of production and consumption, always already globalized, require for their understanding both the specific knowledges produced by Chicano/a, Latino/a, and Latin American studies and their continuous collaboration, translation, and conversation in a contemporary globalized and regionally localized frame.

This concept of a globalized Latino/a America as a specific world-region, I want to insist, is not the belated expression of out-of-touch Bolivarian desires. It is instead one of the possible mappings or articulations demanded by already existing sociocultural processes: from the Puerto Rican *guagua aérea* (air bus) of the circular migration between the island and the continent, to the massive telephone bridge of Dominicans here and there, from transnational organizing, to the place the transfer of immigrants' funds represents in the economies of many of their countries of origin.[29] This latter case of remittances is worth expanding.[30]

In the year 2000 Latin American immigrants sent $23 billion to their families in their home countries. This was the equivalent of one-third of all foreign investment in the region. Considering that it was produced by monthly deliveries of $200 to $300, and it involved eighty million separate transactions, the size of the populations involved in this transnational operation is better understood. Remittances amounted to $6.79 billion for Mexico (equal to the revenues generated by tourism, twice those of agricultural exports, and two-thirds of oil exports), and were also significant for countries like Guatemala ($535 million), El Salvador ($1.58 billion), the Dominican Republic ($1.74 billion), Ecuador ($1.24 billion), and Brazil ($1.89 billion). Remittances constitute over 10 percent of the gross domestic product of six countries: Haiti (17 percent), Nicaragua (14.4 percent), El Salvador (12.6 percent), Jamaica (11.7 percent), the Dominican Republic (10 percent), and Ecuador (10 percent). These figures do not even include the estimated $1 billion Cuba receives annually.

This phenomenon is so clearly critical for the economy of the region that it prompted the Interamerican Development Bank to host a "Remittances as an Instrument of Development" conference in an attempt to structure and improve a monetary flux that generated about $3 billion for the remittance industry.[31] As a material manifestation of the world-regional form that globalization takes in Latino/a America, remittances posit interesting questions about its scope and nature. Although Brazil and especially Ecuador received proportionally significant dollar transfers, and in Colombia they amounted to $612 million or roughly half the revenues for coffee export, most of the money went to Mexico (39 percent of the total) and the Central American/Caribbean region. Do cultural exchanges mirror this economic concentration or are these levels disconnected? How does the incorporation of new developments, such as the Ecuadorian and Brazilian cases, alter the historical patterns of U.S.-Mexico and U.S.-Caribbean subregions? How many subregions does the Latino/a American world-regional circuit encompass?

The significant heritage and distinctive active research of area and ethnic studies as well as their collaborations need to be incorporated into the answers to these and other questions as well as into the critical goals defining a new Latino/a American critical education in the United States. The remittances allow us to identify very specific ways in which Latino/a Americans can produce radical change in the Americas. Grounding these ways of intervention is a dual understanding of what it means to be an educated Latino/a American in the United States.[32] My contention is that in the twenty-first century this means exercising a dual citizenship: an American-based one and a Latin American one, which are conceived not as two schizophrenic positionalities but as the complementary sides of a new politically empowered form of political subjectivity. This equation involves active participation in critically engaging with American politics (voter registration, community organizing, unionizing, and so on) in order to improve working conditions for Latino/a Americans in the United States (both legal and illegal) and in the hemisphere. By way of refusing the minoritizing logic of U.S. mainstream politics, that is to say, by refusing to become just an American minority in the assimilationist sense, this involves and demands from Latino/a Americans an ability to restructure the political agenda of Latino/a representation in the United States toward a more interactive conception of hemispheric Latino/a citizenship.[33] Instead of limiting the political struggle to the American political sphere where much work on bilingualism and representation remains to be done, a new Latino/a American civil society of grassroots and medium-level organizations needs also to be fostered. The political agenda of such a transnational public sphere would crucially include the linked destinies of Latino/a labor forces vis-à-vis global capital. At the hemispheric level Latinos/as would also, as they are already doing through remittances, redirect the schism between places where cheap labor power can be tapped and expended with no attention paid to its conditions of reproduction and places where the profits of capital are invested and enjoyed.

CONCLUSION

I should have said from the beginning, perhaps before it became obvious, that I was in no position to offer a comprehensive and panoramic view of the epochal reasons that have prompted both general disciplinary self-questionings and more specifically those affecting area and ethnic studies. In what preceded, instead, I have tried to frame my rethinking of the possible links between Chicana/o, Latino/a, Puerto Rican, and Latin American studies within the analytical space opened by questions such as how, where, and by whom is knowledge on this population produced? How did the institutional (departments, programs, community centers) aspects of the organization of knowledge and their historical discursive trajectories determine or affect their configuration as knowledges? For whom were/are they useful? How does globalization alter already existing knowledge production maps (see Mignolo, de la Campa, and Perissinotto in this volume)?

In Eric Hershberg's (1998) words, "If the study of Guatemalan culture leads one to conduct fieldwork in Los Angeles, and if the analysis of economic networks in Los Angeles compels the researcher to carry out fieldwork in the Guatemalan highlands, the divide between area studies and U.S.-oriented scholarship becomes very foggy indeed" (124).

It may be too early to decide, when analyzing some important aspects of the Latino/a American world-region, if we can extend Roger Rouse's concept of transnational migrant *circuits* as an alternative to community-based approaches, or refer with Luin Goldring to transnational migrant *communities* where people live their emotional, cultural, and political commitments across nations (Pedraza 1998). Whether circuits or communities, connected Latino/a Americans in the hemisphere represent a challenge to both the national state and the forces of globalizing capital. At this level, it seems important to remind ourselves of the obvious: that the so-called culture wars of the 1980s and 1990s in the United States were the expression not only of an exclusively national American reality but also of a globalizing process affecting in similar ways many other national situations. In other words, American multicultural wars were/are, to an important degree, the specifically American way of manifestation of globalization as a process in a concrete national context (Brunner 1998, 151–64).

Thus, from my viewpoint, a critical Americanism, be it political or cultural or both, is something with which Latino/a Americans can establish key strategic alliances. Nevertheless, that should not be taken as the

defining goal of their new Latino/a Americanist active citizenship. The latter is different from the former in that it sees as its sphere of action the whole
hemisphere, its political economy, and the interconnectedness of its politics, cultures, and societies.[34] In the age of globalization, a critical Latino/a
Americanism interrupts any attempt at severing the Latin American connection of U.S.-based Latinos. On the contrary, it promotes a politics that
seeks to make of those links the center of its political and cultural actions.
It understands that diversity or racial tolerance at the U.S. national level
is not a comprehensive answer to racialized economic inequalities that are
at least hemispheric in scope. This implies a structure of political accountability that, in order to be effective, must coordinate the national and the
transnational levels. New, more varied, faster, and more accessible means
of communication should help Latino/a American citizenship avoid the
traps of what Benedict Anderson (1994) has called "long distance nationalism," whereby new ethnicities are cut off from the sacrifices and direct
accountability that come with old-fashioned national citizenship (Robbins
1998). Therefore, this kind of critical Latinoamericanism[35] does not try to
do away with the national. It does not speak the general language of homogenizing transnationalism but depends for its articulation on a critical
engagement with the national situations, something akin to what Jameson
(1987) once called an internationalism of the national situation, both here
in the United States and south of the border. In this task it applies the
lessons of metropolitan organizing in adverse conditions and the lessons
of metropolitan multiculturalism and interethnic alliances to peripheral
national situations that could thus expand the often limited racist, patriarchal, and bourgeois imaginary presiding over their dominant forms of
political and cultural citizenship. But it also takes from the political south
its anti-neocolonialism stance, its refusal to accept co-optation into an
exclusionary American, English-only, white dream that is poised on opening the world to the mobility of capital while it (tragically, but in the end,
unsuccessfully) erects bigger and higher walls against the movements of
people produced by the same unequal global circulation of capital. Thus,
the discourse on difference demands a discourse on inequality, while the
latter requires a multidimensional understanding of difference.

I am not suggesting that Latinos/as in the United States should relin-
quish the power that their dominant identification as an ethnic minority offers them as a space for political maneuvers in the U.S. political
sphere. Instead, I am proposing that Latino/a Americans should be able
to articulate multiple positionings within which that of an ethnic mi-

nority is just one. Latino/a subjectivity is multivoiced, not least because it is more often than not a bicultural or multicultural, a bilingual or multilingual subjectivity whose cultural and political allegiances extend beyond the confines of national borders.

Some of the discussion on area studies seems to assume that Latin American studies can be done away with as a remnant of the Cold War. Whether it is claimed that area studies is no longer necessary to the U.S. national interest at this point or that it always may have been a bad form of "gringo" interventionism or epistemological imperialism is here immaterial. Some of the criticism of Chicano/a and Puerto Rican studies, on the other hand, seems to be based on the assumption that under new conditions of globalization, these two national/ethnic approaches would have lost most of their explanatory power. These perspectives forget a number of key facts, such as the historically colonial and still existing neocolonial relationship of the United States with Mexico and Puerto Rico as well as the extent to which these two national populations combined account for a significant part of the ever-increasing Latin American immigration to the United States.

In concluding, I would like to stress how, to an important degree, Latino/a American area and ethnic studies, and more specifically their separate traditions and crucial dialogues, are today part of a fundamental matter of citizenship and democracy in the United States. That is to say, the increasing waves of first-generation immigrants and their accumulation in the United States cannot be subsumed under the limited set of topoi that directed the study of ethnic components of the American melting pot. There is no one-way assimilation any more. There is no simple ethnicization of the links of the immigrant with his or her own country, something that was, anyhow, always already inadequate to explain the Puerto Rican and Mexican American experiences. Those lines have become at least a two-way traffic if not a multidirectional cultural and economic process. As such, they affect American ideas of representative democracy in radical ways. Even left-leaning white progressives become nervous when confronted with the standard numbers and statistics about Hispanics. There is something fundamentally unsettling about the prospect of so many millions of Americans belonging not only or not simply to a different social class than most white Americans. What is to be done, from this perspective, when the poor are not only poor but also culturally alien or diverse? From some progressives' viewpoint, this means emphasizing class alliances over ethnic divisions and markers. While class analysis has tended to remain within the limits of national economies, panethnic approaches can sometimes forget the political economy determinations affecting their varied constituencies. The approach I am favoring here calls for a geopolitical understanding of (1) the racialization of the international division of labor; (2) the production of knowledges and the administration of scales, scapes, and scopes on so-called global processes; (3) a cultural and historical understanding of previous globalizing colonial projects; and (4) a critical perspective on the claims of transnationalisms and nationalisms as mutually exclusive projects.[36]

What emerges as a result is a world-region that is culturally and politically specific and whose conceptualization is part of the simultaneous effort to bring forward the historicity of a territory and to reterritorialize history (Coronil 1996, 76–77).

An Overview of This Volume

The first part of the book, including this introduction, focuses on both the plural histories of area and ethnic studies and the views of history that AES have criticized and made possible. Frances Aparicio (responding in an extended interview to Juan Zevallos Aguilar's questions) offers first a quick but excellent overview of the origins of Chicano/a and Puerto Rican studies in their connections to the emergent Latino/a studies field. She lists key activists and academic figures, publications and canonical texts. This information is, of course, important for the reconstruction of social and institutional histories, but it becomes crucial when trying to allow for constructive dialogues between undercommunicated traditions of research, activism, and problematics. Aparicio then moves on to clarify, first, an object of study for Latino studies, Latino communities in the United States; and second, those areas where the new field has made influential contributions to recent metropolitan theoretical debates: immigration, hybridity, racialization, and transculturation processes.

Walter Mignolo develops a historically grounded understanding of Hispanic ethnicity and the cultures of scholarship that have dealt with Latin American and Latino/a issues, especially in the United States. For him, Latino/a studies has provided an interstitial space whence a critique of both Latin American studies and American studies is made possible, revealing the epistemic limits of disciplinary knowledges. Studying the space of Latin Americans and Latinos/as at the margins of Europe and the United States, and emphasizing the connections between Latino/a studies and Latin American social critical thought, Mignolo proposes a reconfiguration of the traditional divides separating identification and objectivity, academic knowledge and social movements and activism.

George Yúdice analyzes area studies in the context of the post–World War II scenario. Here the research university is seen as driven not only by Cold War designs but also by the needs of U.S. capitalism's accumulation strategies. During this period (from the 1950s to the 1970s), difference and social unrest (ethnic movements, feminism, and subsequently gay and lesbian activism) produced institutional responses we now know as ethnic, women's, and gay and lesbian studies. In the new phase of capital restructuring initiated in the 1980s, the university shifted its focus from the absorption of difference at the national level to its study at the global one. In this context, area and ethnic studies become sites for the study of geopolitical and geocultural obstacles to global capitalism's expansion as well as sources for the production of standardized international knowledge. Yúdice's reflections on the impact of U.S. scholarship in the establishment of international research agendas and the responses it elicits from non-U.S. scholars are one of his most crucial contributions to the debate in this book.

The second part of the book, "Different Knowledges and the Knowledge of Difference: Gender, Ethnicity, Race, and Language," opens with Angie Chabram-Dernersesian's critical stance on Latino/a studies as a knowledge formation produced by current globalization studies. Carefully carving a space between her commitment to coalitions both political and intellectual and her refusal of top-down panethnicities, Chabram invites us to think what is at stake in panethnic labels such as "Latino" and "Latinidad." Instead of denunciations of the theoretical work that emphasizes more complex positionalities affected by gender, race, class, and different historical trajectories, Chabram suggests a critical view of native multiculturalisms, panethnic Latinisms, or other forms of totalizing epistemologies and administratively driven top-down megaspaces.

Kirsten Silva Gruesz reveals aspects of "The Occluded History of Transamerican Literature" by emphasizing the existence of two archives that call for a new form of comparative literature, based not on different national traditions but on a transnational critical frame. Those two archives are the written record left by hispanophone communities in border zones such as New Mexico, California, and Texas and the many transamerican cultural and publishing networks developed in the nineteenth and twentieth centuries. Based on these borderlands literary cultures, Silva Gruesz is able to posit important questions about the different forms of cultural and linguistic literacy of the Hispanic bilingual populations and about the space of literature in their everyday life.

Stefano Varese provides a healthy and challenging reminder of the strong connections even in times of globalization between collective memory and space. Commenting on a series of examples of indigenous knowledges and political local, national, and global organizing, he highlights three basic concepts: the aforementioned connection of culture and location, the plurality of understandings of citizenship, and the ethnopoliticization of indigenous struggles for sovereignty. By referring to the transnational dimension of local struggles, Varese's contribution is also an invitation to rethink the limits and possibilities of area and ethnic studies as well as the place of local and indigenous knowledges and social activism in them.

Román de la Campa offers a comparative analysis of two different traditions of Latin American cultural studies that demand further dialogue. The one based in the United States, according to de la Campa, has had a humanistic bent grounded on deconstruction and the analysis of textuality. The one developed in Latin America has been closer to the social sciences and has dealt with socioeconomic daily life. He then proceeds to a critical genealogy of the hegemonic ambitions of the U.S.-based transnational Latinamericanism by analyzing critical discourses on *testimonio,* subalternity, postcoloniality, and modernity, and their distinct loci of enunciation and legitimation.

Giorgio Perissinotto's essay offers a down-to-earth, practical view of the institutional and pedagogical issues involved in the teaching of Spanish language and literature classes in the United States. Providing useful sociolinguistic information on Spanish in the United States, the essay allows a glimpse into fairly common but little talked about tensions between Spanish-, Latin American–, and Chicano/Latino-oriented faculty. His reflections on issues of bilingualism, canonicity, and linguistic standards are fundamental to any rethinking of AES.

In the third and last part of the volume, Juan Flores provides a thoughtful analysis of how recent historical and theoretical developments have altered the context for Latino/a studies. Both globalization and new concepts of race, ethnicity, gender, and nation have fundamentally challenged what was patriarchal and homogenizing in the previous conception of the nation that grounded Chicano/a and Puerto Rican studies in the 1960s and 1970s. At the same time that he emphasizes the diversity obscured by older nationalisms, Flores warns about the multiple dangers of reducing Latinos/as to an ethnic group experience with the concomitant simplified stories of assimilation. In times of globalization, Pan-Latino/a, says Flores, must also be Trans-Latino/a to rigorously incorporate the transnational nature of actually existing Latino/a experiences in the United States. He ends by providing both a comment on possible sources of institutional alliances and a series of methodological strengths stemming from the tradition of Chicano/a and Puerto Rican studies that should orient Latino/a studies now and in the future: interdisciplinarity, collective work, and academic research–community ties.

Tomás Almaguer's essay reminds us of the importance of often conflicting and multiple racializing dynamics affecting Hispanics in the United States. Providing an overview of Spanish colonial and American racial categories, Almaguer reproblematizes the field of Latino/a studies by drawing on the major distinctive feature of the contemporary Latino/a experience: their multiracial status. In his critical assessment, not only the American racial formation and white supremacy but also the Latino/a reactions to them provide the central organizing principles of the curriculum in Latino/a studies at the dawn of this century. Almaguer concludes with an analysis of this problematic in two classic works by Richard Rodriguez and Piri Thomas.

Last, but not least, comes the text of the lecture John Beverley presented as a keynote speaker at the conference that originated this volume. Beverley starts by positing a crucial question in any rethinking of AES: "What is the relation between multiculturalism and hegemony?" He then explores the in/validity of the concept of hegemony itself in postnational and global times via a critique of the limits of cultural studies. He proposes an egalitarian imaginary where the people are not conceived of as a unitary subject but rather as a people-multitude bloc, essentially heterogeneous in character (that is, multinational, multiethnic, and multicultural). This view, we may add, is particularly useful for rethinking AES insofar as it theorizes the concrete political space in which that rethinking is taking place.

NOTES

1. An important tradition missing here, which could have provided relevant contrasting viewpoints, is Cuban studies. Salvadoran, Dominican, and Guatemalan studies, now emerging, could also have been considered. See Fernández (1992), Chinchilla and Hamilton (1999), Jonas and Thomas (1999).

2. The 1960s saw the emergence of the first few ethnic studies programs and departments in U.S. history. By the end of the 1970s there were over 500. By 1996 there were 700, which included 359 on African Americans, 41 on Asian Americans, 127 on Chicanos/Latinos, 144 on Native Americans, and 94 multi-ethnic studies programs or departments. See Yang (2000, 273); Hu-DeHart (1993).

3. Internal colonialism demands are not simply moral but essentially political claims, while demands for justice and equal citizenship are not only political but also important moral and cultural ones.

4. According to Ramón Gutiérrez, in order to overcome the limitations of this alternation between total separation/integration, new comparative models of ethnic studies have emerged. They highlight the need to go beyond vertical models of single-ethnicity-based programs and define themselves as horizontally connecting the histories and cultures of the many ethnic components in the United States, including the particular immigrant experience of white Americans. Also, to overcome the potential for socially and culturally reductive takes on ethnic identities that conceive of them as culturally monolithic and socially homogeneous, comparative approaches pay special attention to intragroup stratification, theoretical lessons of comparative ethnic relations and trajectories, and power dynamics at the internal and external level between dominant and subaltern ethnic groups (see Gutiérrez 1994, 164–65). This, as we will have an opportunity to stress later on, does not necessarily mean, at least in our interpretation, the elimination, and in fact is dependent upon the existence, of healthy programs and specialists devoted to an in-depth investigation of so-called single ethnicity groups.

5. For an excellent critique of multiculturalism, see Beverley (chapter 11 in this volume). In the words of William V. Flores and Rina Benmayor (1997): "The United States has thrived not because of its efforts at cultural homogenization, but despite them. . . . Rather than 'disuniting America' or tearing apart its 'social fabric,' difference produces new cultural forms that, in fact, help define America—and have done so throughout its history" (5). "Pluralism implies that in our private lives we can possess and exhibit different cultural identities, but that in the public sphere, except in these sanctioned displays of ethnicity, we must put aside those identities and interact instead in a culturally neutral space as 'Americans.' By taking for granted that public space can be and is culturally neutral, pluralism endorses the dominant culture as normative. More serious is pluralism's silence on inequality and power relations in the country" (9).

6. Pedro Cabán (1998) states: "The field of Latino Studies occupies a distinct niche in the academic hierarchy and is characterized by a profoundly different set of analytical and political concerns. Latin American Studies was a top-down enterprise promoted by government agencies, university administrators and large foundations. In contrast ethnic studies programs were interested in studying the 'Third World within' the United States, and linking these studies to the 'Third World without'" (202).

7. To say nothing of the vernacular Latin American tradition of continental thinking embodied by authors such as Andrés Bello, Francisco Bilbao, José Martí, José Carlos Mariátegui, Ernesto Guevara, and so on. Throughout this essay I have left this vernacular tradition mostly out of my analysis for two reasons: first, it is broad and complex enough to be the subject of a separate study; and second, under conditions of globalization, this time I thought it best to defer to Latin America–based authors for the analysis of the complex links between U.S.-based Latin American studies and its counterpart in Latin America. For some critical positions, see, for example, Gonzalez Stephan (1996); Mato (1994); Beverley, Aronna, and Oviedo (1995); and Moraña (2000). See also Mignolo (chapter 2) and de la Campa (chapter 7) in this volume.

8. Eric Hershberg (1998), for example, states: "Herein lies what is best understood as the fundamental paradox of the partnership between government and the academy in the establishment and expansion of Area Studies. As often as not, scholars who benefited directly from investment motivated by Cold War agendas proved unsympathetic, even hostile, to those very agendas. Nowhere was this more evident than in the field of Latin American studies" (121).

9. As a result of these American needs a number of immediate solutions were devised during the war. They included two U.S. Army "area training programs": "Foreign Area and Language Curricula of the Army Specialized Training Program (ASTP-FALC) for enlisted personnel (located in fifty-five institutions) and ten Civil Affairs Training Schools (CATS) for officers" (Wallerstein 1997, 199). The rationale for these programs was concisely expressed by the 1943 "World Regions in the Social Sciences" internal report of the Committee on World Regions of the Social Science Research Council: "The present war has focused attention as never before upon the entire world. Interest in Foreign Regions has been intensified and sharp attention drawn to areas over which we have felt little or no concern. The immediate need for social scientists who know the different regions of the world stands second only to the demand for military and naval officers familiar with the actual and potential combat zones" (quoted in Wallerstein 1997, 195). The Cold War narrative also highlights the importance of the federal government support for area studies under Title VI of the National Defense Education Act of 1957, which was partly the result of the Sputnik scare and the red menace of Soviet science and know-how it represented. See Wallerstein (1997) and Gulbenkian Commission on the Restructuring of the Social Sciences (1996, 197–210).

10. A similar logic has been criticized by Norma Alarcón (1991): "The fact that Anglo-American feminism has appropriated the generic term for itself, leaves many a woman in this country having to call herself otherwise, that is, 'women of color,' which is equally 'meaningless' without further specification" (34).

11. For a quick overview of these criticisms, see Shea (1997); A. Hall and Tarrow (1998); and Heilbrunn (1996).

12. For two interesting takes on what—from separate traditions and origins

and based on a certain version of area and ethnic studies—they consider the dangers of Pan-Latino studies to ethnic studies in the current U.S. academic climate, see Chabram-Dernersesian (chapter 4 in this volume) and Cabán (1998).

13. For an explanation on popular and democratic subject positions as different articulations of the political space, see Laclau and Mouffe (1985, 131).

14. It may be added that market forces, while always attempting to create a homogeneous Hispanic market, have often been much more open than political forces to bilingualism and biculturalism. In this regard it is worth mentioning Chun, Christopher, and Gumport's (2000) hypothesis that the social acceptance of fields of knowledge in the U.S. organization of academic knowledges depends on their relative distance to the market and to politics. Proximity to the former helps an emerging field, and closeness to the latter may endanger its institutionalization.

15. Crawford is in fact using the analytical framework proposed by Richard Ruiz (1984).

16. "English Plus" refers to an initiative started in Miami by the SALAD group (Spanish American League against Discrimination) that, while acknowledging the importance of English in the United States, opposes English-only campaigns on the grounds that a bilingual education is essential for success in a global economy. See Crawford (2000, 113).

17. Useful in this context is the concept of "cultural citizenship" elaborated by Renato Rosaldo, William V. Flores, and Rina Benmayor, among others: "Cultural citizenship can be thought of as a broad range of activities of everyday life through which Latinos and other groups claim space in society, define their communities and claim rights. It involves the right to retain difference, while also attaining membership in society. It also involves self-definition, affirmation and empowerment" (W. Flores 1997, 262).

18. The recent attacks on bilingual education may, in turn, provide just such an opportunity for political mobilization.

19. On the issue of managing diversity, see Baker (1996). See also Yúdice (chapter 3 in this volume).

20. From this viewpoint the Ebonics controversy of a few years ago should be seen as expressing the racialized nature of cultural and linguistic distinctions in the United States. Susan Moreno (n.d.) states that the Latino rate of college enrollment nationally was 8 percent higher than that of non-Latino whites in 1994. Latino enrollment in two-year institutions was 51 percent higher than that of non-Latino whites, but in four-year institutions Latino enrollment was 30 percent below that of non-Latino whites at the time, and at the graduate level the rate of Latino enrollment was 50 percent lower than for non-Latino whites.

21. This sentence borrows language from the collectively produced rationale for the Hemispheric Dialogues 2 project at the University of California, Santa Cruz, at http://lals.ucsc.edu/hemispheric_dialogues. These dialogues become particularly important for maintaining the crucial relevance of the multiplicity

of analytical factors (such as race, ethnicity, gender, and class) that the linguistic and historical homogenizing forces of terms such as "Hispanic" or "Latino" tend to obscure or gloss over. See, for example, Chabram-Dernersesian, Varese, Almaguer, and Mignolo (all in this volume).

22. These dialogues should incorporate the theories and knowledges being produced elsewhere in the Luso-Hispanic world as well as the asymmetries between their respective research agendas and those of the metropolitan academics. On this crucial issue, see Yúdice (chapter 3 in this volume).

23. Sometimes these cultural explanations take curious turns, such as in the case of Francis Fukuyama (1998). Fukuyama praises Hispanic immigrants' supposed cultural conservatism (family values, religious practices, strong desire to assimilate, and so on) and attacks American liberals, African Americans, and multiculturalists.

24. For an excellent analysis of the real complexity of those conditions in California, see Pastor (forthcoming).

25. After all, as Vicente Rafael (1999) has reminded us, having started as an offspring of post–World War II modernization theory, area studies has evolved and shifted its "focus from the modernization of local differences to understanding the various strategies for localizing modernity" (1209). Modernization theory is still present only in "those who call for its abolition in the name of grand theories of rational choice and free markets that see local differences as obstacles to be overcome" (1209). See Payne (1998), who calls the proponents of such grand theories "revised modernisation theorists."

26. For useful reflections on the scale and scope of research see Payne (1998), who quotes the work of Björn Hettne (1995): "He [Hettne] argues that the problem for the field [Political Economy of Development] is that it has been 'trapped somewhere between an obsolete "nation state" approach and a premature "world" approach.' A stance needs to be taken, he has suggested, at a midpoint between these two extreme positions, thereby constituting a synthesis that transcends the dichotomy of the successive endogenism and exogenism of previous modernisation and dependency analysis" (265). My own idea of a Latino American world-regional imaginary and space attempts to explore such a midpoint. In this effort it seems essential to bring into the discussion the increasing importance of the transatlantic circuit of Latino American migration to Spain.

27. On collective imaginaries and narratives memories, see the pioneering work of Jesús Martín Barbero (1993).

28. See, for example, Martín Barbero (1993) and Sinclair (1999). Sinclair distinguishes among a world-regional level, a Latin American one, and a global one, which encompasses Latino United States and Spain (27).

29. A globalized Latino America as a specific world-region is then best understood not as the result of a certain area studies research agenda based on the United States but as the confluence of both historical developments that have led to a self-conceptualization as a region and contemporary processes of circuit and

community formation. See, in this regard, Arjun Appadurai's (2000) distinction between "trait" geographies and "process" geographies. In the former, areas are seen as "immobile aggregates of traits," and in the latter, regions are conceived as "precipitates of various kinds of action, interaction and motion—trade, travel, pilgrimage, warfare, proselytisation, colonisation, exile and the like" (6–7).

30. Remittances are defined as "the portion of international migrant workers' earnings sent back to countries of origin." See Interamerican Development Bank (2001).

31. The preliminary report for that conference is the source of my data on remittances (Interamerican Development Bank 2001).

32. It seems critical to understand, first, that many Latin Americans are already virtually participating in a globalized imaginary heavily influenced by American mass cultural production, and second, that migration data show that a Latin American person is always at least potentially a Latino American one.

33. For an account of the ability of Latino Americans, specifically Mexicans and Cubans, to formally influence U.S. foreign policy, see Jones-Correa (1995–96).

34. For an excellent overview of the socioeconomic issues involved in hemispheric interdependence, see Bonilla et al. (1998), especially the essays by Rebecca Morales, Manuel Pastor, and Frank Bonilla.

35. A clarification of my spelling of "Latinoamericanism" is in order for those of you who may think it is only another grammatical idiosyncrasy of my writing in the contact zone. The "o" in "Latinoamericanism" is to function as a defamiliarizing reminder of the conflictual and agonistic quality of Chicano/a Latino/a Latin American cultural studies as disciplinary fields. The "o" that is not present in "Latin Americanism" is the exact homology of what is missing as compared to "latinoamericanismo," its Spanish translation. On the other hand, the repeated "o" in "latinoamericanismo" is the sign of a reassuring, taken-for-granted, and/or never fully questioned repetition of identity of the Latin American object for some Latin American subjects. As such, this "o" functions— that is my contention—as a marker of the conflictual and interrelated nature of difference and identity. It is a surface that both prevents the closing of any possible independent identity and makes possible always provisional postulations. It is this familiarizing effect of the "o" in "Latinoamericanism," within the context of American-based Chicana/o, Latina/o, and Latin American studies, that I have sought to create with my coinage.

36. This formulation benefits from the work of Ramón Grosfoguel (2001) and Walter Mignolo (chapter 2 in this volume).

REFERENCES

Alarcón, Norma. 1991. "The Theoretical Subject(s) of *This Bridge Called My Back*." In *Criticism in the Borderlands: Studies in Chicano Literature, Culture, and Ideology,* ed. Hector Calderón and José David Saldívar. Durham, N.C.: Duke University Press. 28–39.

Alcoff, Linda. 2000. "Is Latina/o Identity a Racial Identity?" In *Hispanics/ Latinos in the United States. Ethnicity, Race, and Rights,* ed. Jorge J. E. Gracia and Pablo De Greiff. New York: Routledge. 23–44.

Anderson, Benedict. 1994. "Exodus." *Critical Inquiry* 20, no. 2: 314–27.

Appadurai, Arjun. 2000. "Grassroots, Globalization, and the Research Imagination." *Public Culture* 12, no. 1: 1–19.

Arguedas, José María. [1958] 1997. *Los ríos profundos.* Ed. William Rowe. London: Bristol Classic Press.

———. [1971] 1990. *El zorro de arriba y el zorro de abajo.* Ed. Eve Marie Fell. Nanterre, France: Université Paris X, Centre de recherches latino-américaines.

Baker, Octave. 1996. "The Managing Diversity Movement: Origins, Status, and Challenges." In *Impacts of Racism on White Americans,* ed. Benjamin P. Browser and Raymond G. Hunt, 2d ed. Thousand Oaks, Calif.: Sage. 139–56.

Berger, Mark T. 1995. *Under Northern Eyes: Latin American Studies and U.S. Hegemony in the Americas, 1898–1990.* Bloomington: Indiana University Press.

Beverley, John, Michael Aronna, and Jose Oviedo, eds. 1995. *The Postmodernism Debate in Latin America.* Durham, N.C.: Duke University Press.

Bonilla, Frank. 1998. "Rethinking Latino/Latin American Interdependence: New Knowing, New Practice." In Bonilla et al., eds., 1998. 217–30.

Bonilla, Frank, Edwin Meléndez, Rebecca Morales, and María de los Angeles Torres, eds. 1998. *Borderless Borders: U.S. Latinos, Latin Americans, and the Paradox of Interdependence.* Philadelphia: Temple University Press.

Brunner, José Joaquín. 1998. *Globalización cultural y posmodernidad.* Santiago: Fondo de Cultura Económica.

Cabán, Pedro. 1998. "The New Synthesis of Latin American/Latino Studies." In *Borderless Borders: U.S. Latinos, Latin Americans, and the Paradox of Interdependence,* ed. Bonilla et al. Philadelphia: Temple University Press. 195–215.

Chinchilla, Norma, and Nora Hamilton. 1999. "Changing Networks and Alliances in a Transnational Context: Salvadoran and Guatemalan Immigrants in Southern California." *Social Justice* 26: 3, 4–26.

Chun, Marc, Susan Christopher, and Patricia J. Gumport. 2000. "Multiculturalism and the Academic Organization of Knowledge." In *Multicultural Curriculum: New Directions for Social Theory, Practice, and Policy,* ed. Ram Mahalingam and Cameron McCarthy. New York: Routledge. 223–41.

Clifford, James. 1986. "On Ethnographic Allegory." In *Writing Culture: The Poetics and Politics of Ethnography,* ed. James Clifford and George E. Marcus. Berkeley: University of California Press. 98–121.

———. 1997. *Routes: Travel and Translation in the Late Twentieth Century.* Cambridge: Harvard University Press.

Cornejo Polar, Antonio. 1996. "Una heterogeneidad no dialéctica: Sujeto y discurso migrantes en el Perú moderno." In "Crítica cultural y teoría literaria latinoamericanas," ed. Mabel Moraña. Special issue, *Revista Iberoamericana* 62: 176–77.

Coronil, Fernando. 1996. "Beyond Occidentalism." *Cultural Anthropology* 11: 1, 51–87.

Crawford, James. 2000. "Language Politics in the United States: The Paradox of Bilingual Education." In *The Politics of Multiculturalism and Bilingual Education: Students and Teachers Caught in the Cross Fire,* ed. Carlos J. Ovando and Peter McLaren. Boston: McGraw Hill. 107–25.

Cummins, Jim. 2000. "Beyond Adversarial Discourse: Searching for Common Ground in the Education of Bilingual Students." In *The Politics of Multiculturalism and Bilingual Education: Students and Teachers Caught in the Cross Fire,* ed. Carlos J. Ovando and Peter McLaren. Boston: McGraw Hill. 127–47.

Fernández, Damián J., ed. 1992. *Cuban Studies since the Revolution.* Gainesville: University Press of Florida.

Flores, Juan, and George Yúdice. 1990. "Living Borders/Buscando America: Languages of Latino Self-formation." *Social Text* 8, no. 24: 57–84.

Flores, William V. 1997. "Citizens vs. Citizenry: Undocumented Immigrants and Latino Cultural Citizenship." In *Latino Cultural Citizenship: Claiming Identity, Space, and Rights,* ed. William V. Flores and Rina Benmayor. Boston: Beacon Press. 255–77.

Flores, William V., and Rina Benmayor. 1997. "Introduction: Constructing Cultural Citizenship." In *Latino Cultural Citizenship: Claiming Identity, Space, and Rights,* ed. William V. Flores and Rina Benmayor. Boston: Beacon Press. 1–23.

Fukuyama, Francis. 1998. "Immigrants and Family Values." In *The Immigration Reader: America in a Multidisciplinary Perspective,* ed. David Jacobson. London: Blackwell. 388–401.

García Canclini, Néstor. 1995. *Consumidores y ciudadanos: Conflictos multiculturales de la globalización.* Mexico: Grijalbo.

Gilman, Sander L. 2000. "Learning a Foreign Language in a Monolingual World." *PMLA* 115, no. 5: 1032–40.

Gonzalez Stephan, Beatriz, ed. 1996. *Cultura y Tercer Mundo.* Caracas: Nueva Sociedad.

Grosfoguel, Ramón. 2001. "Geopolitics of Knowledge and Coloniality of Power: Rethinking the Modern/Colonial World-System from the Colonial Difference." Paper presented at the University of California, Santa Cruz, April 13, 2001.

Gulbenkian Commission. 1996. *Open the Social Sciences: Report of the Gulbenkian Commission on the Restructuring of the Social Sciences.* Stanford, Calif.: Stanford University Press.

Gutiérrez, Ramón. 1994. "Ethnic Studies: Its Evolution in American Colleges and Universities." In *Multiculturalism: A Critical Reader,* ed. David Theo Goldberg. Oxford: Blackwell. 157–67.

Hall, A. Peter, and Sidney Tarrow. 1998. "Globalization and Area Studies: When Is Too Broad Too Narrow." *Chronicle of Higher Education,* January 23, B4–5.

Hall, Stuart. 1992. "The Question of Cultural Identity." In *Modernity and Its Futures,* ed. Stuart Hall, David Held, and Tony McGrew. Cambridge: Polity Press in association with the Open University. 273–326.

Heilbrunn, Jacob. 1996. "The News from Everywhere: Does Global Thinking Threaten Local Knowledge? The Social Science Research Council Debates the Future of Area Studies." *Lingua Franca* (May–June): 49–56.

Hershberg, Eric. 1998. "From Cold War Origins to a Model for Academic Internationalization: Latin American Studies at a Crossroads." *Dispositio/n* 13, no. 50: 117–31.

Hettne, Björn. 1995. *Development Theory and the Three Worlds: Towards an International Political Economy of Development.* Essex, England: Longman Scientific and Technical.

Hu-DeHart, Evelyn. 1993. "The History, Development, and Future of Ethnic Studies." *Phi Delta Kappan* (September): 50–54.

Interamerican Development Bank. 2001. "Remittances as an Instrument of Development: A Regional Conference." At http://www.iadb.org.

Jameson, Fredric. 1987. "The State of the Subject." *Critical Quarterly* 29, no. 4: 16–25.

Jonas, Susanne, and Suzie Dod Thomas, eds. 1999. *Immigration: A Civil Rights Issue for the Americas.* Wilmington, Del.: Scholarly Resources.

Jones-Correa, Michael. 1995–96. "New Directions for Latinos as an Ethnic Lobby in U.S. Foreign Policy." *Harvard Journal of Hispanic Policy* 9: 47–75.

Laclau, Ernesto, and Chantal Mouffe. 1985. *Hegemony and Socialist Strategy: Towards a Radical Democratic Politics.* London: Verso.

Marable, Manning. 1993. "Beyond Racial Identity Politics: Towards a Liberation Theory for Multicultural Democracy." *Race & Class* 35: 1, 113–30.

Martín Barbero, Jesús. 1993. *Communication, Culture, and Hegemony: From the Media to Mediations.* London: Sage.

Mato, Daniel, ed. 1994. *Teoría y política de la construcción de identidades y diferencias en América Latina y el Caribe.* Caracas: UNESCO, Editorial Nueva Sociedad.

Moore, Joan. 1997. "Latina/o Studies: The Continuing Need for New Paradigms." Julian Samora Research Institute Occasional Paper no. 29, Michigan State University. At http://www.jsri.msu.edu/RandS/research/ops/oc29abs.html.

Moore, Joan, and Raquel Pinderhughes, eds. 1993. *Latinos and the Underclass Debate.* New York: Russell Sage Foundation.

Moraña, Mabel. 2000. *Nuevas perspectivas desde, sobre América Latina: El desafío de los estudios culturales.* Santiago: Editorial Cuarto Propio: Instituto Internacional de Literatura Iberoamericana.

Moreiras, Alberto. 1997. "José María Arguedas y el fin de la transculturación." In *Angel Rama y los estudios latinoamericanos,* ed. Mabel Moraña. Pittsburgh: Instituto Internacional de Literatura Iberoamericana. 213–31.

Moreno, Susan. n.d. "US Latinos and Higher Education." Inter-University Program for Latino Research (IUPLR), vol. 1, Briefing Paper no. 6. At http://www.nd.edu/~iuplr.

Nelson, Candace, and Marta Tienda. 1985. "The Structuring of Hispanic Ethnicity: Historical and Contemporary Perspectives." *Ethnic and Racial Studies* 8: 49–74.

Newfield, Christopher, and Avery F. Gordon. 1996. "Multiculturalism's Unfinished Business." In *Mapping Multiculturalism,* ed. Avery F. Gordon and Christopher Newfield. Minneapolis: University of Minnesota Press. 76–115.

Oboler, Suzanne. 1995. *Ethnic Labels, Latino Lives: Identity and the Politics of (Re)Presentation in the United States.* Minneapolis: University of Minnesota Press.

Omi, Michael. 1996. "Racialization in the Post-Civil Rights Era." In *Mapping Multiculturalism,* ed. Avery F. Gordon and Christopher Newfield. Minneapolis: University of Minnesota Press. 178–86.

Ortiz, Renato. 1994. *Mundializacao e cultura.* São Paulo: Editora Brasiliense.

Pastor, Manuel. Forthcoming. *California's Latinos: Assets at Risk.* California Policy Research Center.

Payne, Anthony. 1998. "The New Political Economy of Area Studies." *Millennium: Journal of International Studies* 27, no. 2: 253–73.

Pedraza, Silvia. 1998. "The Contribution of Latino Studies to Social Science Research on Immigration." Julian Samora Research Institute Occasional Paper no. 36, Michigan State University. At http://www.jsri.msu.edu/RandS/research/ops/oc36abs.html.

Rafael, Vicente. 1999. "Regionalism, Area Studies, and the Accidents of Agency." *American Historical Review* 104, no. 4: 1209.

Robbins, Bruce. 1998. "Actually Existing Cosmopolitanism." In *Cosmopolitics: Thinking and Feeling beyond the Nation,* ed. Pheng Cheah and Bruce Robbins. Minneapolis: University of Minnesota Press. 1–19.

Ruiz, Richard. 1984. "Orientations in Language Planning." *National Association for Bilingual Education Journal* 8, no. 2: 15–34.

Said, Edward. 1984. "Reflections of Exile." *Granta* 13: 159–72.

Sandoval, Ciro A., and Sandra M. Boschetto-Sandoval, eds. 1998. *José María Arguedas: Reconsiderations for Latin American Cultural Studies.* Athens: Ohio University Center for International Studies.

Shea, Christopher. 1997. "Political Scientists Clash over Value of Area Studies." *Chronicle of Higher Education,* January 10, A13–14.

Sinclair, John. 1999. *Latin American Television: A Global View.* Oxford and New York: Oxford University Press.

Stevens-Arroyo, Antonio M. 1987. "Toward a Renaissance of Puerto Rican Studies: An Essay of Redefinition." In *Toward a Renaissance of Puerto Rican Studies: Ethnic and Area Studies in University Education,* ed. María E. Sánchez and Antonio M. Stevens-Arroyo. Boulder, Colo.: Social Science Monographs. 123–46.

Tsing, Anna. 2000. "The Global Situation." Paper presented at "Culture and Politics of Place, Locality, and Globalization" conference, University of California, Santa Cruz, October 28, 2000.

Wallerstein, Immanuel. 1997. "The Unintended Consequences of Cold War Area Studies." In *The Cold War and the University: Towards an Intellectual History of the Postwar Years,* ed. Noam Chomsky et al. New York: New Press. 195–231.

Yang, Philip Q. 2000. *Ethnic Studies: Issues and Approaches.* New York: State University of New York Press.

Part I

On the History of Area and Ethnic Studies

CHAPTER I

Latino Cultural Studies

Frances R. Aparicio (interviewed by Juan Zevallos Aguilar)

Translated by Dascha Inciarte and Carolyn Sedway

Frances R. Aparicio is director of the Program of Latin American and Latino Studies at the University of Illinois, Chicago. In the early 1980s, she taught the first course of "Spanish for U.S. Latinos" at Harvard University. Since then, she has developed this course for Stanford University as well as the universities of Arizona and Michigan. She has published numerous articles and books about Latin American poetry, music, and literature in the Caribbean; literary translation; and Latino literature and culture in the United States. In 1999 she answered these questions, presented to her by Juan Zevallos Aguilar.

Over the past decade, Latino studies has been integrated into the American university system. Universities are creating a space for this dynamic field, be it in existing departments of Spanish, Romance languages, or English, or in newly created institutional frameworks. This translates into a greater demand for specialists, guaranteeing work to recent graduates of Latino studies. Could you outline the most important factors concerning the establishment of Latino studies as a field?

Latino studies developed as an academic field in the late 1960s and early 1970s and was triggered by the battles fought by minorities in the United

States who sought to defend their civil rights. While students and activists of Mexican origin in California, Texas, Colorado, and the Southwest demanded programs that would reflect their history and culture in academic settings, Puerto Ricans in New York, particularly under the leadership of the Young Lords, also fought for the inclusion of academic materials that would reflect their culture and language. These demands arose in a political context in which racial and cultural minorities were militantly opposed to social and governmental institutions. Schools and universities were one target of these social movements, since they constituted the primary space in which youth of Latin American descent were colonized with the aim of total assimilation. It is important to remember that these civil battles were not fought in an isolated fashion, but rather within a larger framework of labor battles, such as the organization of the United Farm Workers under César Chávez, political battles such as those of the Young Lords in Chicago and New York, and the formation of the Raza Unida party in Crystal City, Texas.

As a result of the collective impact of the civil rights movement and new legislation beginning in the late 1960s and early 1970s, Chicano studies in the West and Southwest and Puerto Rican studies in New York arose as academic programs. One of the first was the Program for Chicano Studies, founded by Rodolfo Acuña at California State University, Northridge. Acuña is one of the pioneers in this field as well as a radical historian whose *Occupied America* presented for the first time the history of the Southwest from the perspective of those who were subjugated. Alternatively, in New York, not only have programs and departments in Puerto Rican studies been created, such as the one at Brooklyn College, but also the Center for Puerto Rican Studies at Hunter College, CUNY, whose initial controversial premise was to combine academic knowledge with the participation of the Puerto Rican working-class community.

I want to underline the nationalist character of these projects as a first step in the development of Latino studies. This does not imply, though, that the civil battles were fragmented into national groups; more recent investigation points to a collective activism, both diverse and interethnic. Institutional demands, however, required a strategic focus on the cultural construction of a dominant group, be it Chicano or Puerto Rican. Cuban American identity would arise later as one result of the transformation of refugee and exile identity into one of an ethnic minority, according to Eliana Rivero's analysis (1989).

The cultural nationalism of the Chicano and Nuyorican movements has transformed itself, although only partially and in a dialectic manner, into what we call Latino studies. This tendency toward "Latino-ness" arises from various factors. The diversification and redistribution of those of Latin American and Caribbean ancestry in the United States, itself a result of the changes involved in the creation of a global economy, has forced us to transcend nationalist boundaries and to recognize national diversity in the Latino community in the United States. At the same time, the growth of Latino-ness as an academic discipline is due to universities that, for supposed fiscal reasons, consolidated various national culture programs into one unit—not surprising in this age of bureaucratic conservatism. The convergence of the Latino as a social and bureaucratic entity creates a space for Latino studies that itself arose for historical and intellectual, as well as bureaucratic and structural, reasons.[1]

In intellectual terms, cultural nationalism has now been transcended thanks to the revisionist work of feminist Chicanas and Latinas who experienced exclusion and oppression from masculinist ideologies therein as well as critical analyses of gay issues and the recognition of transnational dynamics in the social construction and development of Latino identity.

However, these nationalisms still permeate Latino studies and, in fact, as the field is being shaped daily, it is characterized precisely by dialectical tensions between the hegemonic nationalisms of each group and the strategic need to build a collective identity, which we call "Latino-ness" or "Latinoism." The field of Latino studies is, then, the rubric that has been used to construct this alternative and oppositional space within the academic world. It is made up of Chicano, Puerto Rican, and Cuban American studies as well as more recent studies addressing the diversification and redistribution of the Latin American population within the United States. Dominicans, Colombians, and Central Americans, groups undergoing the greatest demographic growth since the 1980s, add to the complexity of the Latin American and Caribbean populations in the United States. Dominicans and Colombians have transformed identity paradigms of Puerto Ricans in the East, just as the Central Americans have affected the hegemony of Chicanos in California. Rodolfo Acuña, for example, has insisted that the term "Chicano" also cover the Central American experience.

During the past decade we have witnessed a local and regional diversification of U.S. Latinos since cities that are composed of large Puerto Rican populations, such as New York, or Mexican populations, such as

Los Angeles, are experiencing an increasingly diverse presence of other national groups. I had pointed to this phenomenon in a 1990 article regarding Pan-Latin diversification in university student bodies and its pedagogical implications (Aparicio 1993). Until recently, Puerto Rican studies has been dominant in New York, while Chicano and Mexican American studies have been hegemonic in California and the Southwest. Some programs, however, have made changes in their Latino academic programming as well as in their public identity.[2] The Midwest, however, is a region in which the Latino community has been much more Pan-Latino and mixed in both demographic and historical terms. One finds that there has been more of an interchange among national groups. For this reason, programs of study have generally had a Pan-Latino or, at least, a Chicano Rican character. Magazines and program titles from the Midwest clearly reveal this Pan-Latino paradigm. The Program for Chicano Rican studies at Indiana University, Bloomington, directed by Luis Dávila, has been a model program for these more modern tendencies. The *Americas Review,* published in Houston, was the *Chicano Riqueña* magazine that Nicolás Kanellos founded in Indiana. The Latino studies programs at the University of Michigan and DePaul University, the Latin American and Latino Studies Program at the University of Illinois, Chicago, and the Chicano Boricua studies at Wayne State University have served as antecedents to the diversification experienced in New York and California in the 1990s.

This combination of factors stimulated the growth of Latino studies as opposed to the nationalist antecedents of Chicano studies and Puerto Rican studies. Therefore, we cannot define Latino studies in a fixed or isolated manner. Rather, it must be thought of as a field that is constantly transforming itself in response to demographic, social, cultural, and historical fluctuations pertaining to Latino communities in the United States. It is precisely this tension between cultural nationalism, the specificity of each group, and the need to see ourselves as a collectivity with common and analogous experiences that characterize the dynamic of Latino studies.

Clarifying this history, Latino studies was not constituted in the last decade, but rather has become "institutionalized." It has been legitimized by universities as a needed academic field to prepare our students as future citizens of a multicultural and multiracial society in the twenty-first century. The institutional response of American universities, faced with social and militant activism of minority students, was, in part, to co-opt these demands and oppositional values, redefining them as "multiculturalism." Institutional multiculturalism resemanticizes oppositional and communal values of social movements, adapting them and inserting them into the competitive and individualist habitus of Anglo-Saxon academic culture that still predominates in higher education.

Multiculturalism has had major impacts on this field. First, institutional multiculturalism tends to homogenize minority cultures and negate their historical specificity. To change national ethnic programs into programs fashioned as Latino is an obvious example of the way in which these specificities are displaced and diluted toward models and spaces that are more homogenizing. Second, there is a process of "recanonization" that occurs within the university and that is based on an ahistorical and decontextualized vision of the texts being studied. For example, texts circulate and are read in other courses such as women's studies, English, history, anthropology, and Hispanic studies. If these multiple lectures and interpretations are understood from various disciplinary angles, which contribute to a deeper and more complex understanding of the text, then such readings tend to exist outside the political, colonial, economic, and social history in which the text was forged.

The general perception that Latino studies has emerged recently, which informs your question, illustrates precisely the ahistorical vision that exists in both text and field. In teaching and in course development, professors who have Gloria Anzaldúa, for example, on their reading lists tend to include her as the only voice representative of Chicano or Latino experience. Few spaces exist in which to include Chicano or Puerto Rican texts within multicultural courses, so this selection of what I have termed "the mascots of multiculturalism" tends to legitimize certain ones and excludes others that would contribute to a more comprehensive overview of Latino literary production. As this pedagogy is combined with a minimal number of Latino university professors, institutional multiculturalism is reduced to what has been considered touristic voyeurism of various cultural groups in the United States. Finally, another identifiable problematic effect in this institutionalization process is the displacement of the authority of Latinos in this field as well as their trivialization.

The perception that one need not specialize in these subjects in order to teach them prevails in many universities and departments. This perception is even more prevalent in cultural and popular studies, and this accompanies the underestimation of the field, particularly when compared with traditional fields such as that of medieval studies or Western culture. This phenomenon is the result of class prejudice against cultural productions whose subjects and agents are working class and who are considered racially inferior to thinkers of Western culture, as well as the result of the higher appraisal of the past over contemporary and popular culture themes.

The integration of Latino studies into university spaces has also implied the political neutralization of this field so that it has become more "acceptable" and so that it might match the dominant academic values of the United States. Simultaneously, the presence of this field, as well as a new literary, historical, and cultural canon, has destabilized the hegemony of these disciplines and the formative role of traditional understanding. For example, in the field of Hispanic studies the presence of Latino literature in English or in interlingual forms forces questions regarding the fixed relationship between language and culture that itself defines and justifies the institutional space of Hispanic studies. A literary and cultural production such as that of the U.S. Latino one produced by subaltern and racialized subjects also transgresses the privileged place of the Hispanic literary canon. Latino cultural courses in Spanish programs force an interrogation and a critical discourse of Anglo privilege, of racialization in the United States, and of the use of Spanish as a cultural bridge.

This alternative canon has been formed through the effort of pioneering intellectuals in the field and the generations that followed in academe. They not only defied racism in their departments but also contributed to the production and development of a literary, historic, cultural, and critical corpus that is currently part of that emerging tradition. Among them I can think of Edna Acosta Belén, Frank Bonilla, Alfredo Matilla, Luz María Umpierre, Rina Benmayor, Efraín Barradas, Virginia Sánchez-Korrol, Juan Flores, Marc Zimmerman, and Ana Celia Zentella, some of the most important figures in Puerto Rican cultural studies. Chicano studies has developed thanks to many people, among them Luis Leal, Joseph Sommers, Tomás Ybarra-Frausto, María Herrera-Sobek, Vicky Ruíz, Francisco Lomelí, Charles Tatum, Norma Alarcón, José Limón, Américo Paredes, Ramón Saldívar, José Saldívar, Sonia Saldívar-Hull, Angie Chabram-Dernersesian, Rosalinda Fregoso, Juan Bruce-Novoa, Hector Calderón, Norma Cantú, Gary Keller, Yvonne Yarbro-Bejarano, Octavio Romano, Tey Diana Rebolledo, Marta Sánchez, and many more. The field of Cuban American studies has also benefited from the contributions of people like Ofelia García, Alejandro Portes, Carolina

Hospital, Achy Obejas, Gustavo Pérez-Firmat, Lisandro Pérez, Ruth Behar, Silvia Pedraza, Eliana Rivero, and Ana Roca. Publishers such as Arte Público Press, directed by Nicolás Kanellos, Gary Keller's Bilingual Review Press, and Norma Alarcón's Third Woman Press are examples of the pioneering projects that began in the 1970s and have grown over the years, affording visibility to the literature produced by Latino authors and creating a process of distribution, marketing, and publicity for its publication. Also, magazines like *Aztlán,* the *Americas Review* (previously *Revista Chicano Riqueña*), *Third Woman,* the *Bilingual Review,* the *Centro de Estudios Puertorriqueños Bulletin,* and, more recently, *Latino Studies Journal,* directed by Félix Padilla, along with other magazines directed toward a Hispanic context within the disciplines, have helped to foment a critical tradition and knowledge about the Latino experience in the United States.

Fifteen years ago, it would have been impossible to offer courses that examined the history of Latino studies as an academic field, courses that usually function as the central seminar of the discipline. Today, thanks to the vast production of articles, books, magazines, doctoral theses, and university conferences and consortia that have helped sponsor interdisciplinary Latino studies (the Inter-University Program for Latino Research, for example), we can study the development of the field as such, offer seminars about Latino studies, and begin to establish a kind of metacriticism about various cycles, tendencies, and historical transformations of our approaches, ideologies, and methodologies. In history, literature, sociology, anthropology, psychology, and law, among other fields, there now exists a critical body of work as well as a canon of primary texts produced by this sector.

Institutional spaces in which Latino studies is located serve as an excellent metaphor with which to analyze the problematic and complex relationship of the field to academic institutions and to various disciplines. The definition of this program has depended, as we have already suggested, on the political history of each local community. In the last decade, many of the programs or departments of Chicano or Puerto Rican studies and other analogous programs have been consolidated, either as Latino and Latin American or Cuban studies or, along with Asian American or African-American studies, under the auspices of ethnic studies. Since its inception in 1984, Latino studies at the University of Michigan has been placed within the North American studies or American Culture Program, in English. This implies a degree of colonization (as a territory and subprogram) yet also a multiracial, interdisciplinary, and cultural interaction that has been healthy for the intellectual development of both professors and students of every racial and ethnic group. The field of Latino studies, as with other ethnic fields, has destabilized disciplinary, linguistic, and ethnic boundaries of knowledge production.

There has recently been a notable increase in the number of prestigious universities that are initiating these programs, and they have had to deliberate, in difficult and complex discussions, on the placement of Latino studies. Where does it belong? With which other programs should it be affiliated? Because of its interdisciplinary nature and the racial diversity of the Latino population in the United States, the field of Latino studies should converge with African-American studies as well as with Latin American, North American, and women's studies. In my opinion, Latino studies belongs to all of those spaces, including Spanish and English departments, and it should not become the property of any one. We should enjoy bureaucratic autonomy without sacrificing the intellectual dialogue and cooperation that is so important in an academic world that is ever more multidisciplinary and global. The great diversity in which these programs are placed usually reflects existing resources in terms of the national profile and professorial disciplines and in terms of the predisposition, or lack thereof, of certain departments to integrate Latino studies into their programs, following the bureaucratic structures of each university. In many cases, the presence of Latino studies within one department could become very limiting—no single discipline can fully represent this field. Nor should it be articulated exclusively in English or in Spanish, rather in a combination of both. At the University of Michigan, for example, a Spanish requirement for the Latino studies major was implemented. This implied collaboration with the Spanish Department in both the teaching of the language as well as in the development of shared coursework. It is interesting to observe that many Chicano academics have been trained in English departments, while those of Caribbean or Puerto Rican ancestry have greater representation in Spanish departments. As a result, universities must be conscious of establishing Pan-Latino diversity within the faculty as well as diversity in those areas of research.

One of the most obvious potential dangers in the establishment of a Latino studies program is its placement in a space leading to its colonization and lack of autonomy. The integration of Latino studies with Latin American studies or with North American studies, whose history and foundation respond to disparate political realities, could imply a series of obstacles and internal conflicts in terms of administration, decision making, admissions, and other issues of an academic or structural nature. Those universities that established Latino studies as an emergency response to political pressures also established programs and structures before hiring a significant number of professors—professors who should be the ones responsible for designing an academic program based on the profiles of both students and faculty.

One of the accomplishments of the field of Latino studies is the practice of interdisciplinary research that is no longer centered solely on literature. What does the field of Latino studies consist of? Would this be the first field in which cultural studies is practiced? What are the objects of your study? What are its theoretical perspectives and methodological instruments? Who are its most renowned theoreticians and critics?

According to Juan Flores ("Latino Studies," chapter 9 in this volume), pioneer programs established a series of values and practices that were to guide this new intellectual praxis: first, the interdisciplinary nature of the work that would transcend the boundaries of traditional disciplines; second, collective work and collaboration between scholars; and third, the integration of academics with local and regional communities. These ideals characterize the field of Latino studies, although this does not mean that they have been completely fulfilled in practice.

In reality there is great tension around the compromise academics have struck between their original ideals and their more pragmatic need to respond to exigencies of the academic world of North America. For example, Latino studies consists of interdisciplinary studies, but the greater part of research is based on traditional disciplines and is focused on one group in particular, maintaining national paradigms. More than interdisciplinariness, which is hard to attain, this intellectual practice has been characterized by multidisciplinariness. This happens precisely because of the criteria used to evaluate the scholarship, criteria that limit the possibilities of radicalization of the field. The dominant academic world pushes the scholar to publish on his or her own, once again diminishing the possibilities of collaborative work. National consortia, like the Inter-University Program for Latino Research, sponsor this type of interdisciplinary and collaborative work, awarding funds and legitimacy to such projects.

Finally, the integration of academics with local and regional communities is a currently debated issue within the field; many academics are
questioning the concept of community and redefining it exclusively as
the academic community. Others have expressed a commitment toward
working with Latino urban and working-class communities, integrat-
ing them into their investigations as subjects, more than as objects, of
study. The debate has been articulated as the conflict between theory
and community, a dichotomy that suggests that the extra-academic
community does not have the potential to theorize or to be considered
as an intellectual entity. However, one of the more unique characteristics of Latino studies has been the development of theories that are not
divorced from the daily reality of subjugated subjects, in the words of
Cherríe Moraga (1983), theories "from the flesh," derived from the social and human experiences of subordinated sectors. One of the forms
institutional racism takes is the dominant perspective that Latino studies lacks academic seriousness, intellectual complexity, and important
theorization. Latino studies has been marginalized and remains invisible
within cultural studies and postcolonial literature produced in the First
World. Significant contributions by Latinos and Latinas to theories
about the subject, hybridity, and the analysis of colonial conditions in a
supposedly postcolonial world have yet to be recognized. Latino studies
was one of the first spaces in which cultural studies was produced along
with Afro-American, Asian American, and Native American studies. For
Latino studies, the object of study has always been the colonized subject
who has been silenced by dominant institutions, the popular sector, social movements, and women as subjects who are doubly oppressed.

In historiography, Chicano and Puerto Rican subjects from the working class have radicalized official history, while in the humanities, the
analysis of cultural productions of the working class also destabilizes
the paradigms of elite culture. The need to examine the structures of
colonialism among U.S. Puerto Ricans, as well as internal colonialism
among Chicanos, has awarded Latino studies an important role in the
development of the postcolonial. In fact, the gaze toward foreign countries and the so-called Third World that predominates in postcolonial
studies has denied or forgotten the existence of colonialism within the
countries of the First World, marginalizing these spaces that are so significant. This focus on what is "international" and "abroad" has been,
therefore, a way of silencing the analysis of forms of domination and
colonialization within the United States, phenomena that we Latino

critics have always examined in depth as part of our analysis of history, immigration, women, language, and education, among others. The multidisciplinary and, sometimes, interdisciplinary tendency within Latino studies, its convergence with cultural studies, poststructuralism, discursive theories, feminism (convergences and divergences), and the new revisionist historicism, is all part of an intellectual practice called Latino studies. The appearance of the "border subject," its theorizations by feminists such as Gloria Anzaldúa (1987), as well as by immigration historians, literary and cultural critics, and social scientists, has been the most important concept that Latino studies has contributed to cultural studies in the United States, Europe, and Latin America.

In opposition to many dominant ideas that suppose that Latino intellectuals should apply and imitate Western theories, Latino studies has constituted a dynamic and original space precisely because we have worked with and against dominant theories, questioning them and proposing new models of cultural and racial identity. In one of the few articles that exist about the development of the field, Angie Chabram-Dernersesian (1999) observes that pioneer Chicano professors and intellectuals absolutely resisted integration of Western and North American theories in their studies, a position that is explained within the greater context of opposition and battle as well as social positions that are much more connected with the working- and popular-class communities than with the world of academics (Chabram 1991). In fact, these pioneers were trained as professors in traditional disciplines, but they could not build a new field based on traditional disciplines. For example, instead of studying "irony" in a Chicano novel (as some did), which would have been the dominant tendency within New Criticism, Latinos focused on the ways in which the literary text articulated a social critique of the life conditions of Mexican Americans, an approach that at the time was considered very descriptive or merely political.

In contrast, younger generations have had the privilege of being trained with Chicano and Latino professors, and today they can articulate a critique with the theoretical tools developed by their predecessors. In fact, by the 1980s, Chicana feminists such as Norma Alarcón, Gloria Anzaldúa, and Chela Sandoval with her seminal dissertation, "Oppositional Consciousness" (1993), demonstrate that critical and oppositional work can be mediated through academic theoretical discourse, and they began to open the path for the integration of knowledge about Latinos within dominant academic spaces. The articles by Chicana feminists that counteract the exclusion of minority women in Anglo models of feminist liberation had an impact not only on political activities but also in the classroom.

While poststructuralism announced the death of the author, of the historical subject, and of history as such, Chicano and Latino authors were constituting themselves as historical subjects for the first time, articulating in public spaces the history that had not yet been told, what Foucault would later call subjugated knowledge. If European literary theories denied the minority subject, Latino authors and critics found themselves against the grain of what dominant theory proposed. Chicano and Puerto Rican studies, and later Latino studies, have been oppositional precisely because they have focused on the vindication of subaltern and colonized subjects: in history, Rodolfo Acuña's *Occupied America* (2000) presents, for the first time and in a systematic manner, the history of the American Southwest and West from the perspective of those who are subjugated. He begins to transform history into a discourse produced by subaltern subjects instead of by an elite. By the same token, the transformations in social sciences, such as anthropology, that question the forms in which authority and discourse have legitimized themselves by means of colonizing practices and the authority of the critic himself or herself, have not been arbitrary but rather have arisen as a partial result of the new historical visions produced by blacks, Chicanos, Latinos, and Asians in the United States. Literature, poetry, and literary texts produced by the working class in the barrios are being studied. This is a literature that breaks with static normative criteria; it is written in interlingual codes and thus transcends the discursive purity of the national language.

Women who are authors and writers also penetrate public space as historical subjects with their autobiographical narratives, feminist novels, and hybrid texts, such as Anzaldúa's *Borderlands* (1987). In the field of history, feminist historiography has concerned itself with the recuperation of the historical agency of working-class Latina women in particular, their economic and cultural contributions to labor and social movements, and an analysis of women as objects of Americanization and assimilation in the society of the United States.

In this sense, the field of Latino studies has been an intellectual praxis always motivated toward reclaiming historical, social, and cultural validity in the daily practices and the cultural experiences of this subaltern community within the United States, a heterogeneous community that has been relegated to invisibility by the dominant system. One of its main premises is an oppositional and decolonizing praxis.

Besides institutional initiatives that award a space to Latino studies, what are the specialists proposing in order to be a part of departments that have already been constituted or to create autonomous spaces? I ask this question because I identify a tendency to consider Latino or Hispanic culture as being a part of Latin American culture. I remember Joseph Sommers (Sommers and Ybarra-Frausto 1979), who proposed this conception in the 1970s, and, in the present, José Saldívar's (1991) work in which a link is established between both of these cultures. On the other hand, there is a tendency that proposes, in order to grant a specificity to what is Latino or Latino-ness, the existence of autonomous institutional spaces.

Here you refer to the recent tendency in Spanish departments and among Latin Americans to integrate Latino studies into their courses and programs. In part, José Saldívar's *The Dialectics of Our America* (1991) facilitated the consideration of studies in the Americas as an alternative intellectual space that grew out of the colonial model of North American studies, which is based on a homogeneous definition of an American culture bounded by the border with Mexico. If we remember that the United States constitutes the country in the world with the fifth-greatest number of Spanish speakers, we cannot fail to conceptualize the North as a Latino or Latin American space. The realities of immigration, diasporas, and exile (in the Caribbean, the southern part of the continent, Mexico, Central America, and the Andean region) have made it a necessity to recognize the Latino cultural and literary production that is taking place within the borders of the United States. Guillermo Gómez Peña has shown this need to consider himself "of the border" as well as Mexican.

The great Latin American immigration during the 1980s not only transformed the Latino profile in the United States, but also obliged Latin Americanists, as much there as here, to recognize transnational flows in the production and reception of culture. In this sense, Hispanic Caribbeanists who teach in North American universities have had a role to play as predecessors to this dynamic. Before "transnational" became trendy, they had conceptualized these paradigms in analyzing the circular migration of Puerto Ricans. Luis Rafael Sánchez (1994) has called this the *guagua aérea* (air bus). Theorists of immigration have also proposed the term "transmigrant" in order to refer precisely to the impact of the immigrant and of his or her cultural production in their country of origin, a concept that counteracts unidirectional paradigms of assimilation and acculturation that inform traditional studies about immigration. The integration of Latin American studies with Latino studies offers intellectual as well as bureaucratic challenges. I think that the studies of transnational flow, of the processes of racialization, and of cultural studies can be promising conceptual frameworks that will integrate both fields. Of course, the understanding of political and economic relations between the United States and Latin American countries is always necessary in order to be able to study any Latino and Latin American community.

There are many recent works that exemplify the drawing together of Latin Americanists and U.S. Latinos. I am thinking of Silvia Spitta's book, *Between Two Waters* (1995), where issues of cultural hybridity and varied conceptualizations about *mestizaje* in the Andean, Caribbean, and Chicano cultural spaces are analyzed. The term "Latin(o) America," coined by Diana Taylor in *Negotiating Performance* (Taylor and Villegas 1994), integrates both cultural spaces. Suzanne Oboler, whose recent studies compare processes of racialization in Peru with those in the United States, is also contributing to cultural studies in the Americas.

These comparative and transnational approaches analyze important issues that illuminate the many modes of colonization that lead to cultural *mestizaje,* cultural hybridity, transculturation, and the like. For example, how do modes of colonization differ between the Andean region and the Chicano Southwest or Puerto Rico? What sort of politics, cultural forms, resistances, and transformations result from such social violence? According to Oboler, it is in the space of the body of the U.S. Latino where the different processes of North American and Latin American racialization come into conflict. What is or will be the impact of the diverse presence of Latin Americans in the linguistic politics of a country that has been officially colonized, like Puerto Rico, or in the Andean and Central American regions, or in the United States where Spanish has been displaced from a national language to one that is subordinate? All of these are issues that need to be analyzed by means of collaborative work.

However, I do not think that we should establish an opposition between the transnational tendencies of Latino studies, the drawing together of and convergence with Latin America on the one hand, and those who argue for the specificity and autonomy of Latino studies on the other. Intellectual practices don't always need to reflect bureaucratic structures or vice versa. A great number of Latin Americanists in the United States also work in the field of Latino studies, although not all of them consider it their primary area of investigation, a gesture that still reveals the secondary role of this discipline relative to the others. In my own case, I began to write about Latino authors just after I completed my doctorate on Latin American literature. After many years, a colleague recommended that I not stay in the field of Latino studies since, according to him, it would not remain long as a field of study, and besides it was a very politicized field (as if Hispanic studies or other fields of study were free from ideologies and politics!).

Now that some Spanish departments are beginning to include this field of study and the literary canon that produced it, I understand that many candidates who have left Latin Americanist programs present themselves for those positions without really knowing the field in depth. I do not say this to criticize, but rather to demonstrate the secondary role that it still has and the lack of seriousness with which it is defined. It is important to recognize that Latino studies, although it might involve a less extensive tradition, is a field of studies with a vast body of primary texts and academic criticism. It has its own history, its theoretical complexities, and is characterized by great diversity. I have met students who have graduated as Peninsularist literary critics and who never took a course about this literature but who, later, as professors, need or wish to offer these courses without previous preparation. Autonomous spaces, then, are necessary in order to prevent this kind of trivialization of the field, institutionalizing and legitimatizing it.

Besides, as Pedro Cabán (1998) has elaborated, the epistemology and political origins of Latin American studies and Latino studies are very different in a way that makes the convergence of both disciplines, as if they were one, impossible. However, it is obvious that today there are more possibilities and a greater need for transnational studies between what is Latin American and what is U.S. Latino. This convergence, though, must not force a total assimilation of Latino studies within the bureaucratic space of Latin American studies. I say this because in order to be able to produce excellent transnational studies, it is necessary to know both "local" Latin America and the Latino United States in depth. These transnational studies would not be possible without the work of Latino scholars who specialize in certain specific national and ethnic groups and who document regional and social realities.

As an example of what I consider problematic in the convergence of the Latin American and the Latino, let's consider the work of Ilan Stavans, *The Hispanic Condition* (1995). This book tries to offer a hemispheric view of what is Hispanic and examines literary texts as well as figures from popular culture. But the positionality of its author, who obviously ignores the bibliography available on the Latino literary field and on the sociolinguistic elements in the communities, leads him to underestimate the Latino barrio writers and Spanglish as compared to the more "universal" works of Mexican and Argentinean elites. By his lack of insistence on the historical, social, and political differences in the emergence of these literary texts and cultural productions, Stavans offers not a transnational study but a superficial, comparative one from the elitist social position that permeates his entire work. This explains the controversy surrounding the fact that Stavans has become, ironically enough, the Latino studies spokesperson of the U.S. establishment. On the other hand, it is true that transnational studies suggests the possibility of transcending or erasing the boundaries between so-called area studies and ethnic studies.

Epistemological differences, which have to do with problems we assume in each field, converge up to a certain point, for example, when we analyze the impact of immigration politics not only in Latino communities but also in their countries of origin. In other words, in what ways does circular migration, the return of U.S. Latinos to their countries of origin, be it a temporary or permanent return, present the possibility of transformation in the identity paradigms of original communities as well as in the concept of U.S. citizenship? In this context, theories of racialization pertinent to U.S. Latinos could be applicable to the study of said returns. The subject of remittances to Central American countries and Mexico also reveals the need to document the consequences of this infraeconomy in living conditions, in patterns of consumption, and in the national economy of the countries of origin.

In this case, the issue of Latin America's political economy cannot be analyzed without taking into account the presence of U.S. Latinos. In the case of Puerto Rico, which represents, I think, a space in which the problems of both fields converge, we cannot analyze the processes of Americanization on the island without taking into account those that take place in the diaspora. In addition, the political economy of Puerto

Rican sectors in New York cannot be explained without acknowledging colonial and economic relations between the United States and the island, a subject that has traditionally been relegated to Latin American studies.

Again, I insist on the fact that the boundaries between Latin American studies and Latino studies can be transcended on the intellectual level, but it is not necessarily productive at the bureaucratic level. Also, collaborative and collective work would be an ideal structure for transnational and hemispheric studies since the importance of various areas of specialty would be recognized without falling into the dangerous trap of erasing some fields in order to privilege others. The tension you allude to in your question is precisely that which is produced by the interstitial position occupied by Latino studies. In other words, some professors have been trained as Latin Americanists, while many others, in particular the Chicanos, have studied Chicano literature within the literary tradition of the United States. Latino studies belongs to both spaces and to neither in its totality.

The positive thing is that the field nourishes itself with a diversity of perspectives; the students can study the same texts and recognize significant intertextualities that would be different in each discipline and cultural context. The multiplicity of cultural positionalities, then, enriches Latino studies, creating a vast and very complex field. However, as I mentioned before, interdisciplinary study is more of an ideal than an academic reality. The field of Latino studies is multidisciplinary. In other words, it is an amalgam of professors' individual contributions from different approaches. It is the sum of all of the disciplines and of the work that focuses on a national group. There is a great need for more comparative and Pan-Latino work, which is not easy to fill, since each national group has a history, traditions, and an extensive multidisciplinary bibliography. The intersection of cultural theories, poststructuralism, popular culture, and new historicism makes obvious that the field of Latino studies has been one of the most important spaces in the development, application, and questioning of those theoretical frameworks.

There is a general acknowledgment that interesting theoretical formulations are being developed that permit the study of subjectivities in relation to three variables: class, race, and gender. Could you comment, as an example, on the concept of border and which aspects of reality it engages?

I think that the theorization and development of the concept of a border subject and hybrid identity has been one of the most significant contributions of Latino studies to cultural studies. The border, as both cultural concept and metaphor for bicultural experience, has been used since the 1960s by Chicano and Puerto Rican writers and critics. Studies of borders as geographic, social, material, and historical entities have preceded their metaphoric usage. Gloria Anzaldúa's conceptualizations in *Borderlands/La frontera* (1987) of that geographic space as a metaphor of any bicultural or multicultural experience encouraged the wider use of the term in other fields and prepared the ground for analysis of the border or hybrid subject in North American, African-American, and European studies. As usually happens during the process of appropriation and rewriting by dominant entities, the border ceased to be a real and metaphoric space. From this point, the underlying violence of cultural exchange and of historical colonization between the United States and Mexico, or between the countries of the First World and the so-called Third World, could be examined. In Latino studies, the border functions as the "wound" between both worlds proposed by Anzaldúa, as the image of colonial violence that gives way to cultural hybridity; or as a symbol for the immigration process; or as a conceptual basis useful for the analysis of the Americanization of the family by means of the Latina woman's body; or as the suppression of Spanish as a national language: an icon of pain, emotion, and material, social, cultural, and personal repercussions that are imbricated in said movement from one subjugated culture to a dominant other.

It is interesting to distinguish between the use of this term as it has been used by dominant intellectuals and its use among minorities. Hegemonic use tends to dilute both the colonial aspect and the cultural violence that characterizes the border subject, presenting a much more ideal and harmonious vision of the intercultural experience, universalizing the border subject. In contrast, Latino scholars have emphasized what is called *Nepantla* in Nahuatl: that experience of living between two cultures, not always as victims but never completely free as cultural agents or historical subjects. As a result of the dominant discursive tradition that has construed us as victims with neither power nor agency or as invisible beings without identity, Latino academic production has tried to offer an alternative perspective in which Latinos, as border subjects, are not a homogeneous group, but rather a multiple entity whose ideologies are being constantly negotiated, tolerating hegemonic forces and dominant structures as well as resisting and opposing them, while introducing social changes at different levels and producing new and complex positionalities for the cultural subject.

Currently, one of the most interesting aspects in this context is the appearance of hybrid Latinos, not so much in the sense in which Néstor García Canclini (1995) studies hybridity, but rather as Pan-Latino or interracial identities. These subjects are articulating new interstitial positions that critics had not previously been able to theorize, but now we can reflect on new demographic patterns in the redistribution of Latino groups within the United States.

In this sense, the object of Latino studies is those communities that have experienced a history of colonization and subordination by American state institutions and the resistance strategies of those so subordinated. This subordination includes cultural and linguistic colonization, Americanization processes, racialization, economic and social subordination, and discrimination. As a result, historic participation by U.S. Latinos has remained invisible as has our historical agency in terms of the development of what is considered North American culture. Latino cultural studies, in particular, examines the forms of resistance articulated through subaltern cultural production as strategies in which Chicano, Puerto Rican, Cuban American, and other subjectivities are negotiated and then produced through the available multiple discourses. The concept of *Nepantla,* which articulates life between two cultures, need not be exclusively Latino, although it does reaffirm the effects of colonial and neocolonial regimes in the articulation of bicultural subjectivities.

Borders are strategically established and historically contingent. Given the history of Chicano studies, we need to recognize that the concept of border continues to be geocultural as well as postmodern and hybrid. Anzaldúa's work expands its geocultural nature when coining the idea of borderlands even as it reaffirms it. In other words, I do not think that the concept of borderlands is useful in other contexts if we do not recall its roots in the colonial politics of the Southwest, in the history of Chicano oppression in Texas, and in the physical and cultural violence that colonization implies. It is not arbitrary that Chicana authors like Norma Cantú in *Canícula,* Sandra Cisneros in *Woman Hollering Creek,* and Helena María Viramontes in *Under the Feet of Jesus* have insisted on the geocultural and geographic aspect of the border subject faced with his or her universalization. Also, Pablo Vila's work reminds us of the very complex reality of the border between Ciudad Juárez and El Paso, which articulates the processes by which Mexicans on both sides continue to affirm cultural, racial, class, and other borders.

These authors insist on the specificity of the border as a sociopolitical and cultural reality informed by the border subject's experience within the United States. Analogous concepts, such as the *guagua aérea* (air bus), and "tropicalizations" have also circulated as working tools that facilitate discussion about transnational circulation of culture, people, money, and intercultural representations. If "Nepantilismo" need not be exclusively descriptive in the U.S. Latino context—in fact it derives from the colonial Mexican context—then Latino border subjectivities in the United States are unique in the type of colonization they experience and in the inter-Latino configurations that are developing within this particular context. For example, Latino studies has to cover different subjectivities and hybrid experiences negotiated by the diversity of immigrants from Latin America to the United States. Not all Latin Americans in the United States have experienced North American colonization similarly in manner or degree, even as they live in this country and even when relations between the United States and their native countries have been a central factor in their immigration. Differences of class, skin color, education, gender, and access to resources are key factors in the possible economic and social integration of immigrants. These internal differences must be objects of study in Latino studies. The issue is not necessarily the placement of geographic and academic borders in Latino studies, but rather one of widening our knowledge about the hybrid border subject as it changes in history.

The rewriting of the concept of border has had both positive and colonizing repercussions. In the field of North American studies, this concept has permitted a series of transformations in the literary canon and critical corpus that are changing that which is being studied and defined as "American." It has opened doors for the study of the Americas, precisely that which José Saldívar (1991) proposed in his book and which is illustrated today in articles by Oboler, Arlene Torres, and other scholars who integrate analyses of racialization processes in Latin America and in the United States.

Similarly, the concept of border has traveled across disciplinary demarcations with very little, if any, acknowledgment of Latino theoretical contributions. A meticulous review of the bibliographic references of many postmodern, postcolonial, and cultural studies that examine the border subject in other national contexts reveals that the work of

Latino academics is seldom cited, while the texts of postmodern and postcolonial hegemonic theoreticians are privileged even when they themselves are minorities or "ethnic." In this sense, the use of the concept of the border and its academic circulation has duplicated colonial conditions that we Latinos still confront as minority subjects.

What status do cultural contributions by Hispanic minorities enjoy? What status does the production of knowledge about them have in American society? Of what does the canon of literature consist as well as other Latino cultural manifestations such as performance art?

Cultural contributions by minorities of Latin American descent in the United States are very diverse in terms of their visibility and general acceptance within the dominant Anglo society. In 1988, *Time* magazine dedicated an issue to Latino contributions in American society. The title on the cover, "Magnífico: Hispanic Culture Breaks Out of the Barrio," implied that the cultural productions associated with the working class and with the barrio were neither obvious nor significant.

As a socioeconomic identity is diversified, the possibility of entering into the center and dominant spaces becomes evident. Invisibility has characterized U.S. Latino culture, despite the presence and visibility of Latinos in urban centers such as New York, Miami, Houston, Chicago, and Los Angeles, which has increased to the point where they cannot be ignored. In the Midwest, however, the battles fought by Latinos are characterized by the need to establish our presence within the context of interracial relations between whites and blacks, the binary that has been the dominant paradigm of multiculturalism. That this should occur more in the Midwest and the East Coast, although Latino presence has been much more obvious and acknowledged by official discourse in the West, is of interest.

Cultural productions by various Latino populations are not a recent phenomenon, but rather are the result of the long historical presence of Hispanic culture in the Southeast, South, and West of what is today called the United States, a territory that has always enjoyed a Mexican and Hispanic profile, what the Chicano movement has called Aztlán. To describe the vast quantity of Latino cultural production since the conquest and colonization would be impossible. In fact, there is a reigning need to investigate the "Latinidad" of the past, since the greater part of the research on U.S. Latinos has been focused on the cultural production of the 1960s and after, a justifiable focus in terms of the cultural renaissance that arose from the political consciousness-raising in communities. The Recovery of the Hispanic Literary Heritage project sponsored by Arte Público Press, a collective project that sponsors scholars interested in recuperating said heritage, has already had a great impact in filling this void.

In literature as well as in the visual arts, popular music, and movies, the mainstreaming of Latinos within the dominant Anglo society has been clearly visible since the 1980s. There is a recognition, however contradictory, that Latino communities are cultural agents whose contributions to American society are valuable and worthy of study. Everything Latino is more apparent: beginning with "La Bamba," Hollywood has facilitated the production and development of what we would today describe as Latino cinema. In the realm of popular music, salsa and Tex-Mex have acquired recognition and popularity as crossover music, leading to the Latino boom toward the end of the 1990s. In literature, writers such as Sandra Cisneros, Ana Castillo, Helena María Viramontes, Cristina García, Esmeralda Santiago, and Judith Ortiz Cofer, among others, are integrated into the large American publishing houses whose distribution networks are international. Reviews appear in the *New York Times Review of Books* as do articles in popular magazines that allow recognition beyond literary and academic circles. Visual arts exhibits have exposed Latino visual artists to the dominant American mainstream.

This recognition, however, implies a contradictory social construction of Latino cultural production. The polyvalent concept of "tropicalizations," which Susana Chávez-Silverman and I have developed in an anthology of the same name (Aparicio and Chávez-Silverman 1997), illuminates these processes of appropriation and mainstreaming. On the one hand, there is a positive recognition that actually makes national territory international; on the other hand, it implies as well a hegemonic tropicalization in which much of this recognition is delineated through the categorizations and power of American society, which redefines, selects, and determines both the value and significance of these productions for a new intercultural Anglo public. Néstor García Canclini's (1995) work is indispensable in understanding this process of *resemantización* through which Latino cultural production must pass.

Literature is fascinating in this respect, since it is clear that each publisher has selected one Latino writer as its own special, representative figure. Literary works are announced and discussed, in many cases, outside the historical, social, and political context from which they arose. The same happens with popular music, which has been canonized by a very limited number of attractive singers for an American, Anglo, and Caucasian public and which has been reinscribed within a very different set of values from those implied in the political, cultural, and class significance of Latino and Latin American communities.

So these cultural productions are placed in a space that continues to be marginal, permitting a higher degree of oppositionality. This can be seen very clearly in the dramatic and performing arts of John Leguízamo, Mónica Palacios, Carmelita Tropicana, Marga Gómez, Guillermo Gómez-Peña, and Coco Fusco. They are simultaneously resemanticized and reinscribed with more normative and dominant values that make them attractive to a dominant American public whose reception reaffirms its dominance over minority cultures. I do not want to deny, however, the enormous progress that we have experienced in terms of visibility and integration by American culture. I can't help mentioning the presence of salsa and Latino jazz as background music in many television commercials. Once limited to ads touting Latino food or restaurants, today they are background to battery, food, car, and insurance ads. This whole gamut of themes suggests cultural integration yet also transforms them into objects of consumption rather than social and cultural practices. The Grammy awards won by Carlos Santana for *Supernatural* in 2000 demonstrate that Latino music is finally leaving an auxiliary or international music market and that it is being considered an integral part of American popular music. Even more significant is the fact that this recording constitutes a collection of songs and arrangements that articulate social criticism of the American society and its system.

Describe the problems and limitations confronted by Latino studies specialists. How are new foundation and finance policies affecting them? More precisely, how have they been affected by the recent support of globalization studies?

One of the prevailing obstacles to the development of Latino studies is new legislation against university affirmative action programs. This law is already having disastrous consequences in both Texas *(Hopwood v. State of Texas)* and California (Proposition 209). Enrollment of minority students in academic programs has been decreasing. If one of the main functions of Latino studies has been its decolonizing role in the production of knowledge about and by Latinos, then without students who are trained to continue developing the field academically, it will run the risk of disappearance. Without students, there will not be enough registration to justify either courses or professorial salaries. We will see a chain of cause and effect that could lead to the total disintegration of these programs.

Conservative fiscal policies have accomplished the consolidation of many of these programs, combining them with others inside the same units, which leads, inevitably, to greater competition for resources as well as limitations on academic programs, courses, faculty, and admission of graduate students, who constitute the field's future. This fiscal threat reveals the colonized position of Latino studies within the university. Most departments and disciplines are also suffering from budget cuts; however, their very existence has never been threatened to the same extent. In spite of the gradual institutionalization of Latino studies programs, negative and racist attitudes still prevail, the majority of which insist that this intellectual practice does not constitute a serious academic field, but rather the political interests of one group. This suggests a lack of objectivity in our teaching and investigation. These attitudes have serious repercussions on promotion evaluations for Latino studies academics. Forming committees with colleagues who are familiar with the history of the field and who can evaluate the contributions of their Latino colleagues in such a context would be difficult. Numerous cases exist of professors who did not receive tenure because of this discrimination against both the field and its criteria.

Another detrimental idea is that one Latino studies specialist per department is sufficient, as if it were a secondary field that can or should be represented by a lone figure. This implies that the field itself will always be in a precarious situation and dependent on the presence of one expert to offer courses and train graduate students. For six years my graduate courses were categorized as "special topic seminars," as if U.S. Latino literature were a marginal subject, "special," and therefore extraneous to the literary canon of the Spanish program. These examples illustrate the institutional racism that continues to limit the field's progress and development as well as the professional worth of the Latino intellectual.

In terms of financial policies, I agree with you that the new tendency to privilege the global over the national has limited possibilities of investigation for Latinos. I do think, however, that there are positive repercussions, as in the recognition that U.S. Latinos are part of a greater Latin America. This has inspired research that will focus precisely on cultural interchange between migrants, diasporas, and countries of origin. The growing circular nature of international migration has inspired this approach, and global studies could also contribute to this perspective. It all depends on the definition of globalization and the ideology with which it is either greeted or rejected by a particular intellectual. It is impossible to judge, for now, whether this new financial policy will positively or negatively affect Latino studies. It is our responsibility, as intellectuals, to utilize available resources in producing knowledge about U.S. Latino communities, both in immigration, a field in which Latinos have proposed alternative paradigms, and in studies of racialization, hybridization, and transculturation processes. Embarking on collective, interdisciplinary, and comparative projects between Latin Americanists, North Americanists, and U.S. Latinos would also be useful. For example, in 1998 we examined the centennial of the Spanish-American War and the 150th anniversary of the Treaty of Guadalupe Hidalgo. It was a useful reflection on the legacy of North American colonialism in the Caribbean, the Pacific, and the Southwest. Funds for global studies made this type of collaborative project possible.

"Globalization" is a term that encompasses many meanings. The study of global processes between Latin America and the United States could dovetail well with Latino studies—in terms of technology, money, immigration, labor studies, or popular culture. This would be an examination of the ways in which ethnic minorities have had limited access to sources of power as well as economic and social benefits, exactly that which globalization was supposed to have ensured. In other words, if we do not pay attention to power differentials established by globalization as a form of neocolonialism and of ways in which we can resist said inequalities, then those approaches will not be pertinent to Latino studies. This is a central difference in discussing the specificity of Latino studies, since one of the main objectives of this field is, precisely, decolonization in its broadest general meaning.

If the formation of Latino studies is related to the essentializing of a Hispanic minority in the United States, in what way does this essentialization reinforce or counteract specialists who affirm the existence of Latino specificity? Of what do the processes of essentialization such as tropicalization and criminalization consist?

We must distinguish between different kinds of essentializations or social constructions of the U.S. Latino experience. The Latino studies category unites national sectors with different immigration histories as well as different socioeconomic, racial, linguistic, and ethnic profiles. In this sense, "Latino studies" is a rubric that homogenizes social diversity and converges, to a certain point, with the proposal by the federal government in the early 1980s to group us all together under the same term. It was the rise of the "Hispanic" census category, according to Oboler in her book, *Ethnic Labels, Latino Lives* (1995), which served to decrease the impact of nationalist cultural discourse and of the politics of the Chicano and Puerto Rican movements. This strategy gave way to a national nomenclature and a collective definition encompassing various nationalities. Political polls, however, have clearly indicated that individuals primarily identify themselves by national identity, be it Mexican, Chicano, Puerto Rican, Cuban, Peruvian, Salvadoran, or Nicaraguan. According to sociologist Félix Padilla, they identify themselves as Latino or Hispanic for strategic purposes, for example, when they organize politically for necessary services such as better education, housing, and social services. This indicates that these social constructions do not always function systematically, but rather as strategic and functional "essentialisms" that are used in order to organize movements and increase social power. More recent studies, such as that of Mérida Rúa (2001), reaffirm a Latino space formed by interactions, mutual influences, and cultural dialogues between U.S. Latinos of disparate national origins. This inter-Latinism proposes a space that is not politically strategic, as defined by Padilla, nor inevitably homogenizing, but rather a hybrid cultural space, a domestic transnationalism that transcends national borders.

Within Latino studies there are specialists whose research and training have concentrated on a specific national group, such as Chicano, Cuban American, or the Puerto Rican diaspora. This is comparable to Latin American specialists who study only Argentinean or Chilean literature or the Mexican economy. These national tendencies are also evidenced in the United States due to temporal or financial limitations on scholarly interest. There are also Latino studies specialists in comparative studies who focus on historical processes or cultural constructions between different national groups.

The study of popular music illustrates the intercultural, interracial, and hybrid nature of Latino cultural constructions. If salsa still resonates powerfully as a national icon among Puerto Ricans and Cubans, then its structures, its aesthetics, and its music are also a product of exchanges that have occurred among Caribbean musicians, between Caribbean and

African-American jazz, and, in California, among Caribbeans, blacks, Mexicans, and Central Americans. In other words, cultural constructions circulate across national borders and lead to very complex intercultural and interracial dynamics through processes of production and reception. However, the value of culture as a national space will continue to be viable while these groups continue being colonized. National reaffirmation gains popularity as a result of globalization, and therefore the work of younger generations will be critical insofar as the Pan-Latino development of the field is concerned. Will national models be followed, or will comparative, inter-Latino, or interracial studies question previous paradigms? Dangers obviously exist in the creation of superficial scholarship that theorizes cultural, historical, or social processes without possessing a deep understanding of the specificity of any group. Of course, this danger exists in every field and is, unfortunately, preponderant in cultural studies.

These social constructs of "Latino" diverge in their origins and functions. Your question covers processes of essentialization such as tropicalization and Latino criminalization, processes that obviously arise in the dominant society and pit themselves against identity constructions such as Latino studies or that arise from the same communities. In our introductory essay to *Tropicalizations: Transcultural Representations of Latinidad,* Susana Chávez-Silverman and I propose "tropicalizations" as a multiple concept that includes simultaneous but ideologically different processes that constitute cultural identity as a social construct. An example of hegemonic tropicalization would be the vision of Latinos criminalized within the United States through state legislation against immigration, the Latino as an undocumented alien, or the Latino who speaks Spanish like a social criminal. The criminal Latino, according to American institutions, is precisely one who maintains and reaffirms his or her values and cultural identity as well as one who resists assimilation. Many oppositional cultural practices are tropicalized in this way. Hegemonic tropicalization gives way to a discourse that delineates the Latino as an exotic and primitive cultural other, the dominant society's object of desire. These discourses continue unabated in tourism, education, cinema, music, and literature.

In contrast, U.S. Latino communities themselves continue to tropicalize American culture from subaltern positions. The systematic presence of Latin music in official spaces, such as Washington, D.C., in jazz festivals, in night clubs, and in discos, exemplifies the transculturating power of "Latino-ness" within American society. Of course, Latin music is oppositional due to its historical tradition, but that does not diminish either its meaning or its social value. The productive moment, that is, the process of reception on the part of an intercultural audience, constitutes in itself a moment of social significance that may or may not be, depending on the listener, analogous with its oppositional social value. One would have to take into account the complexity and simultaneity of said social construction processes within Latino studies in order to arrive at a less fixed or essentializing conclusion regarding the multiplicity of U.S. Latino/a subjectivities.

NOTES

1. Juan Flores, "Latino Studies: New Contexts, New Concepts" (chapter 9 in this volume), analyzes this structural phenomenon that has limited the growth of ethnic programs established in the 1970s.
2. A recent example of changes in the national paradigms toward what is Latino is the Program of Chicano Studies at the University of California, Berkeley, which has modified its name to Chicano and Latino Studies. This change, however, triggered opposition on the part of the nationalist Chicano student body.

REFERENCES

Acuña, Rodolfo. 2000. *Occupied America: A History of Chicanos.* 4th ed. New York: Longman.
Anzaldúa, Gloria. 1987. *Borderlands/La frontera: The New Mestiza.* San Francisco: Spinsters/Aunt Lute Press.
Aparicio, Frances R. 1993. "Diversification and Pan-Latinity: Projections for the Teaching of Spanish to Bilinguals." In *Spanish in the United States: Linguistic Contact and Diversity,* ed. Ana Roca and John M. Lipski. Berlin, New York: Mouton de Gruyter. 183–98.
Aparicio, Frances R., and Susana Chávez-Silverman, eds. 1997. Introduction to *Tropicalizations: Transcultural Representations of Latinidad.* Hanover, N.H.: University Press of New England. 1–17.
Cabán, Pedro. 1998. "The New Synthesis of Latin American and Latino Studies." In *Borderless Borders: U.S. Latinos, Latin Americans, and the Paradox of Independence,* ed. Frank Bonilla, Edwin Meléndez, Rebecca Morales, María de los Angeles Torres. Philadelphia: Temple University Press. 195–215.
Chabram, Angie. 1991. "Conceptualizing Chicano Critical Discourse." In *Criticism in the Borderlands: Studies in Chicano Literature, Culture, and*

Ideology, ed. Héctor Calderón and José David Saldívar. Durham, N.C.: Duke University Press. 127–48.

Chabram-Dernersesian, Angie. 1999. "'Chicana! Rican? No, Chicana Riqueña!': Refashioning the Transnational Connection." In *Between Woman and Nation: Nationalisms, Transnational Feminisms, and the State,* ed. Norma Alarcón, Caren Kaplan, and Minoo Moallem. Durham, N.C.: Duke University Press. 264–95.

García Canclini, Néstor. 1995. *Hybrid Cultures: Strategies for Entering and Leaving Modernity.* Trans. Christopher L. Chiappari and Silvia L. López. Minneapolis, Minn.: University of Minnesota Press.

Moraga, Cherríe. 1983. *Loving in the War Years: Lo que nunca pasó por sus labios.* Boston: South End Press.

Oboler, Suzanne. 1995. *Ethnic Labels, Latino Lives: Identity and the Politics of (Re)Presentation in the United States.* Minneapolis: University of Minnesota Press.

Rivero, Eliana. 1989. "From Immigrants to Ethnics: Cuban Women Writers in the U.S." In *Breaking Boundaries: Latina Writings and Critical Readings,* ed. Asunción Horno-Delgado, Eliana Ortega, Nina M. Scott, and Nancy Saporta Sternbach. Amherst: University of Massachusetts Press. 189–200.

Rúa, Mérida. 2001. "Colao Subjectivities: PortoMex and MexiRican Perspectives on Language and Identity." *Centro: Journal of the Center for Puerto Rican Studies* 13, no. 2 (fall): 116–33.

Saldívar, José David. 1991. *The Dialectics of Our America: Genealogy, Cultural Critique, and Literary History.* Durham, N.C.: Duke University Press.

Sánchez, Luis Rafael. 1994. *La guagua aérea.* Río Piedras: Editorial Cultural.

Sandoval, Chela. 1993. "Oppositional Consciousness in the Postmodern World: U.S. Third World Feminism, Semiotics, and the Methodology of the Oppressed." Ph.D. diss., University of California, Santa Cruz.

Sommers, Joseph, and Tomás Ybarra-Frausto. 1979. *Modern Chicano Writers: A Collection of Critical Essays.* Englewood Cliffs, N.J.: Prentice-Hall.

Spitta, Silvia. 1995. *Between Two Waters: Narratives of Transculturation in Latin America.* Houston, Texas: Rice University Press.

Stavans, Ilan. 1995. *The Hispanic Condition: Reflections on Culture and Identity in America.* New York: HarperCollins.

Taylor, Diana, and Juan Villegas, eds. 1994. *Negotiating Performance: Gender, Sexuality, and Theatricality in Latin/o America.* Durham, N.C.: Duke University Press.

CHAPTER 2

Capitalism and Geopolitics of Knowledge: Latin American Social Thought and Latino/a American Studies

Walter D. Mignolo

To the memory of Richard McGee Morse, Anglo-Latin historian and a pioneer in building North–South dialogues

"Latinamericanism" is in my view a profession defined and practiced in the United States, in a similar vein to what "indigenismo" was in Mexico before Chiapas. And the reasons in both cases are equivalent and analogous. On the one hand, because it is a way of insertion into the academic and professional market. On the other, because there is a similar "patronizing" mode on the part of the professionals, academics, or state-persons, in both cases. None of that has anything to do with the critique of local and global powers that we practice in Latin America.

—*Anibal Quijano, personal correspondence*

In this essay I will explore the epistemic grounding and political goals of three different but interrelated intellectual and institutional projects: Pensamiento Crítico (PC) in Latin America, and Latino/a studies (LS) and Latin American studies (LAS) in the United States. I am aware, of course, that there are different orientations in each of these three projects, that some of them are mutually critical, that it is difficult to talk about one project in each case, and so on. Yet there are some basic principles, mostly unsaid, that link the variety within and make a particular version recognizable, for example, Latino/a studies not Latin American studies. There are also links across projects, although these links are not necessarily strong enough evidence to say, for instance, that Latin American studies and Pensamiento Crítico (Zemelman 2000) cannot be detached from each other. PC tends to investigate problems while LAS tends to study objects. It would be possible to find that there are cases of studying Latin American issues and taking them as objects in Latin America and in Spanish, and I would guess that the orientation toward Pensamiento Crítico is practically absent from Latin American studies, but it is not, of course, absent from Latino/a studies. My goal in this article is simply to work on the borders of each project.[1]

"Globalization is changing the world" has been a common dictum used to describe, in one stroke, the changes affecting the world after the end of the Cold War, the increasing dominance of neoliberalism, and the increasing tendency to believe that capitalism and democracy are inseparable companions. This image that has been introduced and is maintained from the right works both nationally and transnationally. Nationally, it is at the core of the assumptions and arguments that the United States and countries of the European Union use to deal with the internal economy, with massive immigration, and with the control of dangerous turmoil in the Third World. Internationally, the image reproduces and maintains the global distribution of race, continental divides, and labor. As a consequence, the image of Latin America has been changing, and cultures of scholarship cannot be alien to what is taking place at the level of the economy, the law, and the army. What are the intellectual roles, the ethical and political responsibilities of PC, LAS, and LS when confronted with issues such as Plan Colombia, ALCA, the Gatekeepers in the south of the United States and the north of Mexico?

There is a set of related issues to be explored. Knowledge is currently being evaluated in an ascending chronological order, with certain paradigmatic examples as points of arrivals. At the same time, there is an intriguing parallel between the institutional locations of financial and economic "centers" (as in "shopping center" and not as in "center/periphery") and the institutional locations of epistemic and intellectual centers. Even though a sector of the epistemic and intellectual production goes against the political orientation of the financial and economic powers, the fact remains that intellectual and scholarly global designs, from the right and from the left, emanate from the locations of financial and economic centers. With this picture in mind, remember that while

Latin American and Latino/a studies are located in the United States and written in English, Pensamiento Crítico is located in Latin America and written mainly in Spanish and Portuguese. Furthermore, if we take into consideration French and English in the Caribbean, we notice that there is a significant difference between Caribbean English and U.S. and Canadian English; similarly, with Caribbean French and Canadian French. The difference is not, of course, in the grammar or the vocabulary of the language, but rather in the colonial difference. Racially, economically, and politically French and English Caribbean are marked by the history of the colonial divide.

My argument presupposes that knowledge shall be looked at spatially and not (only) chronologically. Chronological ordering of intellectual and scholarly achievements is one of the most damaging principles of modern epistemology, which runs parallel to the modern economy: what is new is better, and the idea of newness is running the market. If the ideology of the market is to be applied to intellectual and scholarly achievements while geohistorical locations are not being contemplated and the colonial difference forgotten, then there is no possibility of taking knowledge production in Asia seriously. The same argument would be valid for Africa or Latin America as well as for languages that are not English, French, or German. The principles and procedures that underline modern conceptualization of knowledge (e.g., epistemology) tend to locate, for instance, Latin American studies "above" Pensamiento Crítico and Latino/a studies. And, of course, this "difference" (which indeed is a particular instance of the colonial difference) is at the core of my interest and of my argument here.[2]

THE PROBLEM AND THE ARGUMENT

I will argue that the emergence of (intellectual fields such as) Latino/a studies is contributing to making visible and remapping the geopolitics of knowledge. That is, who is producing knowledge/understanding? Where? Under what conditions and to what end? In order to move forward with this argument it is necessary to bring a third party into the conversation, one that doesn't have a proper name in the family of "studies" (as we will see, it is not by chance that this is the case), and that can be called knowledge production or social and philosophical thought in Latin America. This is what I call PC. Estudios de America Latina, in Latin America, has an entirely different meaning than the expression Latin American studies in the United States. For instance, the

Instituto de Estudios Latinoamericanos of the Universidad Autonoma de Mexico organized seminars for several years on "Social Thought in Latin America" that have been published in four collective volumes. Contrary to Latin American studies in the United States, Estudios Latinoamericanos in Latin America doesn't have the obligation to think and write "only about" Latin America but can think about the world (and Latin America) from a particular geohistorical location. These four volumes are indeed an exemplary reflection on the epistemology of the social sciences and are of enormous significance.

There were and still are institutional "branches" or at least institutional connections of LASA (Latin American Studies Association) in several Latin American countries. Journals like *Latin American Perspectives* and *NACLA* have been and are important avenues for intellectuals in Latin America, particularly for the possibility of publishing in English. The journals also offer a wonderful place of encounter between intellectuals and social scientists in Latin America and Latin Americanists in the United States. However, area (and Latin American) studies at its inception was a response to the needs of the Cold War and the needs of the United States to link knowledge of the world with national security (Cline 1966; Rafael 1994; Berger 1995, 66–101; Heilbrunn, 1996). Consequently, area studies is essentially an invention of the United States of America, and it is embedded in the genealogy of Occidentalism and Orientalism, its predecessors in the imaginary of the modern/colonial world. Latino Americanism is a member of this paradigm (Santi 1992). As a matter of fact, the very idea of Latin America was born at the same time that the idea of the Orient was being produced in Europe. For that very reason Latino Americanism is at odds with intellectual production in Latin America, although it is quite marketable in the United States and in Europe.

LAS, however, occupies a particular position that shall be kept constantly in mind. The general frame of area studies is that after World War II higher education in the United States devoted time, effort, and money to train scholars on parts of the world that had been remote, both geographically and intellectually, from mainstream academic concerns. Latin America, however, wasn't remote in either of these two aspects. First of all, the Americas, from the extreme north to the extreme south, have one important history in common: they are constitutive of the modern/colonial world and the extension of the West, or the Western

Hemisphere, as Thomas Jefferson labeled it. Therefore, when Latin America became part of "the areas to be studied," its epistemic location was different from the one occupied by Africa and Asia. The establishment of area studies placed Latin America in a double bind in relation to the United States. On the one hand, there was the common history of colonialism and nation building; on the other hand, the differential history of Europe (e.g., Catholics and Protestants; Anglos and Latins; the North and the South) was being reproduced in the former colonies. The emergence of a Latino population in the United States and of Latino/a scholarship is embedded in this double bind.

The Geohistorical Scenario

Let me prepare the scenario by pointing to and making visible the shadow of an absence. In none of the current Latin American and Caribbean countries would you be able to find an institutional locus of knowledge named "European" or "United States of America studies" that would be the equivalent of Latin American studies in the United States. The United States and Europe are not areas of studies for Third World countries. On the contrary, Europe and the United States provide "models" to study the Third World. If you were able to find institutions in the Third World that studied the First World, their function would not be equivalent to the functions of similar institutions in Europe or in the United States. Consequently, the creation in the United States of centers or institutes labeled North American studies (including the United States, Mexico, and Canada) are interesting new developments in the tradition of area studies. However, I will limit myself here to pointing out that this phenomenon shall be analyzed in the new configurations of capitalism and the geopolitics of knowledge related to emerging regional configurations (e.g., NAFTA) prompted by the last stage (e.g., after the fall of the Soviet Union) of globalization. In general, institutions such as the British Academy or the Alliance Française, say in Argentina, Bolivia, or Brazil, are institutions promoting British or French "culture" in the Third World and not research institutions for studying Europe, Britain, or France. The study of French, English, or German in Latin American universities is not related to Argentina's, Brazil's, or Bolivia's national security!

There are, then, some connections between geohistorical locations and knowledge production and the ratio that links the history of capitalism with the history of Western scholarship. The latter is the issue that will be explored here, taking the particular examples of Latino/a studies and Latin American studies in the United States and social and philosophical thoughts in Latin America. Loci of enunciations are not so much a question of the modern subject as they are a question of the coloniality of power and the structure of power and knowledge in the modern/colonial world. The very imaginary of the modern/colonial world that was built into cultures of scholarship, as well as the configuration of areas as fields of studies, make it look strange and difficult to imagine. The scenario is beyond the "normal" conceptualization and the assumed location of knowledge. Occidentalism, Orientalism, Latino Americanism, and area studies can be understood as a foundational paradigm, with different names, of the imaginary of the modern/colonial world, of modernity/coloniality. All these labels have been construed from the perspective of power by colonial discourses of different periods. They are, in other words, the labels by which coloniality of power, as an epistemic operation, organized and classified the world (e.g., as in First World and Third World, for example). I will also explore how this imaginary runs parallel to the growth and displacement of capitalism from northern Italian city states to the Iberian Peninsula, to the Netherlands and England, and lately to the United States.

There is a straight, albeit complex, connection between area studies (and particularly Latin American studies) and Occidentalism, a connection that cannot be cast in the same terms as Orientalism, although all of them belong to the same paradigm (Mignolo 1995b, 1996b). This is one of the consequences of the place of Latin America within the frame of area studies I just mentioned. Occidentalism became a foundational component of the imaginary of the modern/colonial world with the emergence, from the perspective of historical capitalism, of the Atlantic commercial circuit (identified as the discovery of America from the perspective of Castilian ideology) (Mignolo 2000b, 91–126, 49–60). After the crusades and up to the fifteenth century, what would become Europe was the land of Japheth, the land of Christendom or of the Western Christians. That the destiny of Japheth was to "enlarge" everything falling under his domains was already inscribed in the Bible. Thus, with the emergence of Indias Occidentales in the consciousness of Western Christians, the expansion of the West that was already inscribed in the Holy Scripture became a reality. Since English was not a hegemonic language in the sixteenth century, the current vocabulary was Latin or vernacular languages derived from Latin. So Occidentalis and Occidente were the words inscribed in the imaginary of an emerging modern/colonial world. Occidentalism was grounded and grew out of the writing of Spanish and Portuguese chroniclers to the criticism of French intellectuals in the eighteenth century who wrote about Indias Occidentales and America. Occidentalism, then, is the colonial imaginary locating Indias Occidentales in the world map, while (Latino) Americanism corresponds to the imaginary of nation builders in Latin America in complicity with an ascending French colonialism (Nutini 1996; Pagden 1996). Then it is converted by literary critics in the United States into Latino Americanism as an analogy with Orientalism (Santi 1992). As far as I know, "Latino Americanism" is not an expression used by intellectuals and scholars based in Latin America. In all likelihood intellectuals based in Latin America may feel that they are the object rather than the subject of Latino Americanism.

But let's go back to Indias Occidentales and the early construction of Occidentalism. Although the social sciences are an invention of the nineteenth century, in the sixteenth century the discipline of history was part of the canonical curriculum in any university of the Renaissance (Mignolo 1981, 1982), although history did not have a crucial place within the trivium (the lower division of the seven liberal arts), whose fundamental parts were grammar, rhetoric, and logic (Kiefer Lewalski 1986). It was a subsidiary discipline attached to rhetoric and related to poetics. Not until the sixteenth century did historiography begin to occupy a central role, when a significant number of treatises defined and branded history as an autonomous discipline. This process was simultaneous and parallel to the writing of the numerous chronicles and histories of Indias Occidentales. Thus, Indias Occidentales was the stamp that introduced Occidentalism as a fundamental aspect of the modern/colonial world. Indias Occidentales, or America, was considered from the very inception of this imaginary as the West, the colonial West. The colonial West was described, but no one expected descriptions of European Christendom from the perspective of the colonial West. The description of the colonial West was at the same time a description and self-definition of European Christendom, per genus and differentia specifica. The people of the colonial West were judged as people without history, that is, without a disciplinary foundation for knowledge and without past events relevant in the Christian world history. For that reason, philosophy in its theological/legal version was responsible for defining and describing the people of the Indias Occidentales according to the Christian chain of being, and history was the discipline responsible for telling the story of people without history.

What does all of this have to do with Latin American studies? The situation was different, of course, when in the second half of the twentieth century, area (and Latin American) studies took the place occupied four centuries ago by Occidentalism. Area studies divided the world between Africanists, Asianists, and Latino Americanists, but all of them were scholars based in the United States. Occidentalism and Orientalism were the two dominant epistemic paradigms from the sixteenth to the first half of the twentieth century. (Latin) Americanism (Nutini 1996; Pagden 1996) emerged in between both. It was the successor of Occidentalism, the ideology of imperial Europe, and it was also the affirmation of a subcontinental identity of the Creole elite building the nation-states, when nation-states emerged from the ruins of the independence wars in the early nineteenth century.

While Occidentalism was built upon the disciplinary formation of the Renaissance, mainly philosophical theology, law, and historiography, Orientalism was built on the disciplinary formation of the Enlightenment and the application of philology to the understanding of "oriental" languages and histories. The larger picture on which Orientalism was built was no longer the Christian distribution of people and land according to religion. Instead, the Enlightenment's secular classification of people by color (Eze 1997) became the new version of the coloniality of power as practiced by the new emerging colonial powers (England and France) and a new foundation and distribution of knowledge (Serequeberhan 1997). Northern European countries, Protestant rather than Catholic, were taking over Asia and Africa. The Americas had already been colonized, and, furthermore, there had been evidence since the last quarter of the eighteenth century that the era of colonial domination was arriving at its end. This feeling would be intensified by the independence of the United States from England, Haiti from France, and of several Iberian colonies from Spain and Portugal. However, the emergence of Orientalism presupposed the existence of Occidentalism in the imaginary of the modern/colonial world. They were the opposing ends of the same imaginary that made of the world a place to be described and spoken of. In between both was the invisible locus of enunciation, the knower organizing and naming the known.[3]

The emergence of area studies produced two interesting displacements, although still within the same paradigm. The first was geopolitical. The

United States, formerly a part of Indias Occidentales and, consequently, the known object of Occidentalism, became the locus of the knower, the locus of enunciation. While the locus of enunciation of Occidentalism had been situated in the Iberian Peninsula and that of Orientalism in France, England, and Germany, the locus of area studies was situated in the United States. Once again, the displacement of the locus of enunciation within the same paradigm runs parallel to the history of the displacement of capitalism from the sixteenth to the twentieth centuries. As a consequence, the geopolitical field of forces changed. Area studies contributed to the affirmation of the image of the South that had already emerged in Europe in the eighteenth century as the location of that to be known. One of the missions linked to area studies was to develop and modernize the known, the underdeveloped South. This mission was parallel to the missions associated with Occidentalism and Orientalism respectively, that is, to Christianize the Occident, the extension of Japheth as well as the world, and to civilize the Orient.

Thus, the new mission that accompanied area studies was to develop and modernize the South. As far as Latin America and the Caribbean were concerned, its inhabitants were no longer just Amerindians (as they set the stage for Occidentalism in the sixteenth century). They were Creoles (whites and blacks), immigrants (mainly from European descent), and a wide range of mestizos. LAS had plenty of subjects to deal with and to conjugate with modernizing and developing projects. Furthermore, the world had changed due to the emergence of socialism in the imaginary of the modern/colonial world and its implementation in the Soviet Union and, by the time of the institutionalization of area studies in Latin America, in Cuba. In spite of the distance in time, one element remains in common between Occidentalism in the sixteenth century and Latin American (area) studies in the second half of the twentieth century: the difficulties in recognizing the intellectual and epistemic values of the known subjects. None of the Amerindian intellectuals (Pachacuti Yamki, Alvarado Tezozomoc, Alva Ixtilxochitl), with the exception of Garcilaso de la Vega, were published and considered part of the knowledge being produced in/about Indias Occidentales. In the eighteenth century, Creole intellectuals in Mexico, like Eguiara y Eguren, raised their voices to dispel the accusations of Spanish men of letters about the lack of intellectual sophistication in the New World (Mignolo 1995a, 163–69). During the nineteenth century up to the 1970s, roughly speaking, Latin American intellectuals played into that game by modeling themselves on the scholarship and intellectual achievements of France, England, and Germany. Why did this happen?

Another displacement took place at the level of epistemology. While Occidentalism was founded on the Renaissance distribution of knowledge, and Orientalism on the secularization of philology and hermeneutics (no longer a tool for interpretation of the Holy Scriptures), area studies was founded on the social sciences that indirectly contributed to their consolidation (Heilbron 1995). But once the social sciences were institutionalized and began to replace the role occupied by the humanities—less connected with the conflictive social issues of the Cold War period—they began to be exported/imported to the Third World. The problem of native versus foreign social sciences emerged as social scientists in the Third World became aware that dependency was not only economic but also intellectual (Fals Borda [1970] 1987). Some of the dubious outcomes of this attitude were the overt links established between science and nationalism (Ramos [1955] 1995); a debate that has been reopened (Akiwowo 1999) since the publication of the Gulbenkian report on the social sciences (Gulbenkian Commission 1996). However, there were reasons for the dubious reactions. The creation of social science departments in Latin American universities only happened toward the end of the 1950s. Of course, there were *cátedras* of sociology or of social sciences in general, with a person "representing" the field, but not programs or departments in the contemporary sense of the word. Therefore, if the issue may not be properly framed by talking about foreign and native social sciences, the fact remains that the social sciences moved—a hundred years later—from the industrial countries where they were born to the colonial or excolonial countries during the Cold War. Once this happened, the standards, criteria, and norms of the social sciences in the First World became the measuring stick for the practice of the social sciences in the Third World.[4]

The belief in the abstract universality of science was taken for granted in area studies. Social scientists from their respective departments suspected and criticized that area studies scholars put at risk the rigor and objectivity of the social sciences. Area studies scholars were accused of loosening up disciplinary strictures, of moving toward interdisciplinary knowledge (which of course was suspected of lack of rigor) guided by a given "area" rather than by the questions and methods generated within disciplinary frameworks. Area studies scholars were driven by the interest in acquiring knowledge of a territory rather than the laws or at least regularities of human and social behavior. However, the disputes did not touch the belief in the abstract universality of sciences but rather confirmed it. This is one of the reasons why the "adaptation" of the social sciences in the Third World (Cold War era) was problematic. This is the main reason why intellectual production in the Third World was hardly acknowledged. And this is the reason why the issue of "native social sciences" or "foreign social sciences" emerged. Epistemology did not escape the geopolitics of knowledge. The distribution of scientific labor did not escape the distribution of labor in general. It is important to keep this point in mind, to understand that if ethnic and Latino studies are both a state project and a consequence of global capitalism, then nothing is new, or what is new is a transformation within capitalism and the geopolitics of knowledge in the sense that a new player (under the name of ethnic, Latino, Asian American [Vaidhyanathan, 2000], or Afro-American studies) entered the game and began to claim a piece of the pie.

But let's go back to the double scenario prompted by area studies. On the one hand, there were the debates in the United States between disciplines and areas, and on the other, there was the "absence" of former Third World intellectuals in those debates. The second scenario produced an interesting phenomenon. The social sciences in the (former) Third World, and by extension social scientists living in the situation they were reflecting on, were not allowed the same level of objectivity that was allowed to area studies scholars. As social scientists, they were observers and, as such, did not "belong" to the sociohistorical realities they were studying. This perception from the social scientist in the North about the social scientist in the South was in a sense correct. The most innovative social thought and knowledge in the South were produced at the intersection of sociopersonal interests (which doesn't mean individualistic and subjective) and disciplinary norms. In other words, in the South the most innovative works in social sciences were produced precisely by departing from the disciplinary control of the social sciences imposed in and from its place of origin. That the perception social scientists in the North had about social scientists in the South was correct (that is what happened) doesn't mean that it was right (what happened was bad). The destiny of dependency theory in the United States as opposed to its impact and influence in Latin America is a case in point.

The classic article by Fernando Henrique Cardoso, "O consumo da teoria da dependência nos Estados Unidos" (1977), is a case in point.

Cardoso pointed out that in Latin America dependency theory was the outcome of a political concern and of a dialectical way of thinking, but in the United States it was reduced to method, to constants and variable equations, and therefore interpreted and criticized from a "scientific" point of view. It all happened as if the critics of dependency theory were not personally invested in what they were saying, since they were just following the authorized norms of scientific procedures. In other words, the political investments of social scientists who in Latin America engaged in dependency theory were stripped out in the United States and replaced by the disappearance of the knowing subject in favor of the known. This is not surprising since we are now witnessing similar arguments in the United States against the political bent taken by the social sciences and the humanities, as if the status quo were not a political statement in itself. For Latin American social scientists, their field was a starting point and a point of reference to engage in thinking about specific problems, but for social scientists in the United States the question was centered on method rather than on problems. For this very reason it is quite telling that Frank Bonilla (1998) recalls a discussion at Stanford with Cardoso and members of the emerging field of Chicano studies. One could say that Chicano/a scholars found an echo in dependency theory in Latin America due to a casual encounter at Stanford prompted by a casual visit of a Brazilian sociologist. I believe that the encounter emerged from the profound ethical, political, and epistemic links between Chicano/a (and Latino/a) social scientists and social scientists and intellectuals in Latin America. The encounter at Stanford can explain both the tragic destiny of dependency theory among U.S. social scientists and Latino Americanists and its triumphant reception by a community of Latino/a scholars.

Chicano/a and Latino/a scholars and Latin American scholars (i.e., living and working in Latin America) have one thing in common: the incorporated epistemic relations with their subject matter. Contrary to their area studies counterpart, the subject matters of Latinos/as and Latin American intellectuals (that is, working in Latin America and "studying" Latin America) are not remote but right under their feet. I am not talking here about identity politics but of the politics of identities managed from above by Occidentalism, Orientalism, and area studies. I am not talking about "essences" but about historical living conditions in a planetary distribution of wealth, power, social conditions, and social identities. That is, the politics of identity of Occidentalism, Orientalism, and area studies have worked by identifying people by religions and colors with geographical locations from above. Identity politics have been and still are a reaction and an effort toward disidentification (Muñoz 1999), of moving away from the politics of identity. I am aware that even when successful in dispelling the phantom of essentialism (which is very much a creation and an imposition of modernity itself and not an invention of colonial subalterns), I may still run the risk of creating suspicions of subjectivities that are particular to those scholars who prefer the security of disciplinary norms and having knowledge dissociated from history and from the body, that is, scholars who prefer maintaining a locus of enunciation removed from the geopolitical organization of a capitalist economy. These were the assumptions, I am suggesting, of those scholars who reframed the dialectical and political dimensions of dependency theory to the parameters of scientific and disciplinary norms and were successful in dissociating the knower from knowledge and from the known. The subaltern, in fact, cannot speak on his/her own terms, although the right to speak should not be confused with the truth of the spoken.

Furthermore, while the epistemic choices of Latin American and Latino/a scholars impinged directly on ethical and political issues in their own countries and regions, Latin American studies scholars found themselves in a different position. They lived and pursued their research in the United States and were removed from the ethical and political situations of the country or area in Latin America they were studying. This quarrel has indeed required some Latin Americanists to take a more invested stance toward the "remote" subject matter of their investigation. At the same time, social scientists and intellectuals in Latin America after the 1970s were less interested in establishing dialogues with social scientists in the United States, be they Latin Americanists or not. From the time of the consolidation of the social sciences in Europe and the United States (at the beginning of the twentieth century) intellectuals in Latin America were proud of adopting the sociologist of the day in Europe or in the United States (Romero Pittari 1997). This move was part of the ideal of civilization and of the emerging project of modernization. Around the 1970s, however, with the wave of decolonization in Africa and Asia and the work of Frantz Fanon, sociologists began to call for a "decolonization of the social sciences" (Fals Borda [1970] 1987, 15–86) rather than for an adaptation of civilized or modern theories. This was also the time when Latin American intellectuals directly critiqued area studies in the United States (77–82).

From Occidentalism to Genealogies of Thoughts in Latin America and to Latino/a Studies

If we look at the trajectory from Occidentalism to Latino/a studies, we perceive that a detour was taken, that a change of perspective took place, and, consequently, that Latino/a studies does not stand in the same paradigm as area (and Latin American) studies. I would say that Latino/a studies is on the other side of the colonial difference, since Occidentalism and area studies are in the paradigm of local histories that produce and implement global designs while ethnic studies is not. Latino/a studies, instead, is part of an emerging paradigm of local histories whose raison d'être is to deal with global (epistemic) designs. One could offer another interpretation and say that Latino/a studies is oppositional within the same paradigm of Occidentalism as, for instance, Bartolomé de Las Casas was in the sixteenth century. I would prefer to say that Latino/a studies is oppositional in the sense that Guaman Poma de Ayala (at the turn of the sixteenth century) was with respect to Las Casas, that is, on the other side of the colonial difference, which is why Ayala's voice was not heard. Scenarios like this one can be explained from the perspective of capitalism and the geopolitics of knowledge, while they cannot be articulated in a historical and linear conception of knowledge organized on the principles of Western civilization or of national histories. One could say that Las Casas lost the battle against the Castilian state, but one cannot forget that Guaman Poma de Ayala was out of the battle altogether. These analogies are not perfect, but they are helpful in understanding the point I am trying to make and its historic density. Las Casas, in the last analysis, would be closer to leftist Latino Americanists than to Latino/a studies scholars. Perhaps David Stoll's (1999) take on Rigoberta Menchú may have something to do with being on a different side of the colonial epistemic divide. Perhaps invoking the ethical problem of lying is his excuse to speak the unspeakable as a social scientist, that is, taken by and prisoner of the scientific and not the social concept of truth. Perhaps this event is revealing something wrong with area and Latin American studies that has to be removed from their very foundation rather than debating whether Menchú or Stoll was right or wrong.

Pedro Cabán has described the institutional and political location of Latin American and Latino/a studies in a very useful way:

> The field of Latino Studies occupies a distinct niche in the academic hierarchy and is characterized by a profoundly different set of analytical

and political concerns. Latin American Studies was a top-down enterprise promoted by government agencies, university administrations and large foundations. In contrast, ethnic studies programs were interested in studying the "Third World within" the United States and *linking these studies to the "Third World without." The genesis of Puerto Rican and Chicano Studies departments was virtually the polar opposite of that of Latin American Studies.* The field came into being during a period of social ferment and were parts of an attempt to "uncover the occluded and submerged, to liberate the repressed in the process of shaping people's history. Their project was to redraw the boundaries, to affirm the autonomy of the internal colonies (barrio, reservation, inner cities) and thus recover the space for the exercise of popular democracy." (1998, 202)

There is, however, another aspect that distinguishes Latin American from Latino/a studies, and this is the epistemic one. Latin American studies (and area studies in general) were constructed on the disciplinary foundation offered by the social sciences, which meant that it operated on disciplinary norms and the principles of modern epistemology that detached the knower from the known. In more concrete terms, while Latino/a scholars were linking scholarship with Latino/a social and political issues, Latin American area scholars (in the United States) were far away from the place where social and political issues required the attention of their scholarship. Their best political move was, and has to be, directed toward U.S. government foreign policy in Latin America (Schoultz 1998). There were and still are connections within Latin American (area) studies and Latin American intellectuals, as can be witnessed in the journals *NACLAS* and *Latin American Perspectives.* But the dissidence within the main paradigm is not the same as the emergence of a new paradigm, such as Latino/a studies. That is, while Latin American (and area) studies are part of the larger paradigm of the modern/colonial world, together with Occidentalism and Orientalism, Latino/a studies are part of a paradigm today identified as ethnic studies, which is precisely not the location of the knower but the location of the known. Latino/a studies, in other words, is accomplishing the formidable task of turning the place of the known into the location of the knower. And that was also the achievement of social and philosophical thought in Latin America, particularly as formulated by dependency theoreticians, philosophers of liberation, and critics of internal colonialism. This is why there is so much in common between Latino/a studies and social and philosophical thoughts in Latin America, as is made clear in the narrative offered by Bonilla (1998).

Juan Flores (chapter 9 in this volume) has clearly traced the two stages in the formation of Chicano/a, Latino/a studies, and Agustín Lao-Montes (forthcoming) has offered a detailed history of these developments. The bottom line is that what we call Latino/a studies began as a form of social activism, if not a social movement, while today it is becoming institutionalized. This turn of events should not be taken either as a cause for celebration or as a nostalgic remembrance of good things past. It is, simply, the way it is. Ethnic and Latino/a studies (as well as the social sciences and area studies) did not escape the transformations of the global order after the fall of the Soviet Union. Regarding Latino/a studies, Flores summarized the situation in the following words:

> The main shift marking off the present context of Latino Studies from its previous manifestation twenty-five years ago is perhaps best summed up in the words "global" and "globalization," with all due caution of what [Robert Fitch] has aptly called "globaloney." The economic restructuring of world capitalism that took off in the mid-1970s along with the further revolutionizing of telecommunications have made for radically new levels of interaction and interconnectedness among populations at a regional level. The growing mass migrations generated by these changes are also affected by them, and in their circular and transnational character differ markedly from the migratory experiences of the early 1970s. (chapter 9 in this volume)

In the institutional transformation of Latino/a studies, the links with scholarly discipline were unavoidable. This is precisely my point: the intersection between Latino/a studies and the social sciences has an epistemic configuration that looks quite different from the configuration of area studies. As a matter of fact, it looks very much like the epistemic configuration of intellectual labor in Latin America that had to deal with the introduction of the social sciences and other disciplinary "novelties" in the humanities (structuralism, poststructuralism, postmodernism, deconstruction, and so on). The end result, at both ends of the spectrum, is the emergence of critical social thoughts merging the ethical and political drives of the intellectual or scholars with the disciplinary rules of the disciplines but from the perspective of the former. In other words, the problem precedes the method in the social sciences and the topic in area studies. These are the possibilities and potentials, which doesn't mean that they will necessarily end up producing good results. Possibilities and potential are there for grabs, and they can be used in different ways. And, simply, that is that. However, it is better to have the possibilities and potentials opened up by Latino/a studies than not to have them at all. Ethnic studies, Latino/a studies in the United States or philosophy of liberation, and the pedagogy of dependency theory or internal colonialism in critical social thoughts in Latin America have brought to light the epistemic colonial difference. And that is not a small victory under the present circumstances and the colonial structure of power.[5]

Let's go back to dependency theory to further argue this point. Mark T. Berger (1995) offers a detailed and interesting account of how, in the United States, dependency theory was eroded on methodological and ideological grounds. In that process, the Chicago-trained sociologist André Gunder Frank (1967, 1998) became, if not the owner, the representative (perhaps against his own will) of dependency theory in the United States. There is nothing wrong with Frank's book and the close connections he established with intellectuals in Latin America that were developing and debating on dependency and world capitalism. Indeed, Frank was a good translator of the conceptualization of dependency theory being developed in the Spanish and Portuguese languages in Brazil and several Spanish-speaking countries. However, against his good intentions, his English summary contributed to relegate almost to oblivion the theoretical production in Spanish and Portuguese (for the politics of language and epistemology, see Mignolo 2000b, chapter 6). This is part of Berger's report:

> The emergence and growing power of dependency theory represented a direct challenge to the dominant liberal discourses on Latin America; however, by the mid-1970s dependency theory had met its demise as the radical work on Latin America was accommodated by the liberal institutional structures of the North American university system, by the dominant professional discourses and changing political circumstances. *Dependency theory, as it came to be understood in North America in the 1960s, developed out of the North American Marxism of Paul Sweezy and Paul Baran and Latin American historico-structuralism,* which was initially associated with Raul Prebisch and the United Nations' Economic Commission for Latin America (Comisión Económica para América Latina, CEPAL). (Berger 1995, 106–7; emphasis mine)

That is true, although the problem with this account is that it is as if only the story of what happened in the United States counted. In Berger's account dependency theory doesn't have a life of its own, almost as if it doesn't exist outside of the U.S. academy, where it is part of the story of Latin American studies and Marxism in the United States. And this is precisely why the perspective on capitalism and the geopolitics of knowledge is so crucial. Dependency theory was indeed an intellectual event of enormous impact that was preceded by CEPAL (founded in 1948, two years after the creation of similar commissions for Europe, Asia, and the Far East). As is well known, Argentine economist Raul Prebisch, chair of CEPAL, proposed the differentiation between center and periphery in order to theorize development and modernization in areas that began to be labeled at the time (around 1952) as the Third World (Estay Reino 1994). And center-periphery opposition became a cornerstone (or a key word) in dependency theory.

The center-periphery dyad introduced by Raul Prebisch had re-markable consequences. The first was to conceive of capitalism as an international system of unequal endowment and to understand Latin America within that relation of forces. Second, it became a crucial concept for U.S. sociologist Immanuel Wallerstein in developing his theory of the modern world-system (2000). Third, it created the condi-tions for the development of dependency theory, which, as many of the theoreticians involved in the debate were aware, offered an analysis of capitalism from the perspective of its margins (Osorio 1994). This was not a small achievement. In fact, in 1974 when Wallerstein launched his theory of the modern world-system in terms of center, periphery, and semi-periphery, he (unwillingly) produced an epistemic displacement. That is, in his theory capitalism as an interstate system was no longer seen from the periphery but from the center. Consequently, dependency theory in the United States became absorbed by three kinds of allies: the economic debates originated by Paul Sweezy and Paul Baran (Berger 1995) in their books and in *Monthly Review*; the sociological theory of perspective introduced by Immanuel Wallerstein and developed, years later, in the Center Fernand Braudel at Binghamton (Wallerstein 1979); and Latin Americanists who questioned the methodological accuracy and the ideological underpinning of their proponents (Gereffi 1989).

Nevertheless, the theoretical production between the early 1950s and mid-1970s in Latin America is a story to be remembered. Independent of the destiny of dependency theory in the United States, the debate in

Latin America continued still in the early 1970s. In 1972 a manuscript version of *Dialéctica de la dependencia* by sociologist Roy Mauro Marini began to circulate and be discussed. The book was published in 1973, and the intense debates have continued until recently (Barreda Marín 1994). Parallel to this debate in the social sciences, there was a continuous production and discussion in the emergence (approximately 1970) and growth of the philosophy of liberation, parallel because philosophy of liberation responded to the more general episteme of dependency theory.

In this case, it was not economic but intellectual dependency that the philosophy of liberation began to strive for. The work of Enrique Dussel (1973), until these days, had been a constant adaptation and transformation of his inaugural thesis that he elaborated as a "third position." Dussel's third position is not in between but "next" to the other two. Dussel realized in the early 1970s after reading and interviewing the French/Jewish philosopher Emmanuel Levinas that the displacement Levinas was performing on the ontological toward a dialogical and face-to-face concept of being was not yet sufficient. Dussel realized that for Levinas the "other" face that brings being forward in dialogical interaction and that emerged from Levinas's elaboration on the historical marginality of Jewish people did not include Africans, Amerindians, or even people from Asia. Dussel founded from this differential, which I have called elsewhere the colonial difference (Mignolo 2002), the coloniality of being and consequently the coloniality of philosophical reflections in the Third World. Thus, the coloniality of being is not a hybrid between Heidegger's ontology of Being and Levinas's Otherwise than Being. While Heidegger's conceptualization presupposes the story of the Renaissance concept of Man, and Levinas's the story of the Jewish Diaspora, Dussel's responded from the story of coloniality and the modern/colonial world. He has continued developing and testing this thesis in recent debates with Karl-Otto Appel, Richard Rorty, Paul Ricoeur, and Giovanni Vattimo (Dussel 1994, 1996, 1999; see also Alcoff and Mendieta 2000; Mignolo 2002). The philosophy of liberation and its living tradition made a signal contribution to what today is being conceived as Pensamiento Crítico. And this contribution was parallel in time and shared some of the basic premises that are found in Pensamiento Crítico practice in the social sciences from dependency theory to internal colonialism.

At the end of the 1960s and in the early 1970s, Mexican sociologists

Pablo González Casanova (1965) and Rodolfo Stavenhagen (1965) introduced the notion of internal colonialism. This early step has informed their prolific and influential work since then, and coloniality has constantly been the perspective from which they have talked about modernity (González Casanova 1996; Stavenhagen and Iturralde 1990). It brought to light the fact that colonialism did not end with independence and nation building, but that in fact what happened was, as Peruvian sociologist Aníbal Quijano has explained recently, a reorganization of the coloniality of power. The early conceptualization of internal colonialism (parallel to dependency theory and philosophy of liberation) found its theoretical home in Quijano's theoretical bold move (1992, 1997, 2000). It also found its continuity in Bolivian sociologist Silvia Rivera Cusicanqui's attentive work on the diachronic contradictions in the history of Bolivia and the fact that modernity, in Bolivia, is something to be attained, while coloniality is what shapes everyday life. Rivera Cusicanqui is aware that while the colonial period may be over, coloniality is still alive and well in Bolivia as well as in the rest of the world. Her work clearly shows how coloniality (although she doesn't use this word) has been ingrained and reproduced in the Republican period in the history of Bolivia as well as after the revolution of 1952. She has brought to light, from the perspective of coloniality, many issues of political relevance (1992). For instance, she has persuasively addressed the question of ethnic and gender "rights" in the Andes (1996, 1997). She has pointed out the limitations of the social sciences to understand and foresee historical directions (1992) and has framed the conceptualization of *ayllu* democracy and liberal democracy (1990) in a perspective similar to the one that, a few years later, was taken by the Zapatistas. Finally, she (in collaboration with Bolivian historian Rossana Barragán) initiated a dialogue with South Asian subaltern studies (1997). This places the initiatives of the Latin American Subaltern Studies Group in the United States, still under the invisible umbrella of Latin America studies, into an entirely new light (Beverley 1996, 1998, 1999; Mignolo 1996a). Furthermore, it underlines the difficulties of a South-North dialogue in the scholarly and political domain I am discussing; the question is not just to study the subalterns, but whether you study them from/in the South or from/in the North.

I find it inconceivable that Latin American studies, in its various forms, has been so oblivious to such theoretical explorations in Latin America. I am trying to underline that Latin American studies is different not only from Latino/a studies, but also from the genealogies of social and critical thoughts in Latin America as well. While Latin American studies has offered sound and compelling descriptions and interpretations of Latin American society and history, I cannot think of a conceptual contribution equivalent to the richness of social and critical thought in Latin America. I suggested before that there was no such thing as Latin American studies in Latin American countries. There were, of course, "branches" of the Latin American Studies Association and institutional connections, but of course the projects emerging from the Latin American Studies Association and area studies were not necessarily projects matching the needs and intellectual drives of people living and working in Latin American countries. I am not assuming that living and working in Latin American countries is a warranty to truth, but neither is the academic setting in the United States nor the scientific assumptions of the social sciences there. Therefore, my argument addresses the project of the knower rather than the true rendering of the known. If the known was always already the "same" (e.g., Latin America), the knower would respond to the constraining call of the known rather than to the needs, impulses, drives, desires, and fears of the knower. Of course, this statement is valid from both the right and the left. There was and there still is cooperation between Latin American intellectuals and Latin Americanists in the United States, and publications such as *Latin American Perspectives* and *NACLA* are indeed good examples, as are publications like *Nueva Sociedad* in Caracas, *Casa de las Américas* in Cuba, and *Anuario Mariateguiano* in Peru. Places of interactions are good and are needed, but they do not imply common goals. The recognition of the differences doesn't imply that the "branches" of Latin American studies in Latin America did not have any consequence. They may not have had interesting consequences in responding to interesting intellectual projects brewed in the United States; however, such interactions were fundamental for the transformation of U.S. scholars such as André Gunder Frank, who by studying underdevelopment in Latin America has learned from dependency theory how to think about underdevelopment from the perspective of the Third World. Contrary to the destiny of dependency theory in the United States, Frank recognized in 1970, after his encounter with and participation in the debates on dependency theory, that he was "a schizophrenic intellectual that kept apart his political opinion and his intellectual or professional positions. I was used to accepting scientific theories as they came to me, without criticizing them. I forged my political criteria as responses provoked in me by isolated events. As many of my colleagues (in the United States), I was a liberal intellectual" (Frank 1997, 6; Chew and Denemark 1996).

To recognize the enormous impact of dependency theory in the 1960s and 1970s in Latin America does not imply that we should idealize it or that we should believe that it is in need of redemption. I am arguing that dependency theory is a pillar in the genealogy of social and critical thought in Latin America. I am further arguing that the "scientific" criticism it received in the United States offers further evidence that it was and is a pillar that cannot be erased and supplanted by managerial theories or by humanitarian interventions. ALCA (Area de Libre Comercio de las Americas) clearly shows that that particular version of dependency theory can be criticized, but that dependency is today an issue as valid or perhaps even more valid than it was thirty years ago. Dependency theory along with the philosophy of liberation are as fundamental in the genealogy of social thought in Latin America as are, for example, Marx, Nietzsche, Freud, Durkheim, or whatever you may have in different genealogies of European thoughts or in the genealogy of European (second) modernity.

A Highlight of the Current Scenario

Latino/a studies in the United States and critical social thoughts on Pensamiento Crítico in Latin America have a common epistemic, ethical, and political ground. In the first place, both are tangential to the social sciences in the sense that they cannot avoid them, but at the same time, they cannot submit to them. Submitting to the disciplinary norms of the social sciences would be precisely to lose the critical edge and to bend to the "white" epistemology presupposed in the current constitution and configuration of cultures of scholarship, which are modern and Western. Second, scholars involved in these projects will be more interested in producing knowledge directly related to the problems of their respective communities (ethnic, national, regional). Knowledge production directed to problem solving will take precedence over concerns for the method and adherence to disciplinary norms. This common concern brings the need in Latino/a studies and social and critical thought in Latin America for a recurrent critical reflection on the conditions and possibility of knowledge itself, a concern that has been quite alien to Latin American studies in the United States. The only moment in which the conditions and possibility of knowledge became a problem was when area studies began to be questioned after the end of the Cold

War. Obviously, area studies is not strictly an epistemic problem since neither LAS nor PC belong to the area studies project. Area studies was U.S. scholarship about the rest of the world and Latin America (and, of course, also social and critical thought, and Latin America became either an object of study or a nonexisting intellectual production from the perspective of area studies). And since area studies was about the rest of the world, Latino/a issues were not an international but a national issue. As such, Latino/a issues were part of the transition from the ideology of the melting pot to the ideology of multiculturalism. And thus, Latino/a scholarship was not given much consideration, since Latinos/as belong to the social paradigm in which knowledge is not expected to be produced.

LAS has followed two interrelated and complementary paths. One was the social sciences path (Cabán 1998), and the other the humanities path (Flores, chapter 9 in this volume). The humanities path echoed the trend in literary and cultural studies in the United States. There is, however, one particular aspect I am interested in underlining here: the instance in which Latino/Chicano/a studies intersects with Latin American literature and culture and becomes a theme as well as an issue. A parallel of this instance in PC can be found in the work of Néstor García Canclini (1989) and his interest in border culture. In both cases, however, the interest is in the "other side of the border" but not in the genealogy of social thoughts. LAS tends to draw its philosophical and methodological inspiration from European and U.S. cultural studies, while PC goes back to Marx and dependency theory, mainly, and from there a dialogue is established with current intellectual debates. However, the awareness of the need to remap the idea of critical thought (Pensamiento Crítico in LA) is more and more urgent. The claim is not to be seen as localism or a search for authenticity. On the contrary, it is what modern European intellectuals have done since the eighteenth century and what U.S. intellectuals learned to do beginning in the early nineteenth century.

Two significant steps were taken in the early 1990s to reach out and link Latino/a studies with Latin American intellectual production: José David Saldívar in his classic book *The Dialectics of Our America* (1991; see also Saldívar 1996) and Juan Flores, *Divided Borders* (1993). Saldívar's invitation, for instance, was taken up in Cuba by Roberto Fernández Retamar, who opened the doors of *Casa de las Américas* and the *Premio Casa de las Américas* to Latino scholars and intellectuals. Saldívar offers new avenues for the interconnection between Chicano, Latin American, and American literary and cultural studies. His main argument is the need to include José Martí and Roberto Fernández Retamar in the canon of American (i.e., U.S.) literary history. He makes clear that such claims come from someone who was born and raised in the border between South and North America. One can surmise that Saldívar is not saying that he captured an "essence," the essence of the borders, but that strong imprints were left in his body that later on he (as anybody else) could recast as his experience. Today the argument may no longer be structured in terms of the canon, but rather in terms of the end of an America divided in two, Jefferson's and Bolívar's America, Anglo and Latin America. The legacy of dependency theory reminds us that continental divides are illusions in a world that has been becoming more and more interconnected and interconnected within a particular imaginary (e.g., modernity/coloniality, the imaginary of the modern/colonial world since the sixteenth century). Continental divides are, in the first place, the end product of the imperial and colonial differences. Thus, the divide between Europe and the United States is today an imperial divide, while the divide between Anglo and Latin America is a colonial divide. And colonial differences are there to make sure that people with similar concerns in different locations of the continental divide remain apart, remain foreign to each other.

But this doesn't mean that a Pan-Latin/Americanism should be promoted. Rather, it would be more productive to be aware of the differences between Latinos/as and Latin American intellectual projects and at the same time recognize the similarities within those differences. Pan-Latin/Americanism would end up reclaiming the principles of universality inherited from modern epistemology. Diversality as a universal project would allow, precisely, the overcoming of the "low" market value under which Latin American and Latino/a intellectuals' projects are operating in the current global order. The second reason why Saldívar's book *The Dialectics of Our America* has to be remembered in this context is precisely because the first section is titled "Metahistory and Dependency," and the first chapter, devoted to Gabriel García Márquez, is titled "Squeezed by the Banana Company: Dependency and Ideology in Macondo." It will suffice to remember that 1967, the year of the publication of *One Hundred Years of Solitude*, was also the year in which dependency theory and philosophy of liberation were heavily discussed in Latin America.

Saldívar's book opened up a space for other projects such as Jeffrey Belnap and Raúl Fernández's *José Martí's "Our América": From National to Hemispheric Cultural Studies* (1998). Belnap, a professor in fine arts, and Fernández, a professor of social sciences, have removed José Martí's expression from its "natural" dwelling in Latin (American) memory. Latinidad becomes double here as it underscores the roots of Latin and Latino/a America and at the same time reveals Anglo (America) as necessarily implied in the definition of "Latinidad" (in South and North America). But Saldívar's book also opened the space for making other kinds of alliances between Chicana scholars and activists such as Sonia Saldívar-Hull. In her *Feminism on the Border: Chicana Gender Politics and Literature* (2000), Saldívar-Hull proposes two moves deeply relevant for the argument I am advancing. The first consists in establishing alliances between Chicana and Latin American writer-activists like Gloria Anzaldúa and Cherríe Moraga in the United States, and Rigoberta Menchú and Domitila Barrios de Chungara in Latin America. The second move consists of looking for theories in what Saldívar-Hull calls "the non-places" of theory such as prefaces, interviews, and narratives. That is, Saldívar-Hull is assuming that theories can be independent from disciplines. By underscoring the non-places of theories, she indirectly shows the geopolitical distribution of knowledge, the links between the place of theory in white feminism and the theoretical non-places of women of color and of Third World women (see also Aparicio 1998).

Latino/a studies may indeed be part of a state project that promotes multiculturalism. After all, area studies was a project that promoted both national security and the knowledge of foreign cultures, and before it the social sciences were needed for a project that linked the idea of progress to that of science. Nevertheless, they are not necessarily in the same neighborhood as their predecessors. I see Latino/a studies inhabiting the same neighborhood as critical social thoughts in Latin America (SCTLA), that is, critiquing the state while inhabiting it, but also critiquing certain forms of knowledge that have been detrimental for the emergence and flourishing of critical social thoughts in the form it has taken and still takes in Latin America and in the form it is taking in Latino/a studies. If it makes sense to think in hemispheric terms, this thinking shall not necessarily be promoted in the place of theory, offering an overview of what is going on under the hemispheric sky. It should, rather, provide information to promote links and build theories in order to legitimize academic and political claims from subaltern positions.

In spite of the Internet, intercontinental scholarly and intellectual connections are not yet easy even when they seem obvious. Many of the issues raised by Saldívar-Hull within Chicana feminism have also been raised by Silvia Rivera Cusicanqui and Rossana Barragan (in the past ten years), in the colonial history of Bolivia, and from a postcolonial perspective grounded in the genealogy of social and critical thoughts in Latin America. One of the most prominent issues raised in relation to gender and ethnicity is the future of democracy in Bolivia, of course, but in Latin American countries more generally. Unlike the United States, where democracy may not be perfect but works in certain ways, the situation in Latin America in the past fifty years has been less than satisfactory in this regard and with few exceptions does not promise to get better. For that very reason, scholarly projects (similar to Chicano/ Latino/a studies) are dictated by social imperatives rather than by disciplinary norms. Nevertheless, the similarities between women and indigenous people in Bolivia and Latinos/as in the United States should not be dismissed. Recognition of social similarities between groups of people in the Latin and Anglo America will help in linking intellectual projects by people who belong precisely to those groups.

The legacies of dependency theory can be linked with recent research and publications on globalization and a critique of modernity from the perspective of its alternative versions, that is, of alternative modernities. The reason for following this path is to suggest the connections in the concerns being explored by Latinos/as and Latin American intellectuals. I am also assuming that the differences between them and Latin American studies (in their more traditional forms or in the more recent subaltern and cultural studies versions) are also being revealed. If I am paying more attention to Latino/a and Latin American intellectuals, it is because they are less visible, because their link is totally invisible, and their genealogies generally forgotten. For instance, the most significant works on globalization in Brazil (Santos 1994; Santos et al. 1994; Ianni 1995, 1997; Ortiz 1997, 1998) start from or presuppose the concept of the modern world-system and dependency theory. Both concepts are indeed part of a genealogy in Latin American critical social thoughts that is not a nationalistic one, but rather one that offers scholars on the margins an academic perspective and an ideological location. The fact that Frank Bonilla made a link with this genealogy should not be forgotten. Genealogies and links here reveal common colonial histories for intellectuals in Latin America and Latinos in the United States. The principles underlining Cabán's description of Latino/a and Latin American studies are not far removed from the principles underlying Milton Santos's distance from Anthony Giddens's (that is to say, from official sociology's) conceptualization of space. There is "something else" in Latino/a studies and Santos that prompts the need to take such a distance. That something else, I submit, is the awareness of thinking from the colonial difference rather than doing so from the stricture of disciplinary and institutional norms (social sciences, area studies).

Santos (1994) has argued, for example, contra Anthony Giddens, that the space of our time is not empty but full. Santos distinguishes between "hegemonic time" (the time of larger economic organization and the time of the state) and "non-hegemonic time" that, by the end of the article, he calls "subaltern time." Technology here is of the essence, since Santos observes that for the first time in the history of humankind technology is the same all over, in the East and the West, in the North and the South. Technology is the same yet that does not mean it is equally distributed, for there are hierarchies. However, the hierarchies are not in technology itself but in its economic distribution and social access. Consequently, the temporality of hegemonic actors is not the same as the temporality of nonhegemonic actors on a global scale. There are, today, a global time and a global space, but they only become "visible" in global places hierarchically organized all over the globe. But the question is not between hegemonic space/time and subaltern places. Places are the only thing we have, so to speak, yet there are hegemonic places where the lived space/time coincides with managerial time/space and places where hegemonic space/time has to be negotiated and articulated with nonhegemonic lived time.

> Places *[lugares]* today are different from each other and hierarchically ordered precisely because they are all global *[mundiais]*. Times too (both dominant and subaltern temporalities). The so-called global space is constituted by the relationships thus established between all places *[lugares]*. So-called global time is constituted by the global possibilities actually used and enacted by hegemonic agents. The rest are subaltern temporalities. This is the empirical base of globalized time and space, without which no particular instantiation is intelligible.[6]

Santos is not talking about center/periphery but of hegemonic and subaltern times and places. His argument, however, is not located in the hegemonic time and space but underlies his epistemological subalternity in the global order of things. If technology is the same all over the world, as he argues, the hierarchies are not. Thus the technological network is historical and epistemological simultaneously. However, the legacy of dependency theory and its global perspective on capitalism remains as a genealogical reference for current research on globalization from a subaltern perspective.

Santos's argument can be connected with arguments with different contents but similar logic advanced by Octavio Ianni and Renato Ortiz, both in Brazil. Renato Ortiz made the distinction between globalization and "mundialization" (that is, between the global and the worldly). The fact that such a distinction was introduced by an intellectual in Latin America and not, for instance, in Germany, England, or the United States may have some relevance. The distinction between globalization and mundialization parallels Santos's distinction between hegemonic and nonhegemonic space/time and their interaction with hegemonic and nonhegemonic places. In the first, lived and managed time coincide, while in the second they enter in conflict. Mundialization therefore is the subaltern perspective in which globalization is enacted. But because of the correlation between lived time and managerial time in, say, Germany or the United States, it is more difficult to perceive, from those places, the subalternity of mundialization and of subaltern time/ spaces. Which, of course, doesn't imply that if you are in a subaltern location you will automatically have such a perception. I am saying that subaltern locations enable such a perception, not that they determine or impose it. Furthermore, subalternity and marginalization are not subject matters for Ortiz and Santos, as they can be, for example, for Alain Touraine. They are lived experiences that nourish conceptualization and the theoretical imagination.

Ortiz devoted a chapter in the new edition of *Otro Territorio* (1998) to comment on the social sciences and the historical location of their practice. Let me summarize his argument in three points. First, in the 1990s the perception of "native" and "foreign" social sciences was not the same as in the 1970s, which doesn't mean that hierarchies have been erased just because a postnational take on the issue was being advanced. What distinguishes, for example, French from Brazilian social sciences is not that one is foreign and the other is native, but that they have a different disciplinary memory in the way that the social and historical object was constructed. For instance, the state has been a crucial object in France and in Europe in general but not necessarily in Latin America and in Brazil. Thus a category like "bourgeoisie" is not really universal. It is appropriate for a specific situation of European history, but it is very problematic to understand Latin American oligarchies and the caste system in India (trans)formed by colonialism, or to understand Japanese society in the Meiji era in terms of the European bourgeoisie. Topics like youth or mass media that today transcend national frontiers, precisely because of globalization, are global phenomena that cannot be reduced to a universal concept embracing Chinese and Bolivian youth or mass media in France and in Senegal. Ortiz's distinction between globalization and mundialization points precisely to the irreducible epistemic difference that critical social thoughts should reveal constantly. Otherwise, conceptual universality and knowledge about the world will remain as the indistinguishable similarity between the global and the universal. Latin American critical thoughts and Latino/a studies, although working within the capitalist global design and its geopolitics of knowledge, have the possibility of working toward social transformation and linking their particular and interconnected local histories.

Second, social sciences in Brazil or Latin America should not necessarily be characterized and defined by a series of canonical topics such as *mestizaje,* colonialism, rural tradition, industrial impasses, or popular culture (Ortiz 1998, 186), although these are some of the subjects that made Silvio Romero, Euclides da Cunha, and Nina Rodriguez the precursors of social thought in Brazil. So, if there are no national and foreign sciences, as it was formulated in some cases in the 1970s, it is also true that up to that moment it was as if it were the case. The civilizing mission and modernization ideology came with a string attached and made people believe that "transplanting" social sciences was a civilizing gesture and a modernizing move. In a postnational and global era, however, "social sciences" can only be a "connector" between people in different parts of the world having a more or less common vocabulary, a more or less common way of doing things, elements that can gather together in institutional (regional, national, or international) associations. In that precise sense of being just a "connector," the social sciences are global and, of course, hierarchically organized. There is a new epistemological place for the practice of the social sciences that is not exactly the nation but the nation at the crossroads with the global. The hierarchy depends on the global structure of capitalism and on the relationship between languages (French, English, and German) in relation to the hegemony of knowledge. This doesn't mean that you cannot think in Portuguese.

It means that you are not always heard in the international debate. Contrary to critical social thought in Latin America expressed in Spanish and Portuguese, Latin American studies is an institutional discipline that presupposes English as the official language. Latino/a studies, on its part, operates in a bilanguage register (see Mignolo 2000b, chapter 6, for the distinction between bilingual and bilanguage/bilanguaging). As far as epistemology is embedded in language, the fracture with English as an official language of knowledge is another place where Latino/a studies and Latin American studies meet in confrontation with hegemonic structures and institutions of knowledge.

Third, there are some topics that are more relevant than others to reveal the hierarchical divide and the distribution of scholarly and intellectual labor geopolitically. Dependency theory, for instance, was developed under the force of national and subcontinental ideologies, yet the same could be said about the development of the social sciences in Europe:

> Rarely discussed by European and American authors, since they have no interest in making explicit the limitations of their own thought, [eurocentrism] has marked the social sciences since their origins. I am not only referring to eurocentrism as an ideology, as does Samir Amin, a culturalism whose particular roots are turned into the universalism of "Western Civilization." . . . What I highlight is the existence of a conceptual eurocentrism that impregnates analysis and directs reflection in a completely counterproductive direction.[7]

Ortiz explains this point by analyzing the question: why did capitalism originate in the West? Beyond the fact that the question asks for a historical answer, the question itself is ideologically tainted. It presupposes that the West is an existing entity where capitalism originated and not that the West originated as a consequence of capitalism, as the imaginary of the social actors involved in a given economic restructuration. Eurocentrism is not the ideology of an existing place, but the ideology that makes itself a place. The location of modern epistemology and the social sciences is part of that ideology and, in that sense, a historical and epistemic hierarchy has been established in the complicity between capitalism and the geopolitics of knowledge. These are central issues that have to be addressed to imagine a future in which continental and ethnic divides will continue to keep Latin American and Latino/a studies in the United States apart from social thoughts and cultural critics in Latin America and the Caribbean. The question I am raising is not that of the unified study of the Americas but that of conversations about the complicity between forms of knowledge and the construction of the idea of America and its historical subdivisions.

CONCLUDING REMARKS

First, I would like to stress that Latino/a studies has much more in common at this point with Pensamiento Crítico in Latin America and with its genealogies of thought than with Latin American studies in the United States. The latter draws its epistemic and methodological orientations from the genealogy of the social sciences and from influential thinkers in Europe and the United States. Dependency theory, the philosophy of liberation, and internal colonialism are indeed crucial components of Pensamiento Crítico in Latin America but not of Latin American studies in the United States. Latin American studies in the United States "studies" Latin America, but its thinking frame comes from the genealogy of the social sciences and from contemporary influential thinkers whose foundational genealogy is in Western European legacies. Or, if you wish, it is in the critique of capitalism from its very periphery as dependency theoreticians will have it and all the Marxist tradition thereafter, both of which inform social and critical thought in Latin America and have been and still are alien to Latin American studies. These are, indeed, epistemic subaltern locations in space/time, as Santos prefers to say. Or they are locations of particular subaltern disciplinary memories, articulated with the hegemonic (Eurocentric) assumptions of the social sciences (Ortiz 1997). In every case, the perspective is bottom-up, as Cabán (1998) would like to say. On the contrary, Latin American studies, even when it takes a most radical leftist position, remains a top-down enterprise heavily tainted by Eurocentric beliefs implied in disciplinary norms.

Second, current discussions in the United States about the links between Latino/a and Latin American studies are totally alien to the Latin American intellectuals I have discussed here, and with good reason, since this is apparently not a matter for their concern (García Canclini 1999). Unless the discussion gets beyond the limits imposed by the ideology of area studies and becomes guided by the genealogies of social thought in Latin America and Latino/a studies in the United States, these three worlds will remain detached and suspicious of each other. Latin American studies can still have its function as a top-down academic enterprise in which the study of Latin America functions not to transform Latin American society but, mainly, to transform U.S.–Latin American international relations. That is, Latin Americanists would have to assume that the ethical and political implications of their scholarly work should also be directed toward the United States (for example, Grandin 2000) or mediated between both Latin American intellectuals and Latin Americanists (Cadena 2000; Stern 1998; Starn 1999), mediated in the transformation of U.S.–Latin American relations and in the transformation of cultures of scholarship in the United States rather than in the transformation of Latin American societies, and finally, mediated in their own transformation in contact with progressive intellectual production in Latin America (as Frank's self-description illustrates) rather than the other way round.

Let me close with some examples that illustrate the distinctions I have been arguing for in the three different projects I have loosely identified here as Pensamiento Crítico in Latin America, Latin American studies in the United States, and Latino/a studies in the United States. Let's contrast John Beverley's *Subalternity and Representation* (1999) and Frances R. Aparicio's *Listening to Salsa: Gender, Latin Popular Music, and Puerto Rican Culture* (1998). Beverley opens with the following:

> This book can be read as a conversation with Ranajit Guha, so my first acknowledgement is for the example of his work, and for the friendship and solidarity he has shown me and the Latin American Subaltern Studies Group. My personal introduction to subaltern studies came at a meeting of the South Asian Subaltern Studies Group that Gayatri Spivak organized when she was director of the cultural studies program at the University of Pittsburgh in the late 1980s. . . . Spivak's *A Critique of Postcolonial Reason: Towards a History of the Vanishing Present* (1999) came out as I was correcting the proofs. But at least some of its concerns are anticipated, and sometimes, echoed, here. (ix)

For her part, Aparicio writes the following:

> This interdisciplinary incursion is, first of all, an act of love toward the Latina/o culture and people. I have seen, among those Latinas and Latinos whom I have known and loved, the destruction and pain that cultural displacement, exclusion, and internalized colonialism can create. At the same time, I have also witnessed firsthand the strength that we hold in our power of affiliation, cultural resistance and affirmation. . . .

Simultaneously, this project is a declaration of war. As a porto-riqueña who still resists being labeled a feminist scholar, I cannot but critique from within, the traditional masculine discourse that continues to imbue everyday lives as Latinas-os with blatant objectifications and insidious mutings of women. (xi–xii)

Now let's compare an example from a Latin American project with an example of Pensamiento Crítico in Latin America. In the preface to his edited volume, *Colonial Legacies: The Problem of Persistence in Latin American History* (Adelman and Aron 1999), Jeremy Adelman writes:

> History telling in Latin America has long been about colonial forma-tions and their legacies. Our collection of essays tackles this enduring tradition of writing Latin American history and diagnosing the seem-ingly endemic difficulties of democracy and the rule of law. More than other Atlantic societies, Latin America appears shackled to its past, especially to its colonial heritage. For some, this yields to postcolonial exotica; for others the past is a scourge on the present. What persists is persistence itself. (ix)

On the other hand, distinguished Mexican sociologist Pablo González Casanova and Marcos Roitman Rosenmann, editors of the volume *Democracia y Estado multiétnico en América Latina* (1996), write the following:

> Democracy has not always been the force *[el motor]* on which propos-als for the articulation of political power in Latin America have been developed. Moreover, democracy's different formulations are the result of permanent social struggles that incorporate new subjects and political forces from civil society, subjects and forces that demand a redefinition of political contents. Thus, the emergence of a multiethnic democratic project is the effective demonstration of the existence of a social force that manifests its specific weight in the struggle for democracy by claim-ing the right to ethnic difference and plurality in the construction of truly democratic power in Latin America.[8]

Several observations can be made here. Adelman's paragraph is written in English while González Casanova and Rosenmann's is in Spanish. All the contributors to Adelman's book are based in U.S. institutions, and most of them were born and educated in the United States; all the contribu-tors to González Casanova and Rosenmann's volume are based in Latin American institutions, and all of them were born and educated in Latin American countries, including Rigoberta Menchú (Guatemala), Darcy

Ribeiro (Brazil), and Xavier Albo (Bolivia). González Casanova and Rosenmann's volume built on a long tradition of Pensamiento Crítico about colonialism. González Casanova himself introduced the notion of internal colonialism in the late 1960s; Rosenmann built on Aníbal Quijano's concept of coloniality of power; Darcy Ribeiro is well known for his constant critique of colonialism and Rigoberta Menchú for her testimony as well as her activism. In other words, González Casanova and Rosenmann's volume is not only about the colonial history of Latin America but also about building on the tradition of Pensamiento Crítico and the political dimension these kinds of scholarship have in the countries and (Latin) American subcontinent. When looking at these two volumes, one understands how different Latin American studies projects in the United States are from projects that emanate and continue to expand the tradition of Pensamiento Crítico in Latin America. These are, indeed, two different worlds. But Aparicio and Beverley inhabit these same worlds. Beverley prefers to have a dialogue with Guha and Spivak about the subalterns in Latin America; Aparicio prefers to reflect on her embodied relation with knowledges that have been taken away from her (a form of subalternization of knowledge) and entertains a dialogue about Puerto Rico with Latino/as. That is, her reflections are very much in line with Pensamiento Crítico in Latin America. Indeed, part of the knowledge Aparicio refers to that has been taken away by colonial education is Pensamiento Crítico itself. It was my argument here that it is imperative to strengthen the legacies of Pensamiento Crítico in Latin America, which is the basis on which Latino/a studies has been built. In my understanding, this foundation can be summarized in Aparicio's dictum: "This book originally emerged out of my desire to give a personal and cultural meaning to academic work, that is, out of a profound need to reclaim the knowledge about Puerto Rican culture that had been denied to me through a colonial education" (1998, xi).

While it is necessary to make statements such as this explicit in the United States, I have been suggesting that Pensamiento Crítico, in Latin America, has always operated under these implicit premises. "Political meaning to academic work" is perhaps a more just expression to describe what Pensamiento Crítico has been doing, but it will apply to Aparicio's work, too, and by extension I would say to most of Latino/a creative writing and scholarship. Latin American studies is built on a different set of premises, more respectful of disciplinary norms and more suspicious of the personal and political involvement that is so evident in Latino/a studies and in Pensamiento Crítico. And, of course, disciplinary norms have the prestige that the hegemonic politics of knowledge attribute to disincorporated knowledge. Disciplinary norms, very much like "whiteness" in racial classifications, have the privilege of being the point of reference for the other categories. In a different domain, ethnic food can be classified as such in relation to an unnamed kind of food that is not ethnic and that coincides with the standards set by the discourse of economic and military (but also cultural and epistemic) hegemonic countries.

Perhaps the moment has arrived to open up the debate about Latino/a studies and Pensamiento Crítico in Latin America as guidelines for the transformation of Latin American (and area) studies. The implications of a change of direction in the politics of knowledge are crucial for imagining democratic futures. It is not enough to produce knowledge about Latin America with honesty and high-caliber scholarship. Honesty and quality contribute to reproducing the subaltern position to which Pensamiento Crítico and Latino/a studies have been placed within the distribution of knowledge in U.S. institutions and intellectual life. On the other hand, from the perspective of those who practice Pensamiento Crítico in Latin America, this is not a direct problem within Latin America itself but in the international distribution of intellectual labor. Pensamiento Crítico in Latin America, written in Spanish and Portuguese, doesn't have the influence that, for instance, the Frankfurt School (where German is the language of scholarship) or South Asian subaltern studies (where English is the language of scholarship) does. I am not here seeking recognition or a benevolent inclusion of Pensamiento Crítico in the international canon of the North Atlantic. Recognition and inclusion are always decided from the hegemonic perspective. Only those who are in power can include and recognize. No, I am pointing out a difference that should be taken as the platform for epistemic and political interventions from the perspective of Pensamiento Crítico itself. I see a need to make clear, in the international arena, what Pensamiento Crítico and Latino/a studies have to offer to a planetary scholarly conversation no longer dominated by the intellectual production of England, France, and Germany from the past three hundred years.

Notes

I wish to thank Agustín Lao-Montes for various conversations on these issues and for letting me read the manuscript of his lengthy essay "Latin/o Americanisms: Epistemological and Political Challenges" (forthcoming in *Nepantla:*

Views from South). Second, I wish to thank Juan Poblete for his critical observations on the first draft of this article. I have also benefited from conversations with José Ramón Saldívar, Linda Alcoff, Ramón Grosfoguel, Fernando Coronil, and Eduardo Mendieta in the United States. I am also thankful to intellectuals and scholars in Latin America for a dialogue and a reflection on their own conceptualization of their intellectual, political, and academic projects. These are Edgardo Lander (2000), Zulma Palermo, Enrique Dussel, Catherine Walsh, Aníbal Quijano, and Santiago Castro-Gómez in Hispano-America; and Renato Ortiz and Enrique Rodríguez Larreta in Luso-América.

1. Two important meetings of people who have been developing a set of interrelated theoretical explorations with a political and ethical dimension *in* Latin America and the United States took place in 2002. These meetings were very important for the argument and the suggestions I advance here and for the consolidation of a new *koyne,* a coherent school of thought, across the Americas. Of course, I am not talking about the emergence of a school of thought *in* Latin America *for* Latin America or *by* the Latinos/as and *for* the Latinos/as. On the contrary, I am talking about the emergence of a *koyne,* a conceptual corpus that has gained its place *next to, parallel to,* and *alternative to* existing schools of thought that emerged and prospered in Germany, France, or England, as well as existing and influential schools that emerged and prospered in South Asia and its diaspora. A first encounter took place at Berkeley, in April 2002, organized by José David Saldívar and Ramón Grosfoguel, with the participation of Enrique Dussel, Aníbal Quijano, Norma Alarcón, Laura Perez, Nelson Maldonado Torres, and students and faculty at Berkeley. The purpose of the meeting was to bring into conversation theoretical debates and political issues taking place in Latin America with Chicano/a Latino/a issues in the United States. A second meeting took place in Mexico City the following September, under the auspices of the new Universidad de la Ciudad de Mexico, and in particular under the project of Pensamiento Crítico en América Latina under the leadership of Chilean sociologist Hugo Zemmelman. In both meetings, but particularly in the second, an articulation of Pensamiento Crítico in the sense of critical social thought inscribed in the history of intellectual and theoretical production in Latin America, with a clear political and ethical consciousness, emerged. The new school of critical social thought is being articulated around key concepts such as "coloniality of power, of knowledge and of being," "geopolitics of knowledge," "trans-modernity," and "pluriversality and border thinking," based on the work of Aníbel Quijano, Enrique Dussel, and Walter D. Mignolo, and extended by Ramón Grosfoguel, José David Saldívar, Nelson Maldonado Torres, Santiago Castro-Gómez, Catherine Walsh, and Edgardo Lander, among others. On the other hand, it should be mentioned that the scholarly and ideological perspective that orient the majority of the six thousand social scientists affiliated with CLACSO (Consejo Latino Americano de Ciencias Sociales) has more in common with the majority of social scientists affiliated with LASA (Latin American

Studies Association) than with the school of critical social thought I mentioned here and explore in more detail in the following pages.

2. By "Latin American studies" I am referring to the scholarly work done basically under the principles of the Latin American Studies Association. Academic associations are buildings with many rooms; however, there is something that allows people to recognize each other under that roof, a family resemblance of a sort; everybody knows what the Latin American Studies Association is. On the other hand, there have been several "departures" from the hard-core principles of LASA. The work of John Beverley has opened up a discussion on Latin American cultural studies and on subaltern studies, two topics that are beyond the heavy preference for the social sciences in the LAS. Or, to put it another way, the humanities became more visible in the Latin American Association in the past decade, and it manifested itself under the (sometimes conflictive) rubric of cultural and subaltern studies (Castro-Gómez and Mendieta 1999). Much of the work in this orientation, in dialogue with Latin American–based literary scholars (Angel Rama, Antonio Candido, Antonio Cornejo Polar, Nelly Richard, Beatriz Sarlo, Roberto Schwartz, and so on), has been summarized and organized by Román de la Campa under the rubric of "Latin Americanism" (de la Campa 1999). On the other hand, Agustín Lao-Montes, a sociologist by training and very much invested in Latino/a studies, has offered us a version of Latin Americanism closer to the social sciences and Latino/a studies, also bringing into the conversation certain aspects of a Latin American tradition I am calling here Pensamiento Crítico (Lao-Montes forthcoming).

3. See, for instance, the revealing article by Siva Vaidhyanathan (2000) on the glamour of Asian American studies, particularly India. Asian American studies has one important difference with Latino/a studies: the language. The fact that English is the official language of the United States, England, Australia, and New Zealand offers to India the possibility of being the difference within sameness. While Latino/a studies is mainly manifested in the English language, the fact remains that there are imperial and colonial differences between English and Spanish. The Spanish-American War in 1898, the Mexican frontier in 1848, and the Cuban revolution in 1959 are all historical events that loom large in the geopolitics of knowledge and on the academic market.

4. There are, of course, research centers in the social sciences in Latin America that operate under strict scientific rules, such as the scholarly *Revista Venezolana de Economía y Ciencias Sociales* (see, for instance, the special issue on "Violencia en Venezuela y América Latina," 2, no. 3 [1967]). But even in these cases, the scientific purity of the observer is always marked by a personal concern with the local history. A Venezuelan citizen and scholar writing about the economic debt in Venezuela would always imply identification with the subject matter. I would say that the subject matter is treated as a second person (we, us), while in area (and Latin American) studies the subject matter is almost always them/they. An inverse case would be Colombian anthropologist Arturo

Escobar (1995), working in the United States but conceptualizing a critique on development and modernization that presupposes all previous work in Latin America on the topic since dependency theory.

5. The addition of "cultural" and "subaltern" does not alter the ideological and epistemic foundation of Latin American and area studies, which doesn't question the relevance of these new developments. The point, however, is that the same geopolitical tension that has been set up by Latin American studies is being reframed today and explains the position taken by the authors of some of the articles published in the collection edited by Santiago Castro-Gómez and Eduardo Mendieta (1999). Achugar (1999) and Moraña (1998) reproduce, in a different context and without confronting their own genealogy, Fals Borda's ([1970] 1987) early concern with the colonization and decolonization of scholarship. The debate in terms of exportation/importation of knowledge can reproduce nationalistic views of knowledge production, but it is a moot point today, although that doesn't mean that the geopolitics of knowledge is no longer in effect. It means that because of the geopolitics of knowledge the question needs to be reframed in terms of (the coloniality) power and the epistemic colonial difference (Quijano 1997; Mignolo 2000b). However, this is a topic for a subsequent argument.

6. Os lugares, hoje, se diferenciam e hierarquizam exatamente porque sao todos mundiais. Os tempos também (as temporalidades hierárquicas e as temporalidades subalternas). O chamado espaco mundial é dado pelas relacoes assim tecidas entre todos os lugares. E o chamado tempo mundial é dado pelas possibilidades mundiais efetivamente utilizadas pelos atores hegemônicos. Os demas tempos sao subalternos. É essa a base empírica da construcao teórica de um tempo e un espaco mundializados, sem a qual cada porcao do acontecer nao e inteligível (Ortiz 1994, 47).

7. Poco discutido por los autores europeos y norteamericanos, pues no tienen interés en explicitar las barreras de su propio pensamiento, (el eurocentrismo) marca las ciencias sociales desde su origen. No me refiero sólo al eurocentrismo como ideología, del modo que lo considera Samir Amin, un culturalismo cuyas raices particularistas son travestidas en el universalismo de la "civilización occidental." ... Subrayo la existencia de un eurocentrismo conceptual que impregna los análisis y orienta la reflexión en una dirección completamente contraproducente (Ortiz 1998, 183).

8. La democracia no siempre ha sido el motor sobre el cual se han desarrollado las propuestas de articulación del poder político en América Latina. Es más, sus distintas formulaciones son resultado de continuas luchas sociales que incorporan desde la sociedad civil nuevos sujetos y fuerzas políticas que obligan a una redefinición de los contenidos políticos. Así el surgimiento de un proyecto democrático de carácter multiétnico es la comprobación efectiva de la existencia de una fuerza social que manifiesta su peso específico en la lucha por la democracia, reivindicando el derecho a la diferencia y la pluralidad étnica en

la construcción de un poder verdaderamente democrático en América Latina (González Casanova and Rosenmann 1996, 11).

REFERENCES

Achugar, Hugo. 1999. "Leones, cazadores e historiadores: A propósito de las politicas de la memoria y del conocimiento." In *Teorías sin disciplinas,* ed. Santiago Castro-Gómez and Eduardo Mendieta. Mexico: Porrúa. 271–286.

Adelman, Jermy, ed. 1999. *Colonial Legacies: The Problem of Persistence in Latin American History.* New York: Routledge.

Adelman, Jeremy, and Stephen Aron. 1999. "From Borderlands to Borders: Empires, Nation-States, and the Peoples In Between in North American History." *American Historical Review* 104, no. 3: 814–41.

Akiwowo, Akinsola. 1999. "Indigenous Sociologies: Extending the Argument." *International Sociology* 14, no. 2: 115–38.

Alcoff, Linda, and Eduardo Mendieta. 2000. *Enrique Dussel: Thinking from the Underside of History.* Lanham, Md.: Rowman and Littlefield.

Aparicio, Frances R. 1998. *Listening to Salsa: Gender, Latin Popular Music, and Puerto Rican Cultures.* Hanover, N.H.: Wesleyan University Press.

Barreda Marín, Andrés. 1994. "La dialéctica de la dependencia y el debate Marxista latinoamericano." In *La teoría social latinoamericana: Subdesarrollo y dependencia,* ed. Ruy Mauro Marini and Márgara Millán. Mexico: Ediciones del Caballito. 199–234.

Belnap, Jeffrey, and Raúl Fernández, eds. 1998. *José Martí's "Our America": From National to Hemispheric Cultural Studies.* Durham, N.C.: Duke University Press.

Berger, Mark T. 1995. *Under Northern Eyes: Latin American Studies and U.S. Hegemony in the Americas, 1898–1990.* Bloomington: Indiana University Press.

Beverley, John. 1996. "Sobre la situación actual de los estudios culturales." In *Libro de homenaje a Antonio Cornejo Polarm,* ed. J. A. Mazzotti and U. J. Zevallos Aguilar. Philadelphia: Asociación International de Peruanistas. 455–66.

———. 1998. "Theses on Subalternity, Representation and Politics." *Postcolonial Studies* 1, no. 3: 305–19.

———. 1999. "Writing in Reverse: The Subaltern and the Limits of Academic Knowledge." In *Subalternity and Representation: Arguments in Cultural Theory.* Durham, N.C.: Duke University Press. 25–40.

Bonilla, Frank. 1998. "Rethinking Latino/Latin American Interdependence: New Knowing, New Practice." In *Borderless Border: U.S. Latinos, Latin Americans, and the Paradox of Interdependence,* ed. F. Bonilla, E. Meléndez, R. Morales, and A. M. A. de los Angeles Torres. Philadelphia: Temple University Press. 217–231.

Cabán, Pedro. 1998. "The New Synthesis of Latin American and Latino Studies." In *Borderless Borders: U.S. Latinos, Latin Americans, and the Paradox of Interdependence,* ed. F. Bonilla et al. Philadelphia: Temple University Press. 195–216.

Cadena, Marisol de la. 2000. *Indigenous Mestizos: The Politics of Race and Culture in Cuzco, 1919–1991.* Durham, N.C.: Duke University Press.

Cardoso, Fernando Henrique. 1977. "O consumo da teoria da dependência nos Estados Unidos." In *As idéais e seu lugar: Ensaois sobre as teorias do desenvolvimento.* Petropolis: Editora Vozes. 125–50.

Castro-Gómez, Santiago, ed. 1998. "Latinoamericanismo, globalización y postcolonialidad." *Cuadernos Americanos* 67: 143–255.

Castro-Gómez, Santiago, and Eduardo Mendieta, eds. 1999. *Teorías sin disciplinas.* Mexico: Editorial Porrúa.

Chew, Sing C., and Robert A. Denemark. 1996. *The Underdevelopment of Development: Essays in Honor of Andre Gunder Frank.* Thousand Oaks, Calif.: Sage.

Cline, Howard F. 1966. "The Latin American Studies Association: A Summary Survey with Appendix." *Latin American Research Review* 2, no. 1: 57–79.

de la Campa, Román. 1999. *Latin Americanism.* Minneapolis: University of Minnesota Press.

Dussel, Enrique. 1973. "El método analético y la filosofía latinoamericana." In *América Latina: Dependencia y Liberación.* Buenos Aires: Fernando García Cambeiro. 109–131.

———. 1996. *The Underside of Modernity: Apel, Ricoeur, Rorty, Taylor, and the Philosophy of Liberation.* Trans. and ed. Eduardo Mendieta. Atlantic Highlands, N.J.: Humanities Press.

———. 1999. *Postmodernidad y transmodernidad: Diálogos con la filosofía de Gianni Vattimo.* Mexico: Universidad Iberoamericana.

———, ed. 1994. *Debate en torno a la ética del discurso de Apel: Diálogo filosófico Norte-Sur desde América Latina.* Mexico: Siglo Veintiuno Editores.

Escobar, Arturo. 1995. *Encountering Development: The Making and Unmaking of the Third World.* Princeton, N.J.: Princeton University Press.

Estay Reino, Jaime. 1994. "La concepción inicial de Raúl Prebisch y sus transformaciones." In *La teoría social latinoamericana: Subdesarrollo y dependencia,* ed. Ruy Mauro Marini and Márgara Millán. Mexico: Ediciones del Caballito. 2: 17–40.

Eze, Emmanuel Ch. 1997. "The Color of Reason: The Idea of 'Race' in Kant's Anthropology." In *Postcolonial African Philosophy: A Critical Reader,* ed. Emmanuel Ch. Eze. London: Blackwell. 103–40.

Fals Borda, Orlando. [1970] 1987. *Ciencia propia y colonialismo intellectual.* Bogotá: Carlos Valencia Editores.

Flores, Juan. 1993. *Divided Borders: Essays on Puerto Rican Identity.* Houston: Arte Público Press.

Frank, André Gunder. 1967. *Capitalism and Underdevelopment in Latin America: Historical Studies of Chile and Brazil.* New York: Monthly Review Press.

———. 1998. *ReOrient: Global Economy in the Asian Age.* Berkeley: University of California Press.

García Canclini, Néstor. 1989. *Culturas Híbridas: Estrategias para entrar y salir de la modernidad.* Ciudad de México: Editorial Era.

Gereffi, Gary. 1989. *Rethinking Development Theory: Insights from East Asia and Latin America.* Program in Political Economy no. 82. Durham, N.C.: Duke University.

González Casanova, Pablo. 1965. "Internal Colonialism and National Development." *Studies in Comparative International Development* 1, no. 4: 27–37.

———. 1996. "El colonialismo global y la democracia." In *La Nueva Organización capitalista mundial vista desde el sur,* vol. 2 of *El estado y la política del sur del mundo,* ed. Samir Amin and Pablo González Casanova. Barcelona: Anthropos. 11–144.

González Casanova, Pablo, and Marcos Roitman Rosenmann, eds. 1996. *Democracia y Estado multiétnico en América Latina.* Ciudad de México: Centro de Investigaciones Interdisciplinarias en Ciencias y Humanidades, UNAM (Universidad Nacional Autónoma de México).

Grandin, Greg. 2000. *The Blood of Guatemala: A History of Race and Nation.* Latin America Otherwise. Durham, N.C.: Duke University Press.

Grosfogel, Ramón, ed. 1995. *Puerto Rican Jam.* Minneapolis: University of Minnesota Press.

Gulbenkian Commission. 1996. *Open the Social Sciences: Report of the Gulbenkian Commission on the Restructuring of the Social Sciences.* Stanford, Calif.: Stanford University Press.

Heilbron, Johan. 1995. *The Rise of Social Theory.* Trans. Sheila Gogol. Minneapolis: University of Minnesota Press.

Heilbrunn, Jacob. 1996. "The News from Everywhere: Does Global Thinking Threaten Local Knowledge? The Social Science Research Council Debates the Future of Area Studies." *Lingua Franca* (June): 49–56.

Ianni, Octavio. 1995. *Teorías da globalizaçao.* Rio de Janeiro: Civilizaçao Brasileira.

———. 1997. *A era do globalismo.* Rio de Janeiro: Civilizaçao Brasileira.

Kiefer Lewalski, Barbara. 1986. *Renaissance Genres: Essays on Theory, History, and Interpretation.* Cambridge: Harvard University Press.

Lander, Edgardo. 2000. "El papel de CLACSO en el desarrollo de un pensamiento propio en América Latina." At www.clacso.edu.ar.

Lao-Montes, Agustín. 2001. "Latin American Area Studies and Latino Ethnic Studies: From the Civilizing Mission to the Barbarian's Revenge." American Philosophical Association. *Hispanic/Latino Issues in Philosophy* 2: 38–47.

———. Forthcoming. "Latin/o Americanisms: Epistemological and Political Challenges." *Nepantla: Views from South* 4, no. 3.

Mignolo, Walter D. 1981. "El metatexto historiográfico y la historiografía indiana." *Modern Languages Notes* 96: 358–402.

———. 1982. "Cartas, crónicas y relaciones del descubrimiento y la conquista." In *Historia de la literatura hispanoamericana: Epoca colonial,* ed. Manuel Alvar et al. Madrid: Cátedra. 57–116.

———. 1995a. *The Darker Side of the Renaissance: Literacy, Territoriality, and Colonization.* Ann Arbor: University of Michigan Press.

———. 1995b. "Occidentalización, imperialismo, globalización: Herencias coloniales y teorías poscoloniales." *Revista Iberoamericana* 61, no. 170–71: 26–39.

———. 1996a. "Los estudios subalternos son posmodernos o poscoloniales?" *Casa de las Américas* 204: 20–40.

———. 1996b. "Posoccidentalismo: Las epistemologías fronterizas y el dilema de los estudios (latinoamericanos) de areas." *Revista Iberoamericana* 62, no. 176–77: 679–96.

———. 2000a. "Dussel's Philosophy of Liberation: Ethics and the Geo-Politics of Knowledge." In *Thinking from the Underside of History,* ed. Linda Alcoff and Eduardo Mendieta. Lanham, Md.: Rowman and Littlefield. 27–50.

———. 2000b. *Local Histories/Global Designs: Coloniality, Subaltern Knowledges, and Border Thinking.* Princeton, N.J.: Princeton University Press.

———. 2002. "The Geopolitics of Knowledge and the Colonial Difference." *South Atlantic Quarterly* 101, no. 1: 57–96.

Moraña, Mabel. 1998. "El *boom* del subalterno." *Cuadernos Americanos* 67, no. 1: 187–213.

Muñoz, José Esteban. 1999. *Disidentifications: Queers of Color and the Performance of Politics.* Minneapolis: University of Minnesota Press.

Nutini, Hugo G. 1996. "Contributions of Americanism to the Theory and Practice of Modern Anthropology." In *Le Nouveau Monde/Mondes Nouveaux,* ed. S. Gruzinski and N. Wachtel. Paris: Editions de l'École des Hautes Études en Sciences Sociales. 579–610.

Ortiz, Renato. 1997. *Mundialización y Cultura.* Buenos Aires: Alianza Editorial.

———. 1998. *Otro Territorio.* Caracas: Editorial Andrés Bello.

———. 1994. *Mundialização e cultura.* São Paulo: Editoria Braziliense.

Osorio, Jaime. 1994. "Fuentes y tendencias de la teoría de la dependencia." In *La teoría social latinoamericana: Subdesarrollo y dependencia,* ed. Ruy Mauro Marini and Márgara Millán. Mexico: Ediciones del Caballito. 2: 157–78.

Pagden, Anthony. 1996. "'Americanism' from Modernity to Postmodernity." In *Le Nouveau Monde/Mondes Nouveaux,* ed. S. Gruzinski and N. Wachtel. Paris: Editions de l'École des Hautes Études en Sciences Sociales. 511–22.

Quijano, Aníbal. 1992. "Colonialidad y modernidad-racionalidad." In *Los conquistados,* ed. H. Bonilla. Bogotá: Tercer Mundo. 437–47.

———. 1997. "Colonialidad del poder, cultura y conocimiento en América Latina." *Anuario Mariateguiano* 9, no. 9: 113–21.

————. 2000. "Coloniality of Power, Eurocentrism, and Latin America." *Nepantla: Views from South* 1, no. 3: 533–79.

Rafael, Vincente L. 1994. "The Cultures of Area Studies in the United States." *Social Text* 33: 91–111.

Ramos, Guerreiro. [1955] 1995. *Introduçao Crítica à Sociologia Brasileira.* Rio de Janeiro: Universidad Federal de Rio de Janeiro.

Rivera Cusicanqui, Silvia. 1990. "Liberal Democracy and *Ayllu* Democracy: The Case of Northern Potosi." *Journal of Development Studies* 5: 97–121.

————. 1992. "Sendas y senderos de la ciencia social Andina." In *Auto-determinación: Análisis histórico-político y teoría social.* 10: 83–108.

————. 1996. "Los desafíos para una democracia étnica en los albores del tercer milenio." In *Ser mujer indígena, chola o birlocha en la Bolivia post-colonial de los años 90,* ed. S. Rivera Cusicanqui and R. Barragán. Bolivia: Ministerio del Desarrollo Humano. 17–86.

————. 1997. "La noción de 'derecho': O las paradojas de la modernidad poscolonial: indígenas y mujeres en Bolivia." *Temas Sociales* 19: 27–52.

Rivera Cusicanqui, Silvia, and Rossana Barragán, eds. 1997. *Debates post-coloniales: Una introducción a los estudios de la subalternidad.* La Paz: Sephis/Aruwiyri.

Romero, Mary, Pierrette Hondagneu-Sotelo, and Vilma Ortiz, eds. 1997. *Challenging Fronteras: Structuring Latina and Latino Lives in the U.S.* New York: Routledge.

Romero Pittari, Salvador. 1997. *La recepción académica de la sociología en Bolivia.* La Paz: Plural Editores.

Said, Edward. 1978. *Orientalism.* New York: Vintage Books.

Saldívar, José David. 1991. *The Dialectics of Our America: Genealogy, Cultural Critique, and Literary History.* Durham, N.C.: Duke University Press.

————. 1996. "Las fronteras de Nuestra América." *Casa de las Américas* 204: 3–19.

Saldívar-Hull, Sonia. 2000. *Feminism on the Border: Chicana Gender Politics and Literature.* Berkeley: University of California Press.

Santi, Enrico M. 1992. "Latinoamericanism and Restitution." *Latin American Literary Review* 40: 88–92.

Santos, Milton. 1994. *Ténica, espaço, tempo: Globalizaçâo e meio ténico-científico informacional.* São Paulo: Editora Hucitec.

Santos, Milton, Francisco Capuano Scalato, Maria Adélia De Souza, Mónica Arroyo, eds. 1994. *O novo mapa do Mondo: Globalizacao e espaco Latino-Americano.* São Paulo: Editora Hucitec.

Schoultz, Lars. 1998. *Beneath the United States: A History of U.S. Policy toward Latin America.* Cambridge: Harvard University Press.

Serequeberhan, Tsenay. 1997. "The Critique of Eurocentrism and the Practice of African Philosophy." In *Postcolonial African Philosophy: A Critical Reader,* ed. Emmanuel Ch. Eze. London: Blackwell. 141–61.

Starn, Orín. 1999. *Nightwatch: The Making of a Movement in the Peruvian Andes*. Latin America Otherwise. Durham, N.C.: Duke University Press.

Stavenhagen, Rodolfo. 1965. "Classes, Colonialism, and Acculturation." *Studies in Comparative International Development* 1, no. 7: 53–77.

Stavenhagen, Rodolfo, and Diego Iturralde, eds. 1990. *Entre la ley y la costumbre: El derecho consuetudinario indígena en América Latina*. Mexico: Instituto Indigenista Interamericano/Instituto Interamericano de Derechos Humanos.

Stern, Steven, ed. 1998. *Shining and Other Paths: War and Society in Peru, 1980–1995*. Latin America Otherwise. Durham, N.C.: Duke University Press.

Stoll, David. 1999. *Rigoberta Menchú and the Story of All Poor Guatemalans*. Boulder, Colo.: Westview Press.

Vaidhyanathan, Siva. 2000. "Inside a 'Model Minority': the Complicated Identity of South Asians." *Chronicle of Higher Education* 46, no. 42 (June 23): B4–B6.

Wallerstein, Immanuel. 1979. "Dependence in an Interdependent World: The Limited Possibilities of Transformation within the Capitalist World-Economy." In *Capitalist World-Economy*. Paris: Cambridge University Press and Editions de la Maison des Sciences de l'Homme. 66–94.

———. 2000. *The Essential Wallerstein*. New York: New Press.

Zemelman, Hugo. 2000. "Postdoctoral en pensamiento y cultura en América Latina." At www.clacso.edu.ar.

CHAPTER 3

Rethinking Area and Ethnic Studies in the Context of Economic and Political Restructuring

George Yúdice

There has been much discussion over the past decade about the restructuring of the university in the United States. The root causes of this restructuring are generally seen as follows: economic, to the degree that higher education has to produce the creators of the knowledge that will drive the so-called new economy and the managers who will administrate it; sociopolitical, insofar as the university troubleshoots the social divisions (especially those based on gender and ethnoracial differences) that threaten social order; and geopolitical, as the U.S. university acknowledges its place as the major brokering institution in global knowledge production in the post–Cold War period. With regard to this last point, it is recognized worldwide that the U.S. university system is far ahead in the production of the intellectual property that brings about "wealth creation." The U.S. genomics industry alone, for example, is about the size of the Argentine economy (Enríquez 2000). As capital accumulation increasingly depends on scientific and technological innovation and as commodity production is further devalued, Latin America and other developing regions will decline even further. Under the current neoliberal consensus among Latin American elites, university research agendas are increasingly driven by market criteria, particularly in the spate of private universities that have sprouted over the past decade or two in every country and even in the increasingly underfunded public universities (Gentili 2000, 13). The result is brain drain from public to private institutions within Latin America and from Latin America to the United States, where scientifically competent immigrants are needed to fuel the new economy, according to the depositions before Congress of Alan Greenspan, chairman of the Federal Reserve. Indeed, pressed by Internet and high-tech companies, Congress will raise the number of HI-B visas in 2000 ("Too Many High-Tech Visas"). The problem, of course, is not limited to developing countries in Latin America or to the United States. Germany, which has "an estimated 75,000 to 100,000 jobs vacant in the booming Internet sector, with few Germans apparently qualified to fill them," is courting high-tech-proficient immigrants from India, a policy that is met with protest and greater appeals for increases and changes within the German university system. According to one observer, "German education with its focus on heavy philosophical concepts does not turn out the people we want" (Cohen 2000).

The repercussions for the humanities and social sciences should be evident. To the degree that they can accommodate to the imperative of the new economic order, the humanities and social sciences will maintain a high profile and obtain resources. Latin American studies, Latino studies, and Latin American literary and cultural studies are all affected differently, although significantly, which is the reason why there has been discussion of some kind of rapprochement among them in recent years. Latin American studies, although still supported as an institution at several universities by Title VI federal grants, has lost much of its raison d'être with the waning of the Cold War. U.S. foreign policy has used cultural and educational programs during periods of perceived external threats since the early 1800s when Latin American republics gained their independence, the Monroe Doctrine was declared, and the Smith Chair in Modern Languages and Literatures was established at Harvard a couple of decades after Spanish was introduced into the curriculum at several universities at the behest of Benjamin Franklin and Thomas Jefferson (Fernández 2000, 1961). The Spanish-Cuban-American War (1895–98) and especially the Good Neighbor Policy during World War II provided impetus for cultural programs and research on Latin America, but it wasn't until the 1960s that Latin American studies became a national institution, with funding from major foundations (Carnegie, Rockefeller, and Ford) and the federal government (especially the National Defense

Education Act of 1958, which expanded language programs and curricula in the culture and politics of the region). Indeed, "Latin American studies acted as a direct complement to the Alliance for Progress" (Berger 1995, 87), and Project Camelot, which sought to foster modernization theory and anticipate and control social change in the region, was clearly an adjunct of foreign policy (91). Later in the decade, the Latin American Studies Association (LASA) was founded with funding from the Ford Foundation's International Training and Research Program. In "nonthreatening" periods these cultural and educational programs were reduced or eliminated, as occurred with the Good Neighbor Policy at the end of World War II and then again in the 1990s with the disappearance of the "communist" bogey after glasnost and perestroika. Some of the slack was briefly taken up by interest in NAFTA, but that involved research exclusively on Mexico, or by the war on drugs, which does not seem to have an intellectual or humanistic component. Without the threat of revolution south of the Rio Grande/Bravo, there is little federal interest in sweetening the stick of economic reform imperatives with the carrot of support for intellectual and cultural production, traditionally operative in the Good Neighbor Policy, the Alliance for Progress, USIA, and other Cold War programs.

Something similar might be said about the lack of interest in Latin America among cultural studies scholars. Complementarily, even Latin Americanists in the humanities tend to follow the division of labor established by grand theory itself. Theoretical paradigms are produced in France and the United States (including postcolonialism and subaltern studies), and scholars in Latin American studies and Spanish departments simply apply them to Latin American objects of study. There are universities where students take theory in an English or comparative literature department and then bring it to bear on literary texts in their Spanish classes. For obvious reasons, this is not a practice adhered to in Latin American universities, where a dialogue with theory and cultural studies has taken place just as long as in the United States, as pointed out by scholars like Nelly Richard (2000) and Idelber Avelar (1999, 52). I myself remarked on the claim by some North American Latin Americanists who in the name of decolonization have discouraged Latin Americans from invoking theorists like Deleuze and Foucault (Yúdice 1996).

This sentiment seems to have been shared by (non–Latin Americanist) cultural studies critics, who rarely invoked any Latin Americans in their work. For all the interest in contestatory politics at the "Marxism and the Interpretation of Culture" conference held at the University of Illinois in 1983, only three (Hugo Achugar, Jean Franco, and Fernando Reyes Matta) out of thirty-eight papers published in the canon-setting proceedings (which would constitute the United States as the center of cultural studies) had anything to do with Latin America (Nelson and Grossberg 1988). The same goes for the cultural studies "bible" of 1992, also an outgrowth of a conference held at the University of Illinois in 1988 (Nelson, Treichler, and Grossberg 1992). This time, however, it seems as if Chicano/Latino interests, albeit woefully underrepresented, were stronger than Latin American ones. Earlier on, Latin America provided grist for the European or European-derived theory mills, but after the mid-1980s, and especially with the failure of the Central American revolutions, Latino studies became the filter through which Latin America would increasingly be imagined by those in cultural studies. This state of affairs was partly due to the influence of multiculturalism. Initially a means to "empower" excluded or marginalized minorities, multiculturalism soon became a quick rhetorical fix of symbolic inclusion and very little material gain. By lumping together Latin Americans and Latinos of all classes and ethnoracial backgrounds, multiculturalism homogenized them as part of a U.S. tendency to panethnicization. Consequently, U.S. multiculturalism has been looked on with much caution by Latin American intellectuals, artists, and activists, to the point of discerning in it a family resemblance to cultural imperialism. My "We Are *Not* the World" (Yúdice 1992) was a critique of panethnic lumping, whereby the Latino was used in a U.S. context to represent the Latin American, a practice that inverted the tendency to hire white, middle-class Latin Americans for positions earmarked for disadvantaged Latinos. A sometimes unwitting but often disingenuous opportunism has been at work in this intermediation or brokering of multiculturalism in the United States (Yúdice 1994, 147–50).

It did not take long before the underlying tension between Latin American and Latino scholars broke out as the latter criticized the former for not thematizing their class and racial privilege vis-à-vis the descendants of subaltern immigrants from their very own countries and as the former retorted that the identity politics brandished by U.S. minorities did not represent Latin American realities (Achugar 1998; Moraña 1998; Richard 1998; Sarlo 1997). Latin Americans also reacted to the market character of much of U.S. academic discourse, which had catapulted "brands" like postcolonial and subaltern studies to a high stature, particularly within the humanities and especially in literature and cultural studies programs, so that much of the legacy of Latin American intellectuals was either forgotten or reinterpreted as the (neo-Ari)elitist redemption of traditional intellectuals over and above the "real" needs of the people.[1] The latter is John Beverley's much cited and debated view of what is wrong with Latin American literary and intellectual discourse (1994, 1996). Likewise provocative to many Latin Americans is the insistence by a few U.S.-based Latin Americanists that the "restitution of Martí's *Nuestra América*" must go beyond a still operative Latin American Occidentalism that downplays the role of race and ethnicity. The recognition of racial difference in Latin America is seen by them as fundamental to a nonimperialist knowledge production (Coronil 1998; Mignolo 1998; Rodríguez 1998). Mignolo's characterization of Gloria Anzaldúa's border or interstitial knowledge as the beacon to which we should all aspire, and as tantamount today as Descartes's *Discours de la méthode* in the seventeenth century (54–56), was surely read as a provocation by the likes of Achugar (1998) and Moraña (1998), troubled and unconvinced by the prospect that a Chicana would serve as the broker for ushering in a new epistemological framework for construing and understanding American realities.

Whether or not we can speak of realities in any absolute way, it is current practice nowadays to examine what were national questions in a transnational framework. The debate between Latin American scholars, on the one hand, and U.S.-based Latin Americanists and Latinos on the other, which I have briefly reviewed, is if nothing else a testament to that transnational framework. At the heart of the debate is the category of identity, which became the centerpiece of cultural studies sometime in the late 1980s and 1990s, overlapping with the emergent (and now widespread) discourse of multiculturalism and diversity. Questions of representation were racked by conflicts over interests (such as university positions and institutional capital), and these conflicts were in turn complicated by the permeation of culture by a market logic, as I argue in the conclusion.

At the same time that Latin American studies and Latino studies were locked in this tension, the latter were also fending off attempts by university administrations to eliminate them or fold them into larger cultural or American studies programs. While Latino studies programs, like other ethnic studies programs, have a rich tradition and scholarship that goes back to the 1960s, they do have certain limitations, particularly the masculinism and nationalism of the early phase and until recently a difficulty dealing with transnational contexts. Consolidation—as in the creation of the Comparative Studies in Race and Ethnicity program at Stanford University and the decade-long attempt at CUNY's Graduate Center to create an intercultural studies program that would bring together African-American, Latino, Asian American, women's studies, and gay and lesbian studies is in great part a response to the defunding of the humanities and the weakening of the commitment to ethnic studies, as Albert Camarillo (1997) of Stanford has pointed out. He has also noted that the expansion of the program at Stanford had the advantage of being more relevant to a post–Cold War world by encompassing the ethnic and religious conflicts throughout the world in keeping with the discourse of globalization. The establishment of comparative ethnic studies programs or more inclusive American studies programs at places like the Five Colleges, Wesleyan, Harvard, Michigan, Duke, and New York University are consistent with the Ford Foundation's new Crossing Borders initiative to revitalize area studies by awarding $50,000 grants to thirty colleges and universities (Volkman 1998, 1). Precisely the issues reviewed above—transdisciplines such as cultural studies and postcolonialism that disregard the boundaries of knowledge production; demographic shifts that bring into focus diverse groups' heritages, languages, and other issues examined in ethnic studies departments; the encounter of scholars with the communities they study (Mato 1998); and so on—are all motivating factors in the Ford Foundation's interest in keeping knowledge production consistent with its transnational contexts; in bringing together intellectuals, scholars, and activists who make likely interlocutors; and in influencing government, university administrators, and donors to support the new area studies (Volkman 1999, xi–xii). Area studies has a sizable infrastructure that can be reconverted to accommodate new forms of knowledge production and distribution. This, at least, is the wager of the Ford Foundation, one that those of us in ethnic studies and cultural studies cannot afford to ignore, for our very livelihood is at stake, particularly as universities throughout the country are either forced to retrench (as in the SUNY and CUNY systems) or downsize certain departments and fields as part of a restructuring that I will try to account for in the following section of this essay.

Area Studies and the Cold War University

Area studies is largely a creation of the Cold War. As mentioned above, the U.S. government and various influential foundations—among them

Ford, Carnegie, MacArthur, and Rockefeller—and other policy-making institutions oriented the university to work in the service of greater competitiveness vis-à-vis the Soviet Union. Area studies emerged to deal with the great ferment of decolonization in Third World countries, both to gain knowledge of them as a way of managing their potential challenge to capitalism and as a way of gaining leverage over Soviet influence. Reaction to the technical achievements of the Soviet Union, emblematized in the "surprise" launching of Sputnik on October 4, 1957, led to the passage by Congress of the National Defense Education Act in 1958, later named the Title VI program. Foundations were also a part of this reaction to decolonization and Soviet influence. From 1953 to 1966, the Ford Foundation spent $270 million on area studies. Ford spearheaded a Foreign Area Fellowship Program in the 1950s to provide graduate students with linguistic competency in understudied languages and cultures. In the early 1970s, this program was relayed to the Social Science Research Council (SSRC) and the American Council of Learned Societies (ACLS), where it functioned as the "keystone of area programs at the Councils for nearly three decades until the restructuring of the Councils in the mid-1990s" (Hershberg 1999, 120). These initiatives provided funding to train thousands of scholars in the language, culture, and political practices of countries throughout the world and "brought scholars from diverse disciplines together to support in-depth, multi-disciplinary training and research." There were also efforts to induce scholars from these areas "to visit the U.S., in part to expose them to the realities of this country; in part to modify their attitudes toward a range of social, economic, and political issues" (Heginbotham 1994, 34). There are precedents for such large knowledge-producing enterprises—the New Deal and especially the Good Neighbor Policy—but those do not compare with the Cold War university.

It is a mistake, however, to attribute the entire enterprise of area studies to the Cold War. I think we must look at another contextualizing factor, which is also connected with the Cold War and may even have driven the Cold War mindset as a kind of legitimation. U.S. capital needed huge resources for its accumulation strategies after World War II. The university was one major site targeted as a socialized resource for capital. This is particularly evident in the use of the university as a site for research and development (R and D) for the defense and health industries. What is often overlooked when examining the university is its usefulness as a form of state intervention in the economy. That intervention was not limited to control of the supply of money and the redistribution of wage goods through taxation and welfare. It was also meant to create employment in three ways: by refashioning the state to be a major purchaser of goods and services; by pumping state funds into undercapitalized sectors (e.g., to rebuild the infrastructure of the railroads) only to relay them back to the market; and by subsidizing new technologies and the training of specialists in order to produce continual innovation (Lewontin 1997, 2–3). It is by this route that the U.S. government socialized the costs (i.e., used taxpayer's dollars) for R and D for the defense and medical industries at universities under contract with government agencies such as the National Science Foundation (NSF), the Atomic Energy Commission (AEC), the Office of Naval Research (ONR), and the National Institutes of Health (NIH).

Lewontin further argues that this form of socialization of capital accumulation strategies re-created and patterned the entire university system, particularly the research university, in the image of the entrepreneurial professors with command over research centers. The budget for such enterprises was enormous. From 1951 to 1961, the increases the NSF received from Congress were from $100,000 to $100 million, 85 percent of which went to universities and research institutes. The NSF and NIH instituted disciplinary autonomy and peer review panels that also became the modus operandi of the social sciences and humanities. Even while Congress launched a vicious attack against academic and other radicals, "there was a widespread indifference to political ideology in the research supported by agencies of the state" (Lewontin 1997, 18). Even pro-Soviet scientific researchers like L. C. Dunn of Columbia University did not lose funding.[2] Lewontin's own political activities with the Black Panther Party, collaborations with the Socialist Worker's Party, and the Communist Party, as well as antiwar activism during the Vietnam War did not cause him to lose any funding from the AEC or the Department of Energy, although he later discovered through a request for his file under the Freedom of Information Act that his activities were closely monitored by the FBI (19). Funders with an interest in gaining knowledge of the adversary and potential allies had to tolerate a measure of scholarly autonomy because the need for research in the university gave it the space for insisting on academic freedom. Consequently, funders cast their net widely, funding research areas that had little to do with Cold War goals if they wanted to maintain an agenda within the university (Heginbotham 1994, 35). Furthermore, since American culture was an important terrain of battle during the Cold War, there was funding available for social scientists and humanists to promote forms of American culture that demonstrated our superiority or our cultivation of freedom vis-à-vis the state command of social and cultural life in the Soviet Union. The art and literary criticism that made the argument for the freedom inherent in abstract expressionism or the style of modern dance promoted by Martha Graham, among others, provide good examples (Kowal 1999). The fifties are the period in which former leftists like Sidney Hook took a conservative turn and from the heights of the academy guided a generation of scholars between the twin "evils" of consumerism and totalitarianism.

The point I am trying to make is that the value of the university for both the economic and political strategies of the United States during the Cold War created a structure for both disciplinary and area studies research on unprecedented levels. Throughout the entire Cold War period, and even afterward, the budgets of colleges and universities did not fall. Between 1946 and 1991 these budgets increased twentyfold and the physical plant by 600 percent (Lewontin 1997, 24), and faculty gained institutional collective power. As a body, faculty put limits on the discrepancy between the sciences on the one hand, and the social sciences and humanities on the other. For example, "lower teaching loads in science meant lower teaching loads in the humanities" (30).

All of this began to change in the 1980s as the university was pressured to restructure. The point is not that university budgets will necessarily fall but that a different higher education system is resulting. Political ideology is only one important factor in this restructuring. I might go so far as to suggest that the political arguments for downsizing certain departments and especially reneging on the "compromise" with marginalized groups that was negotiated in the late 1960s and 1970s, significant in themselves, are part of a legitimation strategy for a different role of the university vis-à-vis capital accumulation.

ETHNIC STUDIES AT THE CROSSROADS OF THE COLD WAR AND THE NEOLIBERAL UNIVERSITY

Before elaborating on the restructuring of the university, let me give a very brief account of the incorporation into the university of marginalized groups during the Cold War. This is the context for the emergence of ethnic studies programs. Civil rights generated demands for all kinds of enfranchisement, including affirmative action programs for entry into the university as well as the creation of Black studies programs. At CUNY, Black and Puerto Rican studies programs were created in the early 1970s. The very growth of the university system during the Cold War as well as the strategy on the part of the Great Society government to troubleshoot the radicalized demands of African Americans, Chicanos, Puerto Ricans, and other disenfranchised or underenfranchised constituencies ultimately incorporated them into a system that was as much about managing populations as it was about empowerment. Elsewhere I have written about the similarity in the troubleshooting function of policies of the War on Poverty and the then recently created national, yet decentralized, system of cultural subsidy embodied in the endowments and the state and local arts councils (Yúdice 1999).

Great Society programs cannot be separated from the overarching conflict of the period: the student movement, antiwar protest, and an increasing sympathy for Third World liberation struggles among students, minorities, and intellectuals. It would be inaccurate, in my view, to privilege any single one of these ingredients that make up the flavor of the period. The changes that took place in the sixties cannot be attributed solely to free expression of agency on the part of the social movements (Blacks, other minority groups, women, antiwar protesters, and students) nor to the goodwill (or more likely the will to co-opt) of government that met the turmoil with antipoverty programs, judicial action, illegal surveillance, and punishment of activists. Both the frustration of minorities and President Johnson's need to increase his electoral base served to structure the field of action. Given the "intricate mesh of interactive effects," Frances Fox Piven and Richard Cloward's characterization of what Foucault meant by governmentality, which necessarily channeled politics in the sixties in the form of protest,[3] the government in turn responded by managing the crisis to its electoral advantage, wielding what they call a "distinctively managerial kind of politics" (Piven and Cloward 1993, 249). It was this same kind of politics that the Johnson administration used to manage the vehement protests against the Vietnam War, which encouraged Third World sympathies among students and the intelligentsia. Like the antipoverty program, the National Endowments for the Arts and Humanities were established, among other reasons, to "strengthen the connections between the Administration and the intellectual community," as recommended by Arthur Schlesinger Jr. at the time (Cummings 1991, 49), for not only would this influential constituency help the Democrats electorally, it might also help defuse opposition to the war. These managerial strategies not only continued but were intensified under Nixon, although he also wielded a heavier stick to go along with his sweeter carrot of increased funding for the arts and the university (Yúdice 1999, 20–21).

This "democratization" of learning and knowledge production did not affect Spanish departments and Latin American studies programs immediately. In this early phase, what would come to be known as ethnic studies was largely in enclaves denigrated by the established disciplines. It wasn't until the late 1980s that Chicano and Puerto Rican studies made inroads into Spanish and English departments, largely under a new imperative and legitimation narrative of diversity. Multiculturalism was the name of this new legitimation discourse, to which I now turn in a second phase of my argument. It could be said that the 1990s offer a different mode of absorption of minorities but one that has to accommodate to a restructured university system. In the post–civil rights period of the Cold War, the numbers of women, African Americans, Mexican Americans, and other ethnoracialized groups increased due to political pressures and the government's strategies to defuse protest and to manage populations. The university system in its expanding phase could absorb these demands in the 1960s and 1970s. The establishment of Black studies, Chicano studies, Puerto Rican studies, Asian American studies, women's studies, and subsequently gay and lesbian studies corresponded to the three dynamics I briefly outlined: the expansion of the university under the Cold War, mobilization and protest, and the government's managerial politics.

In the 1980s, with the turn to the right, economic uncertainty, and the beginning of the end of the Cold War, restructuring of the university was on the agenda. Accompanying these changes, there was a recrudescence of racism among many white Americans that facilitated legitimation of reduction in government expenditures in the social sector. Government did not cut its investment in the university as the site of R and D for capital; it reconverted that site along with other sites that needed restructuring so as to "maintain the level that all political forces recognize as essential to the stability of modern capitalism" (Lewontin 1997, 32). The white backlash helped find populist ways to reduce expenditures. I am referring to a populism of the right, which targeted entitlement and redistributive programs for marginalized groups that no longer wielded the power of mobilization that had been met by concessions in the form of the programs mentioned earlier as well as by a relative inclusion in the university and the government workforce. The restructuring of the university in the 1980s and 1990s rendered such concessions unworkable. The very notion of national security, which was used to orient the university to the defense industry and intelligence services, was rearticulated in the aftermath of the Cold War toward the economy. Indeed, although economic war has always been an instrument of U.S. foreign policy since the nineteenth century, throughout the Cold War it was wielded quite openly as a substitute for armed struggle. In the post–Cold War period, it, along with small containment wars, is even more important. Moreover, the rhetoric of war is also intended to legitimize state intervention in the economy (Lewontin 1997, 32). Under these circumstances, minorities are either routed out of high-profile universities by the rescinding of affirmative action or are absorbed into the corporate rearticulation of multiculturalism, which construes culture and diversity as market factors important for economic productivity.

The state has continued to socialize the cost of research and education, but the premises have changed. State subvention is now oriented to enhancing competitiveness in the global economy. It is in relation to this transformation in the legitimation of the university's claim on government funds that we can establish a relationship between the economic and governmentalized structure of the university and the pressures to rearticulate area studies and ethnic studies. Area studies must shed its accommodation to the Cold War and instead orient itself to geopolitical and geocultural obstacles to capitalism, especially its consumerist, mediatic, and market forms, as well as the post-Fordist course it has taken in exporting work to cheap labor markets abroad. Ethnic studies, in turn, is enjoined to rid itself of the "stigma" of entitlement and redistributive logics to quell the demands of marginalized groups. But ethnic studies is given a way out of this dilemma: to emphasize its culturalist orientation (to the detriment of more pointed critiques of capitalism) and to accommodate to a multicultural contribution to U.S. competitiveness.

This culturalist orientation is compatible with the profusion of corporate rhetoric on diversity as an asset. Two reasons are given: (1) it provides diverse knowledges, presumably useful to capitalist enterprises, especially in niche marketing; (2) it provides linkages between U.S. minorities and peoples throughout the world, presumably making it possible for U.S. corporations to have a comparative advantage in a globalized marketplace. The logic behind this reasoning is that U.S. minorities, particularly Asian Americans and Latinos, will serve as the managers of corporate capital abroad, presumably more in tune with the culture of foreign businessmen and consumers. And given the development of translocal migratory patterns among the so-called new immigrants and their children, these minorities will inculcate U.S. consumption patterns abroad. Corporate logic on this ends up sounding a lot like Appadurai's account of the spread of U.S. culture among diasporics and postcolonials in his well-known essay, "Disjuncture and Difference in the Global Cultural Economy" (1992).

The Post–Cold War University

Downsizing, privatization, and other forms of restructuring, not only of national industries but also of public institutions such as hospitals and universities, are part of structural adjustment programs whose purpose is to make the public sector leaner and meaner and to encourage greater efficiency by linking operating budgets to earnings, particularly from industry-related contracts. These changes augur badly for underprivileged students. In the U.S. context, academic capitalism is ushering in corporate managerialist practices and supply-side higher education, which have prevailed in the post-Fordist private sector. Corporate-tested techniques, such as Total Quality Management (TQM), are even being applied to students. Despite protests to the contrary by the president of the University of Rochester, the following diagnosis seems consistent with his "Renaissance Plan": "Students are neither 'customers' nor 'consumers.' They are the 'industry's' 'inputs' and 'products.' The purchasers of the products—private, corporate 'employers'—are the customers. The push, then, is to improve (standardize) the product by 'improving' the input, a strategy that has clear implications (and no place) for access and affirmative action" (Rhoades and Slaughter 1997). Those who bear the effects of historical inequities will only gain entry, on the principles of quality management, if their "diversity" is in some way remunerable or marketable. And since the white middle class and government are reneging on compensation, we are already witnessing the deepening of class differences as students are routed by class (highly correlated with race) into elite and research universities for entry into executive employment or the lucrative production of intellectual property; public colleges and second-tier private institutions to qualify for middle management; community colleges and private diploma mills for vocational training in the service sector; or into workfare, chronic unemployment, and prison. An official of the National Science Foundation has gone so far as to ask whether or not "in light of the worsening job market for Ph.D.s, we can afford to continue pro-active recruiting and special programs aimed at retaining graduate students from underrepresented groups?" (Burka 1996).

The crisis in higher education, which affects "developing" countries as much or more than it affects the United States, is less a crisis than a planned restructuring by capital in keeping with a model of global competitiveness (i.e., exporting jobs to "free-enterprise zones" where workers are underpaid and receive no benefits and where corporations pay little or no taxes). The emergence of this model, like some of the other phenomena reviewed here, goes back to the beginning of the 1980s with the winding down of the Cold War, the passage of legislative changes aimed to make the United States more competitive in the new global economy of information and knowledge, and the rise of a new political coalition oriented to the marketization of knowledge (Rhoades and Slaughter 1997). The most salient changes have to do with the shift in academic science and technology from basic research toward a commercial competitiveness paradigm. As the Cold War began to wane, the Reagan and Bush administrations redefined national security in terms of national commerce. This shift prompted a reconversion of defense industries and related R and D, with concomitant changes in contracts with universities. In order to fully integrate universities in commercial ventures with the private sector, intellectual property laws, such as the Bayh-Dole Act of 1980, were passed. These enabled corporations to write off taxes on profits made in partnership with universities and the latter to claim proprietary rights over inventions made with federal R and D funds. The vast university system, already accustomed to partnerships with the defense industry in the Cold War era, could now be used to produce the intellectual property that would enable the United States to counter increasing European and Japanese industrial competitiveness and to win control of global markets in the new knowledge, communications, and biomedical and medical technology industries (Rhoades and Slaughter 1997).

The bipartisan political coalition that made these changes possible in the 1980s was also instrumental in designing Bush's Enterprise of the Americas Initiative, which eventually became NAFTA. Like the GATT, this and other free trade agreements pushed to get trading partners to honor intellectual property laws on patents, trademarks, and copyrights. Free trade essentially means the disenfranchisement of citizens as transnational capital prevails over state jurisdiction by means of deregulation. Deregulation means the elimination of barriers (tariffs) to trade but also the elimination of state support of industry or the protection of labor, resulting in the lowering of wages and benefits, the reduction of welfare services (health care, education), the rollback of environmental safeguards, and so on. These changes not only ensure greater profits for corporations, particularly multinational enterprises, but guarantee that there will be little interference with the conduct of business since the organizations that manage trade (those that negotiate tariffs *and* regulations on production and distribution) are not subject to oversight by any electorate. In effect, the General Agreement on Trade and Tariffs (GATT), the World Trade Organization (WTO), the North American Free Trade Agreement (NAFTA), the World Bank, the International Monetary Fund (IMF), and so on, have not been empowered by voters and yet impose their policies virtually unchecked. It is against this model of U.S.-led globalization that concerned organizations (from trade unionists to farmers, church groups, consumer activists, environmentalists, animal rights and human rights activists, supporters of the Zapatista rebels in Mexico, and the Free Tibet movement in China) mounted an unprecedented protest against the "new round" of the WTO in Seattle in December 1999.

The repercussions of this restructuring, although presumably generated at the transnational level in trade agreements and structural adjustment policies, are experienced acutely at the local level, as in the changes in higher education. Observers of the transformations that U.S. higher education is undergoing note that three areas of expansion will ensure its dominance: globalization, culture, and transdisciplinarity. For example, Steven Muller, a specialist in international education, waxes enthusiastic over the benefits of globalization:

> These benign motives [the two-way partnership between industry and research universities] tend to be mutually supportive, and they go hand-in-hand with the globalism of the marketplace and the information society, insofar as both industrial corporations and major research universities have equivalent multi-national or international interests (1995, 70).

In his review of the transition of social science research to a post–Cold War paradigm, Stanley Heginbotham, vice president of the Social Science Research Council, noted that "[t]he collapses of the Soviet bloc and the Soviet Union have accelerated a reassessment among federal, state, and private funders of their program priorities in a changed international environment." If research during the Cold War focused on in-depth understanding of adversarial societies, now it is oriented to "themes or problems associated with the challenges of building more effective social, economic, and political systems." Chief among these themes Heginbotham lists the development of viable markets and market institutions, the fostering of civil society institutions, the building of independent, merit-oriented educational institutions, and the adaptation of technologies responsive to public needs. All of these, moreover, are believed to enhance "questions of performance—especially in the international economy—of the United States relative to the other advanced market democracies" (Heginbotham 1994, 36).

Several years before, then Social Science Research Council president Frederic Wakeman convened a meeting of advisers to orient the council toward a new policy to subsidize "transnational and comparative research." Among the issues he reviews are "such issues as the global emergence of an underclass, the spread of English and the access to power associated with speaking English, and differences among nations in how they use the same technologies, [none of which] accord with ordinary discipline- or area-oriented committee agendas" (Wakeman 1988, 87). It is evident, then, that research into the crossing of national boundaries also requires a crossing of disciplinary boundaries. And at the heart of transnationalism and transdisciplinarity is culture. Wakeman invokes the problem of "deterritorialization" and its impact on state-oriented analysis; "micro or substate level" activity, such as the NGO movement; and "cultural factors not in the state sphere that impinge upon the international sector." "Culture," indeed, has become more central even for the kinds of problems studied by economists and political scientists.

> "[C]ulture" is itself no longer the sort of thing anthropologists once took it to be: homogeneous, local, well-bounded, and in clear one-to-one correspondence with distinct social units. Culture now leaks across national boundaries, and this transnational flow is intimately tied not only to the many diasporas that characterize national populations, but also to the incredible force of media (movies, magazines, cassettes, videotapes, computers, and the like) which close the cultural distance (and accelerate the traffic) between overseas populations and their home societies. (88)

It should come as no surprise, then, that the Council decided, in the very same issue in which Wakeman makes his report, to announce the financing of *Public Culture,* a journal in transnational cultural studies. After all, Arjun Appadurai, coeditor with Carol Breckenridge, was among the advisers convoked to give the Council a new direction. By the time of Heginbotham's more programmatic essay for the Council in 1994, a transnational and transcultural approach to economic, political, and social issues was on the agenda. We see the importance that social scientists now give to culture even in the hardest of the social sciences, economic activity. "The emerging interest . . . is in international scholarship that is context-sensitive: that helps us understand how the globalizing aspects of contemporary society are shaped, refracted, altered, and redefined as they encounter successions of local contests" (Heginbotham 1994, 37). Heginbotham even makes room for traditional disciplines within his scheme:

> Disciplinary departments in the humanities and social sciences will increasingly engage with, and become fuller partners in, international scholarship. The themes and problems they explore will increasingly be seen as common to a wide range of global settings, but will take very different forms. Many of those themes and problems will increasingly be seen as having important transnational components. (38)

What we are seeing here is a pitch for the continuing relevance of the social sciences, and even the humanities, as higher education is establishing partnerships with business and declaring economic competitiveness to be the sole concern. Heginbotham argues that area studies refashioned as transnational transcultural studies will enable "understand[ing of] how the culture, history, and language of a local context shape its interaction with, for example, the evolution of market institutions and engagement with international market forces" (37). He then goes on to aggrandize American scholarship to the proportions of what elsewhere I have called a "We Are the World" syndrome. "The boundaries between American, comparative, and international scholarship will increasingly be seen as arbitrary and impediments to effective inquiry" (37). In a universe of globalized knowledge production under U.S. hegemony, foreign students trained in the United States will measure their own societies against ours and "acquir[e] an understanding of the distinctions between American society and their own society" (38). The comparison with the United States will presumably enable them to manage change at home: "Their educational goals will be to understand the difference between how a globalizing force is refracted in the United States and in their own society so that they can better manage change at home" (38).

It comes as no surprise, then, that even this enterprise of transnational, transcultural studies will serve to maintain the comparative advantage of the U.S. system of higher education, perpetuating the economic differential that accrues to the more global system. Note that Heginbotham is speaking obliquely to funders:

> The interests of funders will be less directed at building a community of U.S. scholars who can represent and reflect American society in contrast to that of the Soviets, and more at playing a leading role in promoting international scholarship that has shared norms, standards, problem definitions, and methodologies. . . . By virtue of the size and excellence of our educational institutions, U.S. scholarship will undoubtedly play a strong influential role in the building of an international scholarship. Given the challenges that we face in our own society, it should be clear, however, that we will benefit from, as well as shape, the internationalization of scholarship. (39)

PROSPECTS FOR A RAPPROCHEMENT OF LATIN AMERICAN STUDIES, LATINO STUDIES, AND CULTURAL STUDIES

The unparalleled competitiveness of the U.S. university system is cause for both the increasing presence of Latin American academics in the United States, not only as permanent professors but also as occasional workers supplementing their salaries back home, and also for their resentment at the power of this university system to establish research agendas to which they must accommodate. With the likely rapprochement between ethnic studies and cultural studies and their protagonist role in helping to reconstitute area studies, i.e., Latin American studies, a U.S. approach to dealing with questions of social stability, markets, and diversity is likely to gain ground in Latin America. In fact, it has already established some beachheads. And there is opposition, as in the debates over the direction of scholarship on Latin America to which I referred in the introduction. These critiques do not come from reactionary conservative points of view, not even from left conservative perspectives such as the Marxist critique of identity politics with which we are familiar in the United States. It has to do with the asymmetry in the establishment of research agendas rather than a critique of the identity politics evident in the approach of U.S. Latin Americanists for a more democratic culture and society, which in any case is a common desideratum of all involved.

Reconciling the differences that this asymmetry opens up is not easy.

One strategy, which would be to invite Latin American academics to participate in the design of research agendas, is not necessarily workable, if we imagine that there will be continued resentment that those invitations are at the disposition of U.S. actors, be they Euramericans or Latinos. The underdevelopment of foreign university systems by the dominance of the U.S. university system engraves this unequal situation in the structure of knowledge-producing institutions on a global level. Another tack might be to create transnational academic circuits with the goal of influencing the educational policy of international bodies and trade agreements as well as international foundations in order to strengthen the university systems in Latin America, which national governments are downsizing due to pressures to cut public expenditures, and also to adjust the educational sector to business, trade, and technological innovation. The Ford Foundation has an initiative to make this partnership more feasible, and those of us who are negotiating the relations among area studies, ethnic studies, and cultural studies should make recourse to it as a means to help defuse some tensions between Latin American and Latino scholars. The Ford Foundation's architect for the Crossing Borders initiative referred to earlier writes that:

> The fund will complement the grant making [to rethink area studies in the United States] by supporting international collaborations through grants made jointly to academic institutions in the U.S and overseas. The Foundation hopes that the impetus for such collaborations will originate largely overseas so that the historical imbalance—whereby scholars in the West studied the "rest"—may truly begin to shift. Without that change, revitalization of Area Studies will inevitably be limited. (Volkman 1998, 3–4)

And I would add that without that change, the reconstitution of ethnic and cultural studies will also be limited.

Conclusion: The Critique of Culture

The post–Cold War creates a situation that is difficult, however, for reworking the relations between Latino studies, area studies, and cultural studies. All of these transdisciplines have prioritized the role of culture—the recognition of cultural differences—as the sine qua non of democratization. It is this notion of culture, for example, that underpins the concept of cultural citizenship introduced by Renato Rosaldo (1989; Rosaldo and Flores 1987). At odds with conventional notions of citizenship, which emphasize universal albeit formal applicability of political rights to all members of a nation, the usefulness of the concept of cultural citizenship is to emphasize that groups of people bound together by shared social, cultural, and/or physical features should not be excluded from participation in the public spheres of a given polity on the basis of those features. In a juridical context that enables litigation against exclusion and a cultural-political ethos that eschews marginalizing the "nonnormative" (considered as such from the perspective of the "mainstream"), culture serves as the ground or warrant for making "claim[s] to rights in the public square" (Rosaldo 1997, 36). Since culture is what "create[s] space where people feel 'safe' and 'at home,' where they feel a sense of belonging and membership," it is, according to this view, a necessary condition for citizenship (Flores and Benmayor 1997, 15). Consequently, if democracy is to be fostered, public spheres in which deliberation on questions of the public good is held must be permeable to different cultures. The relativist strain in anthropological theory—according to which "communal culture" as an ensemble of ideas and values provides the individual with identity (Sapir 1924)—is mobilized here for political ends. Culture is thus more than this anchoring ensemble of ideas and values. It is premised on difference, which functions as a *resource* (Flores and Benmayor 1997, 5). One drawback is that the content of culture recedes in importance as the instrumental usefulness of the claim to difference as a warrant gains legitimacy. It might be said that previous understandings of culture—canons of artistic excellence, symbolic patterns that give coherence to and thus endow a group of people or society with human worth—give way to the expediency of culture. In our era, *claims to* difference and culture are expedient insofar as they enable the empowerment of a community.

Because the expediency or instrumentality of culture is increasingly evident, appeals to cultural difference do not carry the legitimizing force that they once did. It is no longer invoked only by minority groups seeking greater inclusion but also by governments, international nongovernmental organizations, the corporate sector, and even multilateral development banks. With the inflation of culture, its value in the project to democratize society wanes partly because of its absorption into the strategic gambits of capital and politics. Like ideology, in Larry Grossberg's formulation, cultural politics are increasingly beside the point. Grossberg's "end of ideology" is premised not on the demise of communism but on the rearticulation of political economy. Unlike Fukuyama's formulation, however, the new global conjuncture of today does not portend the end of history. Modernity required ideology to camouflage the instrumentality of cultural management. But today, as Larry Grossberg argues, the globalization of culture has led to an "increasingly cynical inflection to the logic of ideology," such that it no longer operates unconsciously. If ideology implies that "people don't know what they are doing but they are doing it anyway," then the expediency of culture as instrumental performativity implies that "they know what they are doing but they are doing it anyway" (Grossberg 1999, 43–44 n. 52). Once we are all aware that cultural identity is wielded as a form of strategic essentialism, it loses its power to open up space, or the space that it opens up is functional for the neoliberal university or a Benettonian representation of cultural democracy compatible with consumerism. The Gramscian view of culture as a terrain of struggle may only extend the reach of the market and other forms of instrumentality on this view. Therefore, ethnic studies and cultural studies need to articulate their goals with a critique of culture.

Bill Readings (1996) elaborates further on the transformation in the experience of culture. In the so-called post-Fordist era, culture no longer mediates between the ethnic nation and the rational state to produce a distinct national identity. This does not mean that culture disappears but only that it is reconverted; it becomes instrumentally useful but no longer legitimized as the medium through which subjects are civilized or, to use the language of early twentieth century cultural policy, become "ethically incomplete" (Miller 1998). Ethical incompleteness, indeed, is a variant of that performative force that requires subjects to come into being by reiterating norms. According to Readings, the emerging global system of capitalism no longer needs "a cultural content in terms of which to interpellate and manage subjects" (cited in Grossberg 1998, 5), which is not to say that subjects do not consume culture more voraciously than ever before. In other words, as culture expands and becomes ever more central to the economy, its importance in establishing a Bourdieuian distinction wanes. Capitalism now is committed only to "monetary subjects without money" who are merely "the shadow of money's substance." Consequently, "if the sphere of the ideological [and I would add, the cultural] has become visible (not only in critical theory and the academy but literally everywhere), this is because it is not where the real game is being played anymore" (Grossberg 1998, 5).

It is not so much that power dispenses with culture; it no longer needs it to shape ethical subjects of the nation. Culture is freed, so to speak, to become a generator of value in its own right. And it is increasingly traveling speedily along the same media as finance capital, which seems to have become a virtual source of value. Neoliberal capitalism may also be understood as the "post-development organization of international capital" now that in the post–Cold War period there is no need to develop the so-called underdeveloped world (Grossberg 2000). Emblematic of this situation is the recent turn to culture by multilateral development lending institutions like the World Bank and the International Monetary Fund. They ask questions like the following: What kind of rationality can economic agents rely on for investment in culture? What kind of structure of incentives will get results? The answer we get is that incentives can provide a stable environment for private investment in culture rather than the episodic nature characteristic of public investment in culture. But even then we are told that "we have to limit the model of financing of culture to specific segments of culture because the demand for resources is too large and wide-ranging" (Santana 1999).

> Return is the sine qua non of investment. Why else should economic agents invest? How can you persuade them? It all depends on how we define return. One thing we can say with certainty is that the financing of culture for culture's sake has a low probability of success. The different kinds of return are: (1) fiscal incentives, (2) institutional marketing or publicity value, (3) conversion of nonmarket activity to market activity. As far as multilateral development banks are concerned, the major kinds of cultural funding are for projects that provide a political return (e.g., help defuse political problems and hence give greater security to investment), and projects that develop human and social capital (e.g., education) that increase the GDP and enable governments to repay their loans. (Santana 1999)

To be sure, education must be financed and curricula developed to expand the GDP, but this is not its only usefulness. Culture and identity, as the lynchpins of the rapprochement of Latin American studies, Latino studies, and cultural studies, have largely been reconverted for the benefit of the neoliberal project. Therefore it is important to understand the degree to which a new phase of institutionalization in the university may not solve the frustrations that all three endeavors have produced in their constituencies. Such understanding requires large doses of critique. For critics like Richard, only the disruptive force of certain aesthetic practices continues to repel the omnivorous reach of the market and the instrumental discourses of cultural legitimation. While this is no doubt true, particularly in countries like Chile where she resides, it is important to recognize that disruption is not produced exclusively by culturalist or aestheticist resistance. Other significant forms of disruption are given by the solidarity protests in Seattle in December 1999 that brought about the collapse of the talks at the meeting of the World Trade Organization. The protestors laid bare the undemocratic manipulation of the international trading system by the major powers against the interests of developing countries, the poor, the environment, workers, and consumers. The rapprochement of Latin American studies, Latino studies, and cultural studies could become complicit with a university system beholden to the corporate world. On the other hand, this new endeavor can work to undermine the very premises under which universities are fostering it. To do so requires examining the transnational context in which the ground of culture and identity is already structured for its absorption. The fact that so many of the abuses of the new world economic order are practiced in Latin American countries (e.g., the abuse of workers in sweatshops, the creation of a huge "reserve army of unemployed labor," the rise of new private universities at the expense of public institutions) is an opportunity to examine and intervene in the very conditions that shape our institutional practice. This is also an opportunity to factor class back into the projects of ethnic studies and cultural studies and extend its relevance to a transnational framework in which these projects can be part of a heterogeneous yet global critique of the ways in which neoliberalism has structured the terrain in which we act.

NOTES

1. The term "Arielism" is based on José Enrique Rodó's *Ariel* (1967), originally published in 1900. It is a call to Latin American intellectuals to eschew the allure of U.S. instrumental culture and instead model their politics on a quasi-Kantian, disinterested aesthetics. Were Rodó to have taken an activist role in educational policy, it would be possible to see in him an analogue of Matthew Arnold, in whose *Culture and Anarchy* ([1869] 1961) culture is characterized as the atmosphere in which an aesthetic technocracy would rule more effectively than either the aristocratic or capitalist classes.

2. "Dunn was an organizer or officer of a number of Soviet-American cooperation and cultural exchange organizations. He was highly visible on the letterheads and at the rallies of Left and pro-Soviet groups and, although he was not a member of the Communist Party, he was active in many organizations

supported by the party. He was the classic 'fellow traveler' of the McCarthyites and his application to be scientific attaché in the American embassy in Paris was denied, presumably for political reasons. Nevertheless, during the entire period of his political activity, his research was supported by an AEC contract" (Lewontin 1997, 19).

3. This mesh or field of action that channeled sixties politics in the medium of protest was structured by "[weak] working-class organization . . . , [flawed] electoral representative institutions . . . , and state structures that inhibited the translation of popular interests into policy" (Piven and Cloward 1993, 422).

REFERENCES

Achugar, Hugo. 1998. "Leones, cazadores e historiadores: A propósito de las políticas de la memoria y del conocimiento." In *Teorías sin disciplina: Latinoamericanismo, poscolonialidad y globalización en debate,* ed. Santiago Castro-Gómez and Eduardo Mendieta. Mexico: Miguel Angel Porrúa and University of San Francisco. 271–85.

Appadurai, Arjun. 1992. "Disjuncture and Difference in the Global Cultural Economy." In *The Phantom Public Sphere,* ed. Bruce Robbins. Minneapolis: University of Minnesota Press. 269–95.

Arnold, Mathew. [1869] 1961. *Culture and Anarchy.* Cambridge: Cambridge University Press.

Avelar, Idelber. 1999. "The Clandestine Ménage à Trois of Cultural Studies, Spanish, and Critical Theory." *Profession,* 49–58.

Berger , Mark T. 1995. *Under Northern Eyes: Latin American Studies and U.S. Hegemony in the Americas, 1898.* Bloomington: Indiana University Press.

Beverley, John. 1994. "Writing in Reverse: On the Project of the Latin American Subaltern Studies Group." *Dispositio* 46: 271–88.

———. 1996. "Estudios culturales y vocación política." *Revista de Crítica Cultural* 12.

Burka, Maria. 1996. "Education and Training of Graduate Students." Meeting of the Council for Chemical Research (CCR), January. At http://www.chem.purdue.edu/ccr/news/jan96/news2.html.

Camarillo, Albert. 1997. Presentation for "Rethinking America and the Americas: A Five College Conversation." Mount Holyoke College, South Hadley, Massachusetts, March 25.

Cohen, Roger. 2000. "Germans Seek Foreign Labor for New Era of Computers." *New York Times Online.* April 9.

Coronil, Fernando. 1998. "Más allá del occidentalismo: hacia categorías geo-históricas no-imperialistas." In *Teorías sin disciplina: Latinoamericanismo, poscolonialidad y globalización en debate,* ed. Santiago Castro-Gómez and Eduardo Mendieta. Mexico: Miguel Angel Porrúa and University of San Francisco. 121–46.

Cummings, Milton C., Jr., 1991. "Government and the Arts: An Overview." In *Public Money and the Muse: Essays on Government Funding for the Arts,* ed. Stephen Benedict. New York: Norton. 31–79.

Enríquez, Juan. 2000. "Technology and the Future of the Nation State." Paper presented at the "Recentering the Periphery: Latin-American Intellectuals in the New Millennium" symposium, New School for Social Research, New York, April 7.

Fernández, James D. 2000. "Fragments of the Past, Tasks for the Future: Spanish in the United States." *PMLA* 115, no. 7 (December): 1961.

Flores, William V., and Rina Benmayor, eds. 1997. *Latino Cultural Citizenship: Claiming Identity, Space, and Rights.* Boston: Beacon Press.

Fukuyama, Francis. 1992. *The End of History and the Last Man.* New York: Free Press.

Gentili, Pablo. 2000. "The Permanent Crisis of the Public University." *NACLA Report on the Americas* 23, no. 4 (January–February): 12–18.

Grossberg, Larry. 1998. "The Victory of Culture: Part 1: Against the Logic of Mediation." *Angelaki* 3, no. 3: 3–29.

———. 1999. "Speculations and Articulations of Globalization." *Polygraph* 11: 11–48.

———. 2000. "The Figure of Subalternity and the Neoliberal Future." *Nepantla* 1, no. 1 (spring).

Heginbotham, Stanley J. 1994. "Rethinking International Scholarship: The Challenge of Transition from the Cold War Era." *Items* 48, no. 2–3: 33–40.

Hershberg, Eric. 1999. "From Cold War Origins to a Model for Academic Internationalization: Latin American Studies at a Crossroads." *Dispositio/n* 49: 117–31.

Kowal, Rebekah. 1999. "Modern Dance and American Culture in the Early Cold War Years." Ph.D. diss., New York University.

Lewontin, R. C. 1997. "The Cold War and the Transformation of the Academy." In *The Cold War and the University: Toward an Intellectual History of the Postwar Years,* ed. Noam Chomsky et al. New York: New Press. 1–34.

Mato, Daniel. 1998. "Remarks on New Approaches to Area Studies." Paper presented at the Twenty-first International Congress of the Latin American Studies Association, Chicago, September 24–27.

Mignolo, Walter. 1998. "Postoccidentalismo: El argumento desde América Latina." In *Teorías sin disciplina: Latinoamericanismo, poscolonialidad y globalización en debate,* ed. Santiago Castro-Gómez and Eduardo Mendieta. Mexico: Miguel Angel Porrúa and University of San Francisco. 31–58.

Miller, Toby. 1998. *Technologies of Truth: Cultural Citizenship and the Popular Media.* Minneapolis: University of Minnesota Press.

Moraña, Mabel. 1998. "El *boom* del subalterno." In *Teorías sin disciplina: Latinoamericanismo, poscolonialidad y globalización en debate,* ed. Santiago

Castro-Gómez and Eduardo Mendieta. Mexico: Miguel Angel Porrúa and University of San Francisco. 233–43.

Muller, Steven. 1995. "Globalization of Knowledge." In *International Challenges to American Colleges and Universities: Looking Ahead,* ed. Katharine H. Hanson and Joel W. Meyerson. Phoenix: American Council on Education/ Oryx Press. 63–75.

Nelson, Carey, and Lawrence Grossberg, eds. 1988. *Marxism and the Interpretation of Culture.* Urbana: University of Illinois Press.

Nelson, Carey, Paula Treichler, and Lawrence Grossberg, eds. 1992. *Cultural Studies.* New York: Routledge.

Piven, Frances Fox, and Richard Cloward. 1993. *Regulating the Poor: The Functions of Public Welfare.* 2d ed. New York: Vintage.

Readings, Bill. 1996. *The University in Ruins.* Cambridge: Harvard University Press.

Rhoades, Gary, and Sheila Slaughter. 1997. "Academic Capitalism, Managed Professionals, and Supply Side Higher Education." *Social Text* 51 (summer): 9–38.

Richard, Nelly. 1998. "Intersectando Latinoamérica con el latinoamericanismo: Discurso académico y crítica cultural." In *Teorías sin disciplina: Latinoamericanismo, poscolonialidad y globalización en debate,* ed. Santiago Castro-Gómez and Eduardo Mendieta. Mexico: Miguel Angel Porrúa and University of San Francisco. 245–270.

———. 2000. "Globalización académica, estudios culturales y práctica crítico-intelectual: nuevos desafíos." Paper presented at "Recentering the Periphery: Latin-American Intellectuals in the New Millennium" symposium, New School for Social Research, New York, April 7.

Rodó, José Enrique. 1967. *Ariel.* Cambridge: Cambridge University Press.

Rodríguez, Ileana. 1998. "Hegemonía y dominio: Subalternidad, un significado flotante." In *Teorías sin disciplina: Latinoamericanismo, poscolonialidad y globalización en debate,* ed. Santiago Castro-Gómez and Eduardo Mendieta. Mexico: Miguel Angel Porrúa and University of San Francisco. 101–20.

Rosaldo, Renato. 1989. *Culture and Truth: The Remaking of Social Analysis.* Boston: Beacon Press.

———. 1997. "Cultural Citizenship, Inequality, and Multiculturalism." In *Latino Cultural Citizenship: Claiming Identity, Space, and Rights,* ed. William V. Flores and Rina Benmayor. Boston: Beacon Press. 27–38.

Rosaldo, Renato, and William V. Flores. 1987. "Notes on Cultural Citizenship." Unpublished manuscript. Stanford Center for Chicano Research, Stanford, Calif.

Santana, Elcior. 1999. "Cultural Investment by Multilateral Development Banks." Paper presented at "The Transnationalization of Support for Culture in a Globalizing World" conference, Rockefeller Foundation and the U.S.-Mexico Fund for Culture, Bellagio, Italy, December 6–10.

Sapir, Edward. 1924. "Culture, Genuine and Spurious." *American Journal of Sociology* 29: 401–29.

Sarlo, Beatriz. 1997. "Los estudios culturales y la crítica literaria en la encrucijada valorativa." *Revista de Crítica Cultural* 15 (November): 32–38.

"Too Many High-Tech Visas Doled Out Last Year." 2000. *New York Times Online.* 7 April.

Volkman, Toby Alice. 1998. "Crossing Borders: The Case for Area Studies." *Ford Foundation Report* (winter 1998). At: http://www.fordfound.org/ QR.29.1/crossing/index.html.

———. 1999. Introduction to *Crossing Borders: Revitalizing Area Studies.* New York: Ford Foundation.

Wakeman, Frederic E., Jr. 1988. "Transnational and Comparative Research." *Items* 42, no. 4: 85–89.

Yúdice, George. 1992. "We Are *Not* the World." *Social Text* 31/32: 202–16.

———. 1994. "Globalización y nuevas formas de intermediación cultural." In *Mundo, región, aldea: Identidades políticas, culturales e integración regional,* ed. Hugo Achugar and Gerardo Caetano. Montevideo: Ediciones Trilce.

———. 1996. "Cultural Studies and Civil Society." In *Reading the Shape of the World: Towards an International Cultural Studies,* ed. Henry Schwarz and Richard Dienst. Boulder: Westview Press. 50–66. Spanish version: "Estudios culturales y sociedad civil." *Revista de Crítica Cultural* 8 (1994): 44–53.

———. 1999. "The Privatization of Culture." *Social Text* 59 (summer): 17–34.

Part II

Different Knowledges and the Knowledge
of Difference: Gender, Ethnicity, Race,
and Language

Latina/o: Another Site of Struggle, Another Site of Accountability

Angie Chabram-Dernersesian

As a political identity "Latina/o" has captured the inter/national imagination, and it continues to do so as we edge into the twenty-first century. Within the popular imagination as well as the academy, Latina/o is a site of social identification that is associated with new(er) hemispheric movements and forms of community as well as new(er) understandings of geography, ethnicity, history, class, race, gender, sexuality, culture (and cultural production), the economy, and social alliance.[1] In the very decade where a conservative agenda issued devastating statewide and national propositions and actively distorted civil rights and immigrant legacies, Latinas/os were visibly and strategically linked to a variety of progressive movements for social change. They waged struggles on behalf of disenfranchised transnational populations for better health benefits and working conditions, political and educational representation, decolonization, language, "social space," and citizenship. They waged struggles against nativism, the border, the border patrol, environmental toxicity, AIDS, and globalization. And they waged struggles against linguistic, sexual, gender, and racial discrimination; homophobia and heterosexism; class exploitation; police brutality, high(er) incarceration rates, and ethnic profiling.

Latinas/os also launched a broad spectrum of cultural productions from popular culture to *dichos,* to Spanish-language television shows, to bilingual virtual cultures. Within the academic arena Latina/o identifications generated a number of anthologies, books, articles, journals, statistical and economic profiles, as well as area studies (Latina/o studies; Chicana/o, Latina/o studies; Latino/a Latin American studies, Latin critical theory, Latina/o cultural studies). Like their counterparts in other social political arenas, together these combined Latina/o (cultural) productions do not bespeak a common political position or cultural-ideological aesthetic. In music, for example, we see huge differences between songs that celebrate panethnic nationalism and suggest to their Latina/o listeners that all we need to do is "come together" in "*hermandad*/brotherhood" (and we'll progress: *echar pa delante*) and songs that offer contested narratives of travel from *el subdesarrollo* to unrealized citizenship and that speak counterinterrogations to the INS and the anti-immigrant rhetoric of the 1990s.[2]

Because Latina/o is not only a site of struggle but also of "accountability," in this essay I will engage what might be construed as a problematic form of panethnic nationalism (or panethnic multicutural nationalism) that resurfaced in the 1990s in response to a worsening of social conditions, a restructuring of the global economy, increased immigration to *el norte,* anti-Latino agendas, and the need for another site of collective identification. To a certain extent this engagement reaffirms what history has taught us over and over again, namely, that we[3] should be attentive to the pitfalls of "ascendant," seemingly transparent forms of panethnicity and panethnic nationalism. In a nutshell these problematic forms of panethnic identification reorganize social subjects around seemingly transparent racial, linguistic, ethnic, political, or geopolitical unities or blocs, and they also forebode a return to single discursive registers of social analysis. In addition, they maintain the centrality of preconstituted racial categories or national paradigms, thus obscuring a number of important social divisions and/or important lines of affiliation. Finally, they usher in a number of "guarantees," including the idea that the panethnic umbrella or mode of representation can guarantee our (progressive) politics and (firm) connections to important social movements and marginalized social groups in the Americas.

Recently, the perils of these panethnic forms of identification were graphically displayed for the American public in the televisual arena by the saga of the Elián Gonzalez case and the Bush election and in the divisions these events provoked within various Latina/o communities. But these perils are not restricted to mediatized portraitures; they can also be found in the clashes at international borders, the transnational factories of the global economy, the platforms for social reform and revolutionary change, and the shelters that house the victims of (Latino) domestic abuse. These perils can be found in the social relations that are reproduced within highly prestigious academies of the United States.

Within this sector alone, these perils become painfully evident as we move beyond the glossy catalogs of the academe into the time-honored curricular practices of traditional departments that appeal to *la hispanidad.* These traditional (Spanish) departments often appeal to an overarching unity of Spanish-speaking peoples while delivering curriculums that selectively foreground elite Spanish, Latin American, and Latino traditions. Other legacies considered to be too popular, indigenous, domestic, working class, or too American for Spanish (American) Eurocentric tastes are ignored, underrepresented, or directed to ethnic studies departments.

But these departments are the only ones that ruffle the vesture of the seamless Latino. Other perils of panethnic nationalisms can be found in academic sites that appeal to a hemispheric identification and do so in the English language. Speaking in reference to a classic scenario within a Latin American studies department at the university, the late Chicana critic Lora Romero (1997) forcefully suggested to us, her readers, that

> in the recent past, scholars doing postcolonial work under the auspices of (US) Latin American studies have demonstrated no more interest in Chicano culture and history than those working in what is called "American (literary) studies." . . . Even now, as Chicano studies gains recognition and prestige in American studies and American literature programs, Latin American studies programs rarely house scholars working on Chicano studies. (246)

Clearly, what is at stake here in this academic scenario is not just token representation or invisibility or just another unsettling example of academic subordination. What is also at stake are the historical as well as social *differences* that have produced these very disparate forms of hemispheric and interdisciplinary study—not to mention the difficulties of bringing these disparate spheres of intellectual production into a productive conversation, let alone an academic interface.

Chicana/o studies programs that house those context-specific forms of knowledge that are erased from the Latin American spaces described by Lora Romero are not immune from the social and intellectual contestations that are being waged by subalternized groups. Increasingly, the very Chicana/o programs that continue to struggle against the erasures of authoritative high-brow traditions are under scrutiny from a variety of Latina/o and indigenous groups that also do not find welcome in traditional departments and seek a presence and an alliance that can shed light on transnational resistance movements. In response to this demand, many Chicana/o studies programs across the nation are adding Latina/o courses to their curriculums or assuming a "Chicana/o Latina/o" naming practice. But clearly not everyone is interested in this type of an umbrella or connection. Some groups seek an autonomous intellectual space on campus. (And in some cases they aim to create other ethnic-specific programs just like Chicanas/os have done before them.) Of course, there are any number of responses to this charge from Chicana/o programs that range from strong support to angry silence, to direct counterchallenges, to concrete proposals for building strong ties of alliance from multiply situated areas of study and politics.

Then there is another reality to be considered: in an era when Latino studies programs and departments are surfacing all over the country as a way to meet the challenges of globalization, many Chicana/o studies programs that are already in existence and engage "the border" do not favor the idea of being subsumed into a Latino studies umbrella that does not foreground those historical specificities of Chicanas/os that took years of institutional struggle to represent.

To return where this list of perils began (the televisual arena), Spanish-language television news shows that promote "the unifying power of the Spanish language" and Latino panethnicity have generated "intra-ethnic tension" among viewers who critique the privileging of news broadcasters with fair skin and light hair or the blatant overrepresentation of certain Latino populations in news broadcasts (Rodríguez 1999, 83). Together, this combined list of perils speaks to the importance of revisiting the constructed nature of *latinidad* (Latinoness) from its diverse positionalities and contestations. In the contemporary period this labor is important because *Latinidad* (Latinos) is on the cutting edge of a variety of globalization studies and social movements and because panethnic nationalisms encourage a passive acceptance of metalanguages under the premise that they are more representative because they are restructured according to the logic of a native (Latino) form of multiculturalism or panethnicity. Here "Latino" purports to represent us in a seamless fashion across nations, nationalities, borders, cultures, barriers, classes, genders, sexualities, and political interests in a decade that witnessed a full-blown rearticulation of a new politics of difference, an ongoing reflection on the pitfalls of universalism, and a proliferation of social contradictions and antagonisms! Clearly, not only the disjunctures and extensions of this claim to representation need to be scrutinized but also the premises that support this claim. One of these premises is the age-old strength-in-numbers argument, which equates an increase in population or a bigger (ethnic) scale with social or political empowerment, and another is the premise that our big scale *alone* can fully attend to the biggest scale promoted by capitalism in the global era.

Those who seek to affiliate "Latina/o" to a variety of progressive social movements also encounter a number of disturbing ways in which some panethnic models of Latino studies can dovetail with the social practices and narratives produced by the dominant forces of globalization: the ones that are distinguished by their homogenizing tendencies, a penchant for "static totalities"—to use a phrase coined by Néstor García Canclini (1996)—and a tendency to run over identity formations that emerged as a result of protracted struggles for another place to stand in and speak from (Hall 1997a, 184). When Latino identity is prefaced by the abbreviated term "U.S." as a way to distinguish between an identity or scholarship base produced over here (in the United States) and over there (the Latino in the Americas outside of a U.S. space), other types of troubling resonances with what Stuart Hall (1997a) has described as a "global mass culture" are set into motion, and so are a series of potential "dangerous liaisons" that provoke one to raise the question of what kind of politics lies behind this "U.S." political (Latino) subject that foregrounds the nomenclature and cultural capital of the United States in its alternative political imaginary even before naming its counteridentification (the other half of the couplet). Admittedly, in the best-case scenario this political form of identification is assumed as a way of positioning oneself within a particular location and set of circumstances as opposed to the alternative of pretending to speak for everyone in the American hemisphere *a lo yankee imperialista*. However, what cannot be denied because of its visibility is the presence of a dominant language and symbolic force of globalization that is recognizable to peoples from all over the world. What is also visible here is an affirmation of the borders and the boundaries of the nation (as a category of social identification) that is contrary to the sensibilities of oppositional forms of transnational Latina/o social identification that posit a decolonizing, antiracist, antisexist, antiglobalization (anticapitalist) movement from below.

For those willing to continue down this painful path of critical self-reflection, there are other ways in which these seemingly disparate Latino and globalization narratives can dovetail. As Frances Negrón-Mutaner (2000) aptly suggests in her essay "Not an Academic Subject," "Due to the globalization of capital, people and culture, never before today has it been more convenient to embrace 'Latino' as an enjoyable transnational strategy to remap America" (117–18). In the context of "market expansion," "political consolidation," the "internal shifting of community settlement patterns," and a "transnational commodity culture that is Latinizing el norte," Negrón-Mutaner poses the question of "whether a shared bicultural public sphere will emerge throughout the Americas in the global period or whether Latinos will be fundamentally mobilized as consumers" for a market economy (118).

Initially Negrón-Mutaner seizes on the "contradictory" meanings of "Latino" (here "the national currency of empowerment and exploitation"), and she argues that it demands our attention in order "to both appreciate its potential and in order to address its limitations" (117). While she acknowledges that communities remain identified in specifically ethnic terms (Mexican American, Tejano, Puerto Rican, and Cubano) and that "Latino" is fundamentally linked to the need to create a subject of politics, her audience-based distinction flattens and dilutes Latino ideological fields. For Negrón-Mutaner the term "Latino" allows non-Latinos "to simplify their cognitive operations, remain in blissful ignorance over the country's colonial past, present, and classify a diverse group under a seemingly transparent category" (118). In her contrast, for Latinos "the term universalizes key demands within the racialized idioms of American politics, while it masks the fact that Latinos do not constitute a coherent, cultural, political, or economic block" (118). In the non-Latino case the hegemonic "Latino" engenders appropriation, assimilation, and false consciousness, and in the second case it engenders a form of strategic essentialism and a homogenization of alternative knowledges that is also indebted to a logic of panethnic nationalism, even as it is rendered with an acknowledgment of "unity in difference." In both cases contradictory Latino expressions are erased from the sphere of intragroup identification.

Among those who have called into question a number of assumptions about the Latino block and "what it means to us" and seek another kind of discursive specification of "Latino" is Juan Flores. In the introductory pages of his book *From Bomba to Hip-Hop* (2000), he takes the position that "while there is a certain inevitability in the formation of pan-ethnic concepts like 'Latino' or 'Asian-American,'" the sociological validity of these constructs "depends overridingly on the attention paid to the specifics of each group and their historical placement within U.S. society." Thus, he posits that within this space "[t]here is 'Latino' only from the point of view and as lived by the Mexican, the Puerto Rican, the Cuban, and so forth" (8). In this way, for him, "Latino" or "Hispanic" only holds up when it is qualified by the national-group angle or optic from which it is uttered; thus "there is a 'Chicano/Latino' or 'Cuban/Latino' perspective but no meaningful one that is simply 'Latino'" (8). Flores also argues that there are certain drawbacks to the usage of this term, but in his case they lie with its convergence with familiar scenarios of appropriation and assimilation. He further explains this position:

> For the generic, unqualified usage, aside from generating and perpetu-
> ating stereotypes of a derogatory or otherwise distorting kind, also is
> employed to mislead the public into thinking that all members and con-
> stituents of the composite are basically in the same position in the society
> and all progressing toward acceptance and self-advancements from the
> same starting line and at the same place. (8)

For Flores, this model of Latino articulation evades a rigorously comparative structural analysis (i.e., "how each group is positioned within the existing relations of power and privilege of U.S. society" and its usage can function as a "tool of exclusion and internal 'othering'" [8]).

Chon Noriega and Alma M. López (1996) provide different types of relational readings and specifications of "Latino"—contrasts between the political traditions of "Latino" versus "Hispanic." For them "Hispanic" emerges both as a professional self-designation within middle-class political and professional activities and as a U.S. census category. "Hispanic" also "reflects various attempts to acquire institutional, economic, and political power through homogenization" (xii). By contrast they see "Latino" as emerging "out of the efforts of civil rights struggles and grassroots social movements to achieve 'radical' change at the national level through the articulation of a collective identity by the Latino intelligentsia" (xii). Notwithstanding this notable difference, which to a certain extent sidesteps the possibility of Latino homogenization/Hispanization/

commodification, the authors admit that "there are too many contradictions within the diverse cultures and political strategies grouped under the terms 'Hispanic' or 'Latino.'" In the final instance, for them "Latino" is a highly conflicted term—a term that is "the product of a racial politics played out at the national level" (xii). In this way, for them, "Latino" becomes a "politically constructed category" that "has been used for competing purposes at various levels of social organization" (xii).

In her book *Telling Identities* (1995), Rosaura Sánchez further disarticulates the racial politics behind an early form of panethnic (Latino) identification: ethnicism. This was "a strategic discourse that was meant to transcend class, generational, origin, gender, and linguistic differences, especially during periods of xenophobic violence against Latinos" (268). Sánchez explains to contemporary readers that while the politics of ethnic identity was a significant strategy and catalyst for consciousness-raising, it proved "inadequate for a committed identification with a Latino imagined community" (269). In the case of the population at hand (the Californios), ethnicism was a problematic form of social organization because "class, political orientation, and even generational and regional differences proved again to be major stumbling blocks in establishing long-term alliances in nineteenth-century California" (269).

Another type of political disarticulation of contemporary Latino ethnic identification is proposed by Alicia Arrizón in *Latina Performance: Traversing the Stage* (1999). Here she suggests that the term "Latina" is the site of multiple "contestations" that reimagine and restage gendered ethnic, class, and sexual communities in ways that escape male-centered heterosexist representations as well as mainstream representations. As she explains in her introductory chapter, "My aim here is to use Latina as a broad category that embraces a political and cultural movement in the United States, where the politics of identity are crucial" (4). For her as well as for some of the Chicana feminists of the 1980s who rejected the inherited models of Latino and feminist articulation, "Latina" is a critical site of gender deconstruction and counterhegemonic subject formation (4). In her particular case, "Latina" is also a "performative" practice that deals with not only "the subcultural claiming of public agency" and a reclaiming of the Latina/lesbian body, but also a gendered experience of double marginality and a "desire to become powerful and conspicuous" (4). (This is against a backdrop of invisibility and marginalization.)

Lisa Sánchez-González tells another side of the Latina feminist story in her discussion of how the Latina critic is faced with a set of contradictory impossibilities. Concretely, she argues that merely positing the layers of Latina oppression (the "exponential effects of multiple, simultaneous disempowerment") is not enough. In her words:

> [T]he sort of humanist premise that merely articulat[es] our experiences or mov[es] from silence to speech . . . often fails, because we speak and speak and speak and, though we might get louder and more analytically astute, or call for backup, people around us do not care, refuse to listen, or, in public protest, simply have us incarcerated, most especially when we make perfect sense. (2001, 138)

Aside from voicing these "difficulties of co-articulation," Sánchez-González suggests that the very existence of a Latina studies articulation that "connotes not so much an individualist will to power as a counter hegemonic will to a collective and collectivizing empowerment" (135–36) is itself made problematic in the context of the growing commodification of (elite) Latina writers; a worsening of the material conditions of Boricuas, Chicanas, and Mexicanas, and their children outside the academy; the exigencies of a publishing industry's profit motives; and the erasures of minoritized academic practices. As she explains:

> Gone are the days when Latina writers were clearly outside the realm of commodification, when their significance, by virtue of this literature's historical moment and modes of production, automatically sidestepped and outmaneuvered the distortion of mainstream marketing. . . . Furthermore, as public universities are cutting budgets in library staff and acquisitions, the last safe place for recuperating and archiving Chicana and Boricua women's literature is under threat. . . . We might accept all this as an unfortunate effect of the publishing industry's vested interest in marketing culture but as cultural critics . . . we know there is more at stake, that literary self-representation is institutional self-preservation as well. (137)

In *Boricua Literature* (2001), where this excerpt appears, there is another troubling reality to be confronted: the publishing industry's commodification of ethnic market niche Latina writers who are socially upward bound, "white," and offering troubling "renegotiations with the overt ideological challenges issued by earlier generations" (135). For Sánchez-González the effects of this literature's "political migration toward a conservative epistemological center" can be felt in the academy "despite the efforts on the part of more progressive educators to establish Boricua studies as a 'legitimate' but definitively contestatory academic discipline" (135). For her, addresssing this fact is part and parcel of the crisis of the Latina public intellectual who seeks to theorize Latina studies as an expression of subalternization, yet finds few possibilities for doing so in an academic space that promotes not only cultural commodification but also a normative conceptually hegemonic expression of mainstream feminism that makes Latina feminism seem almost like a contradiction in terms and a practical oxymoron (139).

When reviewing the contradictory Latina/o expressions accessed thus far in this essay, it is useful to remember Stuart Hall's "Subjects in History," where he offers this take on his idea of no guarantees while speaking of the politics of cultural difference, the diaspora, and how it is rerouted within Black contexts:

> If you open yourself to the politics of cultural difference, there is no safety in terminology. Words can be transcoded against you, identity can turn against you, race can turn against you, difference can turn against you, diaspora can turn against you because that is the nature of the discursive. I am trying to persuade you that the word is the medium in which power works. Don't clutch on to the word, but do clutch on to certain ideas about it. (1997b, 299)[4]

Hall's is a cautionary tale that can remind us of the importance of critical reflection in relation to the way power works through language and the way words that are supposed to liberate us can do just the opposite. (Thus the necessity of remembering the significant meanings we attach to them.) This lesson is often reaffirmed in the corridors and coffee houses of major conference sites where glimpses of the *tertulia* can be found and where, indeed, many of the most interesting and passionate exchanges take place. While people want to make coalitions that can address a number of social crises and forms of oppression/exploitation, they do not always appreciate the way the authoritative panethnic term "Latino" lends itself to a kind of Eurocentrism (*Latin*-idad) and can impose a kind of unwelcome *deterritorialization* and alliance with upper-class, elite, or patriarchal hemispheric cultures in the making.

What is less prominent in these exchanges is a discussion of the ways in which diverse populations residing in the Caribbean and Central and South America articulate this term—the ways they alter or contest "Latino" or invest it with other types of meanings (oppositional or otherwise). This type of focus is important because we are living in an era of increased transnational migration flows where not only people but also cultural productions do much to circulate contradictory forms of transnational identification. Arlene Dávila's (2000) observations on Spanish television networks provide an important scenario for our consideration on this count. She argues that transnational Spanish TV networks can help to "validate dominant norms of good American citizenship in ways that reproduce rather than challenge dominant race/class and gender norms at play in U.S. society" and that these networks often marginalize local "Latina/o issues" while privileging "Latin America" as the source "of cultural authenticity" in Latino/Hispanic culture (84).

Along with transnational Spanish media, Latina/o restructurings of ethnic area studies need to be scrutinized, particularly those that depoliticize Latina/o studies, erase the ethnic-specific dimension of the panethnic political struggle, or deprive ethnic-specific area studies of their global and transnational character. Without denying the fact that Latina/o studies emerges within what might be characterized as the global moment, it does not do so alone; other knowledge formations, including the ones that are often contained within its overarching composite, are not exempt from these changes. Let us remember that these knowledge formations are not cast off the face of the map when the composite Latina/o appears and that they do not dwell apart from the dynamics of the historic present. In fact, these formations are in conversation with a contemporary formation of Latina/o studies even as their founding canons are being unearthed and renegotiated in ever more complex ways through any number of recovery projects and panethnic associations.

While some might see Latino studies as a kind of megaspace that asserts its hegemony over all ethnic-specific area studies, there are other conjunctural models of affiliated Latina/o studies that build from the bottom up, model grassroots collectivizing associations, and strive toward formulating dialectical relations between ethnic area studies such as Chicana/o, Puerto Rican, Cuban, and so on. This does not mean that all ethnic-specific programs necessarily should acquire a panethnic institutional affiliation *a lo* "latina/o" or that panethnicity always means "Latina/o," but that, as Juan Flores (chapter 9 in this volume) has pointed out, different kinds of programs surface in different areas and different forms, depending on (geopolitical) context and historical circumstances at hand.

If it is true that the promise of "Latina/o" lies in its ability to access multiple social identities and their realities in political study, it is equally true that these aspects of its articulation remain difficult to access within global articulations of Latino studies that do not allow us to see "the differentiation along the lines of gender and sexuality," "the specific identity positions of 'Black Latinos'" and "mixed Latino backgrounds," "the critical understandings of translocality," and the no less important and often obscured differences of social class (the very elements that "have drawn increasing attention and have done much to sunder the more or less monolithic and essentialist tenets of inherited conceptualizations" [Flores, chapter 9 in this volume]). This is in part due to what might be construed as a settling down of semantics and poetics in the language of many emergent Latino studies. That is, the oppositional languages of alternative identification are displaced or cleaned up by the new Latino composite, which appears to be divested of their multiple and contestatory expressions and their slashes, vocalizations, intellectual graffiti, and complex serial listings/partnerships.[5] These are the social markings that can (in the best of instances) at least let us know that naming oneself at the beginning of the twenty-first century is productive if not risky business. While there are no guarantees, these markers can suggest to us that interruptions in speech are necessary to interrupt erasures that do not allow one to begin to visualize the presence of intersectional social movements, social identities, or analytical categories (the ones that mark social relations, socially nuanced forms of oppression, exploitation, and imaginings of counterscenarios).

With regard to the ways Latina/o studies get articulated in the academy, I would agree with those who propose that what is required is "numerous entrances, exits," and "escape routes"[6] as well as "collaboration versus subsumption." Already the trend of Latina/o studies is toward dispersal of the lines of affiliation, not the promised self-contained overarching umbrella. (The study of Latinas/os can be found in a number of diverse departments including women's studies, law schools, feminist studies, ethnic studies, Native American studies, Black studies, cultural studies, gay and lesbian studies, border studies, and community studies.)

Notwithstanding this Latina/o positionality, at the university there is an institutionally sanctioned practice of modeling administratively driven top-down academic megaspaces that are politically and intellectually regressive in 2001. (The correlate in this case would be the erasure of historic sites of community building in the name of a globalized Latinization.) It is important to be attentive to the social and institutional consequences of our academic designs, particularly inasmuch as they concern institutional rethinkings of contested areas of study secured through years of active struggle, not individual or academic blueprints.[7] Any rethinking of social academic identifications—be they Chicana/o, Latina/o, Latin American—needs to be articulated from the purview of social conditions and the engagements they might proffer, not with the logic of hegemonic institutions that have historically denied Chicanas/os and Latinas/os and other indigenous peoples a meaningful presence and a place at the negotiating table. In the final instance, these engagements are what propel us to either affiliate or disaffiliate with social identifications and ethnic area studies. These are the engagements that propel us to move forward or regress as we maneuver the fault lines of the social terrain and decide which coalitions, agendas, and forms of ethnic and political identification can meet the demands of social justice and which cannot.

In view of the importance and the timeliness of this enterprise, critics have affirmed that "the very complexities of Latinidad may be the crucial starting point for Latina/o culture and identity in the Americas" (Román and Sandoval 1995, cited in Arrizón 1999, 3). While I would add that the complexities of Latinidad are to be found in a space of social reproduction, I agree that there is much to be done and that we are only at the beginning of a larger searching critique. After all, as is suggested elsewhere, identification is "a process of articulation, a suturing" (Hall 1996, 3), not a cosmic fusion on a grand (hemispheric) scale. As a social as well as a signifying practice, identification requires discursive as well as political work, particularly in this interval of its (re)emergence. Without belaboring the social or conceptual difficulties of the task at hand, it is also important to situate the debates about identity within those historically specific developments that are generating radical transformations, including the "processes of forced and 'free' migration which have become a global phenomenon in the so-called 'post-colonial' world" (4).

Notes

I would like to thank the organizers of the "Latino/Latin American/Chicano Studies and the Rethinking of Area and Ethnic Studies" conference, University of California, Santa Cruz, February 26–27, 1999 (especially Juan Poblete), for the invitation to participate; Zare Juan Dernersesian "for the ride"; the vibrant Chicana/o Cultural Studies graduate group at Stanford for the intellectual exchange; and the professors in the Spanish section at the University of California, San Diego for their critical thinking.

1. See, for example, Arlene Dávila (2000); Clara E. Rodriguez (1997); Frank Bonilla et al. (1998); Norma Alarcón, Ana Castillo, and Cherríe Moraga (1989); Gustavo Leclerc, Raul Villa, and Michael J. Dear (1998); William Flores and Rina Benmayor (2000); Juanita Ramos (1994); Jose Quiroga (2000); Antonia Darder and Rodolfo Torres (1998); Richard Delgado and Jean Stefanic (1998); Roberta Fernández (1994); Juan Gonzalez (2000); Mary Romero, Pierrette Hondagneu-Sotelo, and Vilma Ortiz (1997); and Richard Chabrán and Rafael Chabrán (1996).

2. See the song "Latino, Latino," Orquesta Silva, on *Latino, Latino: Music from the Streets of Los Angeles,* various artists (1991, Priority Records).

3. In this case "we" includes people interested not only in making coalitions but in rethinking the areas of ethnic study.

4. To his description I might add that gender can also turn against you.

5. These are elements that confuse census bureaus and social scientists alike.

6. This idea is inspired in Anzaldúa's (1990) formation of alternative knowledges.

7. The idea is to build and to think about what an antiglobalization intellectual agenda that is multiply situated might look like at the academy.

REFERENCES

Alarcón, Norma, Ana Castillo, and Cherríe Moraga, eds. 1989. "The Sexuality of Latinas." Special issue, *Third Woman* 4.

Anzaldúa, Gloria. 1990. "Haciendo Caras: Una Entrada." In *Making Face, Making Soul—Haciendo Caras: Creative and Critical Perspectives by Feminists of Color,* ed. Gloria Anzaldúa. San Francisco: Aunt Lute Books. xv–xxviii.

Arrizón, Alicia. 1999. *Latina Performance: Traversing the Stage.* Bloomington: Indiana University Press.

Bonilla, Frank, Edwin Meléndez, Rebecca Morales, and Maria de los Angeles Torres, eds. 1998. *Borderless Borders: U.S. Latinos, Latin Americas, and the Paradox of Interdependence.* Philadelphia: Temple University Press.

Chabrán, Richard, and Rafael Chabrán, eds. 1996. *The Latino Encyclopedia.* New York: Marshall Cavendish.

Darder, Antonia, and Rodolfo Torres, eds. 1998. *The Latino Studies Reader.* Oxford: Blackwell.

Dávila, Arlene. 2000. "Mapping Latinidad: Spanish, English, 'Spanglish' in the Hispanic TV Landscape." *Television and New Media* 1, no. 1: 75–94.

———. 2001. *Latino, Inc.: The Making and Marketing of a People.* Berkeley: University of California Press.

Delgado, Richard, and Jean Stefanic, eds. 1998. *The Latino/a Condition.* New York: New York University Press.

Fernández, Roberta, ed. 1994. *In Other Worlds: Literature by Latinas of the United States.* Houston: Arte Público.

Flores, Juan. 2000. *From Bomba to Hip-Hop: Puerto Rican Culture and Latino Identity.* New York: Colombia University Press.

Flores, William, and Rina Benmayor, eds. 2000. *Latino Cultural Citizenship: Claiming Identity, Space, and Rights.* Boston: Beacon Press.

García Canclini, Néstor. "Cultural Studies Questionnaire." *Journal of Latin American Cultural Studies* 5, no. 1 (June): 83–88.

Gonzalez, Juan. 2000. *A History of Latinos in America: Harvest of Empire.* New York: Penguin.

Hall, Stuart. 1996. "Introduction: Who Needs Identity?" In *Questions of Cultural Identity,* ed. Stuart Hall and Paul du Gay. London: Sage.

———. 1997a. "The Local and the Global." In *Dangerous Liaisons: Gender, Nation, and Postcolonial Perspectives,* ed. Anne McClintock, Aamir Mufti, and Ella Shohat. Minneapolis: University of Minnesota Press. 173–87.

———. 1997b. "Subjects in History: Marking Diasporic Identities." In *The House That Race Built: Black Americans, U.S. Terrain,* ed. Wahnemma Lubiano. New York: Pantheon Books. 289–99.

Leclerc, Gustavo, Raul Villa, and Michael J. Dear, eds. 1998. *Urban Latino Cultures: La Vida Latina en L.A.* Thousand Oaks, Calif.: Sage.

Negrón-Mutaner, Frances. 2000. "Not an Academic Subject: Latino Media Aesthetics." In *Future of Latino Independent Media: A NALIP Sourcebook,* ed. Chon Noriega. Los Angeles: UCLA Chicano Studies Research Center. 117–23.

Noriega, Chon, and Alma M. López, eds. 1996. *The Ethnic Eye: Latino Media Arts.* Minneapolis: University of Minnesota Press.

Quiroga, Jose. 2000. *Tropics of Desire: Interventions from Queer Latino America.* New York: New York University Press.

Ramos, Juanita. 1994. *Compañeras: Latina Lesbians: An Anthology.* London: Routledge.

Rodríguez, América. 1999. *Making Latino News: Race, Language, Class.* Thousand Oaks, Calif.: Sage.

Rodriguez, Clara E., ed. 1997. *Latin Looks: Images of Latinas and Latinos in the U.S. Media.* Boulder, Colo.: Westview Press.

Román, David, and Alberto Sandoval. 1995. "Caught in the Web." *American Literature* 67, no. 3: 553–86.

Romero, Lora. 1997. "Nationalism and Internationalism: Domestic Differences in a Postcolonial World." In *Articulating the Global and the Local: Globalization and Cultural Studies,* ed. Ann Cvetkovich and Douglas Keller. Boulder, Colo.: Westview Press. 244–48.

Romero, Mary, Pierrette Hondagneu-Sotelo, and Vilma Ortiz, eds. 1997.

Challenging Fronteras: Structuring Latina and Latino Lives in the U.S.: An Anthology of Readings. New York: New York University Press.

Sánchez, Rosaura. 1995. *Telling Identities: The Californio Testimonios.* Minneapolis: University of Minnesota Press.

Sánchez-González, Lisa. 2001. *Boricua Literature: A Literary History of the Puerto Rican Diaspora.* New York: New York University Press.

CHAPTER 5

The Occluded History of Transamerican Literature

Kirsten Silva Gruesz

La tormenta umbría
En los aires revuelve un océano
Que todo lo sepulta . . .
Al fin, mundo fatal, nos separamos;
El huracán y yo solos estamos.

Near the beginning of the century in which nationalism in the Americas assumed its fateful form, the Cuban-born writer José María Heredia penned these lines from "En una tempestad: Al huracán," which was first published from his political exile in New York City in 1825. A few years later, the editor and poet William Cullen Bryant translated "The Hurricane" and another poem for publications he edited, from which they were liberally reprinted around the country for the next several decades. A partial inventory of the subsequent appearances of original and translation is both telling and tantalizing. In 1854 *DeBow's Review,* an adamantly proslavery monthly in New Orleans, cited Heredia as an example of the high accomplishments of Cuban culture in order to support their argument that the rich island was languishing under Spanish rule and would be better served by U.S. governance. Across town, the

Spanish-language weekly *La Patria,* which had raised one of the sole protests in New Orleans against the expansionist war on Mexico, used Heredia to stir up the sentiments of Cuban expatriates in *favor* of the Spanish empire and against such foreign influence. In far-off San Francisco, *El Nuevo Mundo,* an urbane daily paper published for the city's Mexican and Chilean elites, used an epigraph from "Al huracán" to introduce an original poem comparing the French intervention in Mexico to Spain's continuing grip on Cuba, thereby making Heredia's struggle a corollary to their own. "Al huracán" was also reprinted in various anthologies and newspapers in Mexico, where Heredia had lived out the rest of his short life; when Bryant visited Mexico City in 1872— perhaps the only *yanqui* of the period to be received there with genuine popular enthusiasm—his translation of the poem was distributed in broadside. Two decades later, the poem appeared next to advertisements for sarsaparilla and bilingual lawyers in the daily *El Nuevo-mexicano* of Las Cruces, where a hurricane must have seemed as novel as an iceberg, but Heredia's prestige was nonetheless recognized.

Finally, in the flurry of enthusiasm for Pan-Americanism that swept the United States after its acquisition of an empire in the Pacific and the Caribbean, the Bryant-Heredia exchange was resurrected in at least three anthologies as an example of the fraternal ties that allegedly bound the hemisphere. I'll mention just one: in the U.S.-occupied San Juan of 1903, Francis (Francisco) J. Amy made this pairing one of the center-pieces of his curious textbook, *Musa Bilingüe,* which sought to foster "the intellectual Americanization of Porto Rican youths" through parallel readings of English and Spanish poems. One Professor Brau contributed an introductory apostrophe that makes clear the civilizing mission that an education in the English language and its high culture is meant to have for Puerto Rico:

> The task of directing our social destiny having devolved onto the great republic of Washington, she has brought us, in the folds of her revered flag, the irradiation of her democratic spirit; but alas! the spirit without the speech can accomplish no redemption. . . . This means that perfect homogeneity does not exist between directors and directed, owing to divergencies *[sic]* in language which must be done away with by both. . . . Take this book; study its cohesion, analyze its component parts, fathom its syncretism that blends together the intellectual genius of two empires to which you are bound. (Amy 1903, 6–7)

Amy's book of facing-page poetic translations is presented as the path toward a desirable cultural "syncretism" that would bow to an inescapable political reality: the exchange of a new "empire" for the old. Despite *Musa Bilingüe*'s hopeful gesture at the *mutual* education of English and Spanish speakers, their relationship is as unequal as that of "directors" and "directed." Brau continues, revealingly, "without voice it is impossible to call for help, and we are virtually mute, since we find no one to understand us." Translated language follows, if not precedes, the accomplishment of *traslatio imperii,* and the voice of power now speaks in English. Puerto Rico, as Brau senses, is alone with the hurricane, that naturalizing force of U.S. culture that occludes all things behind its own forceful presence.

What ties together these discrete uses of a poetic text, jointly expressed as "original" and "translation" by two politically engaged writers who despite their former fame today seem antique, relegated to the peripheries of academia? As the early publishing history of "Al huracán" suggests, the ideal of a transamerican culture—of a bridgeable, thinkable communion between the anglophone and hispanophone worlds—is rooted in a revolutionary and cosmopolitan Romantic ethos that Bryant and Heredia, whatever their other differences, shared. But this ideal was from the beginning beset by the powerful engine of U.S. territorial expansion. By the time of the "neighborly" U.S. occupation of Puerto Rico and Cuba at the beginning of the nineteenth century, it had disintegrated into a strained awareness of the structural imbalances between the former colonies of the hemisphere: imbalances that encouraged the more overt forms of U.S. domination that would be perfected (and tiresomely repeated) throughout the course of the twentieth century. "The spirit without the speech can accomplish no redemption," Brau writes, reiterating the nineteenth-century commonplace that speech—and heightened literary speech in particular—might do what mere economic forces and political proclamations could not: transform subjects into citizens and strangers into compatriots. This utopian will of the word is generally recognized as a corollary project to nation building. Yet the relationships of imagined community at this time also extended across porous and contested national boundaries to establish and strengthen other alliances: between slaveholding interests in the U.S. South and their Cuban partners and rivals in the sugar trade; between radical republicans from Mexico and the Caribbean, who made New Orleans a convenient locus from which to plot the overthrow of Spanish and European colonial powers; or between liberal procapitalist coalitions across Greater Mexico from Northern California to Veracruz's Caribbean port—to mention just the examples offered by "Al huracán." Transnational alliances all, and yet they also gesture toward a slowly evolving Latino presence *within* this national sphere.

"Transnational" does not fully describe the relationship of disparate groups of Spanish speakers living in the United States to each other: the sense of confraternity, whether deeply felt or merely wished for, that might explain how Heredia's tropical storm came to be offered as entertainment for the relatively conservative mestizo/Hispano population of Las Cruces. This longstanding Latino presence, which has grown both in quantity and visibility at the edge of a new millennium, invites us to revisit the history of transamerican cultural contacts. It encourages us to take seriously the possibility that the "divergencies" between English and Spanish that Professor Brau sadly noted might in fact eclipse a *common* tradition: common without being unitary or imperially reductive; common, perhaps, in the very nodes of their divergence. This tradition is currently accessible to us in two forms, each contained within a particular discipline and its knowledge structure. The first is composed of the preserved voice of hispanophone communities in zones of border contact such as New Mexico, California, and Texas, and in urban spaces of great ethnic diversity such as New York, Chicago, New Orleans, and Los Angeles: the record currently being identified and cataloged by one of the most ambitious archival efforts ever of its kind, the Recovering the U.S. Hispanic Literary Heritage (RUSHLH) project. This vast archive is made meaningful through the lens of an ethnic studies genealogy; it aims to produce knowledge about the historical contributions of different Latino populations to their particular communal identity (as Chicanos, Puerto Ricans, Cuban Americans, or under the larger umbrella of "Latino") and secondarily to U.S. culture at large. The second way in which we might consider the common history of anglophone and hispanophone American culture invokes the larger frame of transamerican and transatlantic cultural contact: networks of publication and transmission; relationships of patronage, influence, and translation; and the institutions of pedagogy, canonization, and official sanctification that allow texts to live or die in the public imagination. Such contacts fall within the scope of comparative literature, which has historically been seen, at least within U.S. studies, as a footnote to the more pressing issue of the *national* imagination. To the extent that these two frames differ—for at certain points, they do not—both are essential components of a cultural history of the Americas and need to be simultaneously rendered visible.[1] Such a vision is necessary not only to provide a historical grounding for contemporary Latino identity, but to imagine a new form of U.S. cultural history in general: one that would unseat the fiction of American literature's monolingual and necessarily Anglocentric roots, and one that would question the imperial conflation of "the United States" with "America."[2]

Although written by a Cuban—more accurately, a discontented Spanish subject with ties of birth and property to Cuba, who cemented these into a Byronic aura of political idealism and longing—"Al huracán" does not signify exclusively in the context of that island's tradition, nor does it figure solely in the development of an ideally unified Latin American culture, along the lines of José Martí's vision of *Nuestra América*. Rather, each of the poem's appearances in periodicals from rural or urban border spaces contextualizes local issues of autonomy and agency by placing them in broader contexts, and marks lines of affiliation that now might be called global or diasporic, without the postmodern simultaneity that is usually implicit in such terms.[3] Each iteration of the poem can be understood as a social performance, a summons to discrete groups of readers who impose on it the filters of their own positioning within the transamerican sphere and create, if not a "new" poem, a distinct *transaction* of it. The travels of a written work such as this one may seem less historically resonant than the movements of troops, tribes, or tourists across the hemisphere, particularly since the historical record of reception is relatively thin. We can only speculate on the full range of the text's movements; its presence in a publication from San Francisco or from Santiago de Cuba hints at—but never fully documents—the ways in which it was heard, understood, or misunderstood in those places, and passed along to others in the form of an imitation, a few lines lifted or memorized, or a distant echo. The kind of transamerican literary history I begin to imagine here would fill in some of those forgotten transactions and speculate critically on the missing, invisible ones.

In traditional literary history, the textual transmissions that matter are those that take place between canonical figures (Emerson's letter of blessing to Whitman, Sarmiento's argument with Bello over American language differences) or that seem to emblematize a larger cultural pathology (the conversation, for instance, in which General Winfield Scott told historian William H. Prescott that his *History of the Conquest of Mexico* had inspired Scott's occupying troops, urging Prescott to write a sequel glorifying the "new conquest" of Mexico by the Yankees [Johannsen 1985, 248]). My effort here is to broaden the range of textual movements that we consider vital and meaningful. This process involves, in part, a movement away from canonical scenes of transmission and toward an expanded set of texts that we take to be relevant; more profoundly, however, it involves an amplification of the domain of the term "American" into other languages and other spaces aside from the obvious metropolitan centers of political and artistic activity. How do we codify the relationship between a famous poet like Heredia and an all-but-anonymous literary citizen like the editor in Las Cruces in a way that will illuminate the cultural values distinct to the immediate world of each, as well as the affiliations they shared?

As the work of the RUSHLH project to date has demonstrated beyond doubt, the presence of Spanish-language periodicals published in the continental United States calls for new critical paradigms that are both local *and* transnational in scope.[4] Far from being isolated records of local sensibilities, such publications consistently referred to other periodicals in distant places: reprinting pieces from them, taking issue with their editorial stances, or simply mentioning them as reassuring proof that their readers were not stranded in a linguistic desert. The global sphere, in other words, was as important to these organs as the local one, and thus the significance of the work they published was inseparable from an overlapping set of larger cultural contexts: the forsaken *patria* with which most of the local readers identified, the hispanophone world as a whole, and the anglophone United States that surrounded them. More specifically, the existence of a borderlands literary culture begs pressing, and much understudied, questions about the place of belle-lettristic forms in the daily lives of a whole range of nineteenth-century readers of English and Spanish—from the barely literate (who might "possess" a text read aloud to them despite this handicap) to the hypereducated. Although many studies in both U.S. and Latin American literature have interrogated the work of fiction in the construction of certain forms of identity—gender, citizenship, local, and racial affiliations—we know little of the ways in which the more common periodical genres, such as poetry, *crónica,* and essay, might have had formative influences on individual lives as well as on the movements of communities. Responding to these questions would require Americanists both north and south to unloose, at least imaginatively, the geographical and linguistic boundaries traditionally associated with the history of their *national* cultural formations, allowing the organizational categories that would transform this random information into *knowledge* arise from the evidence itself, rather than presupposing them. The peregrinations of "Al huracán," so inadequately accounted for by U.S. literary history, call for new geographies of regional and national cultures alike: geographies that would emphasize their formation within and around the imaginary field of América.

One model for such a comparison derives from liberal historian Herbert Bolton, who in 1932 set out his controversial argument for a common history of the Americas, while another arises more recently from the world-systems model of Immanuel Wallerstein. The Bolton thesis relies on a suggestive list of similarities: the fact that following the wars of independence, native-born property holders in all the American nation-states struggled to escape European colonial domination, most inherited economies based on slave labor and their attendant paradoxes, and all confronted a residual indigenous presence by imposing internal colonial structures based on racial and linguistic divisions. Yet to the eyes of later historians, these similarities pale next to the sheer diversity of national experience in the hemisphere, not least the gaping disparity between their modes of economic development: the United States had by 1820 built a coherent political economy on competitive capital and by 1870 was already making a transition into monopoly capital, while Latin American nations largely continued in dependent economic relations with Europe. Thus, such comparative histories seemed destined, at best, to conclude that Latin America was slow or deficient next to the Anglo world in fostering democratic institutions and economic "progress," and, at worst, to downplay the increasing role of the United States itself in the relations of external dominance that hampered Latin American self-determination (Hanke 1964). Quijano and Wallerstein's 1992 essay "Americanity as a Concept" gave this discredited hemispheric thesis a new currency by arguing for the pivotal role of early colonial practices in the Americas to the constitution of European modernity: "the creation of this geosocial entity, the Americas, was the constitutive act of the modern world-system. . . . there could not have been a capitalist world-economy without the Americas" (551). Shifting the focus definitively from global political relations to economic ones, they identify such historical events as the violent territorial expansion of the United States into the rest of the continent and its imitation of European colonial relations later in the century as phenomena requiring a transnational framework for investigation.

Likewise, comparative literary studies that rely on the superficial similarity of historical "themes" suggested by the Bolton thesis, rather than the complex imbrications of power and influence in the Americas, seem to exist in an odd vacuum. The traditional disciplinary model of Goethean *Weltliteratur*, with its emphasis on personal relationships of influence and a shared Greco-Roman tradition, has yielded remarkably little fruit in this hemispheric context; Stanley T. Williams's 1955 *The Spanish Background to American Literature* and Luis Sánchez's 1973–76 *Historia comparada de las literaturas americanas* were virtually the only efforts in this field for many years.[5] Only when we turn toward more global patterns of migration, diaspora, and exile—in all their racial and linguistic specificity—does a transamerican cultural history begin to make a serious argument for its usefulness, and textual events like the multiple versions of "Al huracán" can become intelligible through their own geometries of distribution, reception, and influence. Illustrating the possibilities of such a cultural history, Hortense Spillers remarks that "the historic triangular trade [in African slaves] interlarded a third of the known world in a fabric of intimacy so tightly interwoven that the politics of the New World cannot always be so easily disentangled as locally discrete moments," and goes on to produce an insightful reading of an artifact of culture produced and distributed—like any other form of capital—within that triangle (9). Hers is just one of a number of recently proposed cultural geographies that expand beyond the bounds of the nation, like Paul Gilroy's "Black Atlantic" stretching from London to Georgia and to Santo Domingo and Jamaica, and Joseph Roach's "circum-Atlantic" performance trajectory dotted by New Orleans, the Antilles, West Africa, and London.

In a parallel move away from the national frame—this time moving *inward* rather than *outward*—the "New Western history" of the past decade has emphasized the contested spaces of border areas and contact zones. Following Bolton's rejection of Frederick Jackson Turner's national-destinarian terminology of the "frontier," the current historiographical trend examines local relations of conflict and cooperation among ethnic and linguistic communities, and the relative autonomy and heterogeneity of their cultural practices with respect to national centers of power. Such critical formulations as Gloria Anzaldúa's "borderlands/*frontera*," José Limón's "Greater México," José David Saldívar's "*transfrontera* contact zone," and Walter Mignolo's episteme of "border gnosis" all echo this fundamental reformulation, and reversal, of dominant national allegories. The critical potential of borderlands theory lies not merely in its insistence on local expressions of difference or resistance, but in the implicit dialogue with the national that it calls forth: the very concept of the border is unintelligible without the nation. Such a theory needs to ask (for instance) not only how the community of San Antonio may have maintained an identity as part of Greater Mexico long after its incorporation in the United States, but how that identity may have simultaneously altered other forms of U.S. nationalism. It would consider not only the central role that New York played in the shaping of a national culture during the nineteenth century, but that city's other identity as a "border city" with a polyglot, chaotically changing, and ambivalently assimilated society. With regard to the history of print culture, and its role in the evolution of literary genres as well as forms of community affiliation and identity formation, Spanish-language periodicals provide a counternarrative to the national focus: just as the print traffic between New York and St. Louis—to follow one of Ronald Zboray's classic mappings of the dissemination of U.S. national identity—played a significant a role in the flow of ideas and expressions that created communities of thought and feeling, so too did the traffic between Mexico City and late-century Santa Fe, New Mexico (Zboray 1993, chapters 4–5).

Yet perhaps the most important application of this dual frame of border/nation has to do with tradition. The challenge posed by the changing demographics of the United States, I argue, is not so much to accommodate Latinos to an existing national tradition as to reconfigure that tradition to acknowledge the continuous presence of Latinos within and around it. That presence—like the systematic eradication of indigenous peoples and cultures in the service of continental expansion—acts as a repressed national memory, but one that is well on its way to an uncanny return. Part of what has been repressed in the United States is its location within a hemisphere *also* known as América, a name it has appropriated synechdochically unto itself. This imperial conflation of "America" with the United States operates both spatially—imagine the surgically isolated silhouette of the forty-eight contiguous states, indelibly imprinted into the minds of schoolchildren—and temporally, as certain events are chosen over others to emblematize turning points in a shared national memory.

The conventional landmarks of nineteenth-century history offer instructive examples: the rise of Jacksonian individualism as the prominent expression of national character; the debates over sectionalism, slavery, and expansion that led to the Civil War; and the triumph of urban industrial capitalism toward the end of the century are widely taken as the key interpretive clusters through which political and social life are to be understood. They are crucial not only to historiographic debates about the period, but to broader paradigms of contemporary literary history and American identity as well.[6] We could, however, as readily focus on pivotal moments in the history of the United States *as it belongs to the Americas* and stage them in ways that are equally suggestive of significant patterns in intellectual and cultural life: the origins of the Caribbean slave-and-sugar trade at the beginning of the century; the Monroe Doctrine of 1823; the Eastern demand for land that resulted in Texas's independence and, eventually, the U.S. invasion of Mexico in 1846; the rampant filibustering in Central America and the Caribbean that began in the 1850s, motivated both by the engine of territorial expansion and by U.S. desires to control a transcontinental waterway; the systematic disenfranchisement of formerly Mexican *californios* and *tejanos* of their citizenship rights under the Treaty of Guadalupe Hidalgo during the 1870s and 1880s; the uneasy standoff of the first Pan-American Congress in 1889 and the U.S. interventions in Puerto Rico, Cuba, and Panama that followed. Thus, the foundational moment in U.S. literary history, the so-called American Renaissance of the late 1840s and 1850s, would be read less exclusively through the lens of the Civil War and Reconstruction, and more pointedly in terms of the development of national expansionism after its war on Mexico in 1846–48.

This alternate set of emblematic moments in nineteenth-century history both follows on and challenges another recent trend in cultural criticism: the argument that the development of canonical U.S. literature cannot be separated from the climate of its transformation into an imperial state. Modernist culture, according to this thesis, must be read within the context of the push for global influence and colonial counter-struggles unleashed in 1898 (see, for instance, the essays in Kaplan and Pease 1993). As William Appleman Williams points out, however, 1898 might be a convenient watershed for discussions of a U.S. empire—the point at which they spilled into daily discourse—but the history of interventionism begins a full century earlier, with a small military landing in what is now the Dominican Republic (Williams 1980, 73). "Imperial," then, may be a problematic term, but it is useful for describing certain *modes* of relations, both political and cultural, which developed in an uneven but recognizable way over the course of the century as Manifest Destiny was transformed from slogan into reality, and as private and public institutions from the North increasingly sought to constrict Latin American sovereignty. Whatever fraternal rhetoric may have marked Monroe's famous 1823 speech decrying European interference in the hemisphere, that protective claim was contorted, just over two decades later, into a justification for President James K. Polk and congressional warmongers, both Whig and Democrat, to occupy Mexican territory on thin pretexts. At the same time, however, these events did not unfold without significant protest from within the United States about its evolving tendency toward an imperial politics in the hemisphere, particularly in the early 1850s, when a concern over the sovereignty of other nations and their borders entered the consciousness of many writers, both prominent and obscure. That protest was largely caught up in, and to some extent muffled by, more immediate questions of abolition and separatism, but they returned in full force by the end of that century (when Mark Twain, for instance, mustered all his authority to denounce U.S. policy in the Philippines). And just as these developments had a profound effect on national culture, so too did they influence Latin Americans: the key texts advocating cultural autonomy at the turn of the century—Darío's late political poems, Rodó's *Ariel,* and Martí's *Nuestra América*—make the recognition and rejection of this imperial power their core epiphany.

If the critical, anti-imperialist perspective of *Nuestra América* is indispensable to U.S. literary study on a national scale, it is also a necessary background to a deep understanding of more localized productions. A full accounting of the significance of Spanish-language periodical culture in the U.S. borderlands would be grounded not only in a particular regional community—as are, for example, the careful reconstructions of nineteenth-century New Mexican print communities by Doris Meyer and Gabriel Meléndez—but in Martí's transnational geography as well. As recent scholarship in the history of book and periodical distribution networks has suggested, patterns of trade and traffic in printed artifacts mark out relationships between metropolitan centers and rural peripheries that are highly revelatory of culture's relation to other fields of economic and political power. Spanish-language periodicals complicate such nation-focused models with their utter reliance on transnational networks of distribution and readership: for instance, an early issue of *La Patria,* which was published from 1846 to 1851 in New Orleans, lists sales agents not only along the U.S. Gulf Coast (from Terre aux Boeufs, Louisiana, to Baton Rouge, Mobile, and St. Augustine) but also across Cuba (in Havana, Matanzas, Trinidad, Puerto Príncipe [Camagüey], and Santiago), as well as throughout Mexico and the Yucatan (Veracruz, Mexico City, Jalapa, Orizaba, Puebla, Tampico, Mérida, and Campeche). Later issues listed sales offices in San Antonio, Matamoros, and Corpus Christi, Texas, in New York City and in Caracas, indicating a gradual geographical extension of this particularly ambitious newspaper's sphere of influence in ways that paid little attention to the formal boundaries of nationhood. Most extant hispanophone periodicals from the nineteenth century demonstrate a similar geographical reach, if not through their records of subscription and sales offices then through the common practice of cut-and-pasted articles from "sister" publications all over the hemisphere.

In addition to these correctives to the nationalist geography of current studies of the relationship between print culture and ideological formations, borderlands print culture also forces an interrogation of other ways in which language measures power: the distribution of degrees of literacy among various social classes, the mediation between Spanish and the institutional loci of English, and of course the implicit suppression of indigenous languages. The acquisition of literacy in a colonial European tongue, and its consequent forms of affiliation through educational institutions and readerly participation in imagined print communities, has long been considered central to the formation of modern political subjects in the Americas. Yet, as the work pioneered by Walter Ong shows us, literacy is anything but a stable concept; it is a process, not a portal. Medievalist Katherine O'Keeffe's formulation of "transitional literacy" provides a useful way to codify the variable skills and needs of both anglo- and hispanophone reading communities in the borderlands: when one assumes that "the conditions 'orality' and 'literacy' are the end points on a continuum through which the technology of writing affects and modifies human perception," the ephemeral medium of periodical texts seems not a testimony to writing's dominance in a given community but rather a valuable source of evidence about "the ability of the reader and the function of the manuscript," along with "the conditions under which the physical text was received" (O'Keeffe 1990, 13–14). The notion of a literacy continuum insists that the practices of "reading" published texts we allow ourselves to assume or imagine be consistent with different stages in this transition. Measuring various indices of Spanish literacy among classes of nineteenth-century Californians, historian Lisbeth Haas labels it an "oral residual culture" in which reading was profoundly *performative,* and this shows signs of being broadly true across borderlands print culture (Haas 1995, 115–25).

Since not all of the genres found in such periodicals were equally consecrated by the standards of metropolitan arbiters of high culture, the pages of any given newspaper spoke to and called forth different levels of language skills and interpretive dexterity. We can extrapolate from these materials a set of reading practices that move well beyond the romanticized portrait of reading as a direct, one-on-one encounter between a well-educated writer and a leisured reader settled on a cozy sofa: native speakers who are still learning the written language through reading; children and non-native speakers whose command of even the oral language is limited; and people who are literally being read *to,* for whom the experience of listening to the written word evokes not only daily speech but the connotations of religious ritual or certain occasions of communal celebration in which they are accustomed to forming a listening audience. All these groups form part of the community of a text's interlocutors, and each brings to the experience a slightly differ-ent set of expectations and reading practices. Just as nineteenth-century periodicals passed through a number of hands, with the buyer sharing a single copy with multiple individuals, the words printed inside them passed through a number of *minds.* On the pages of a periodical, in par-ticular, a poem is staged among competing articles, editorials, and other pieces, set against the noise of announcements and advertisements. The possibilities for transmitting poems under such a dynamic model are numerous: reading aloud between lovers or confidantes; reading to the family circle; reading within the institutional setting of the schoolroom; reading to groups like the Sociedades Literarias in the New Orleans of the 1850s or the New York of the 1880s; and even, as the existence of cigar-factory *lectores* in South Florida at the turn of the century suggests, reading in the workplace. Thus, the archive of hispanophone periodical literature insists on a *performative* dimension to the written word that is occluded in traditional narratives of American literary evolution.

For all the ways in which Latin America, as its intellectuals have pointed out for years, has suffered for being marked as the local testing ground of U.S. experiments with extranational power, its role in the past and future shaping of U.S. identity narratives—both local and national, both vernacular and high cultural—remains disturbingly understudied and undertheorized. Given the increasing proportion and significance of Latinos to the nation's body politic—whether as assimilated citizens, as a largely invisible underclass, or as binational workers—this neglect seems even more irresponsible. Through the example of poetic production in borderlands periodicals, I have tried to sketch some revisionist geographies of reception and influence that would stretch the silhouette of U.S. national identity—in both its spatial and temporal dimensions—out of recognizable shape, making way for a transnational historical framework that will accommodate the peculiar subject-position of Latinos from the nineteenth century to the twenty-first.

NOTES

1. The RUSHLH project, under the direction of Nicolás Kanellos and funded by a ten-year, $20 million grant from the Ford Foundation (among other sources), represents an even greater public investment than the similar Schomburg Project to recover works by nineteenth-century African-American writers. Yet its sense of the community for whom this tradition is being recovered is necessarily more murky, and this lack of clarity about individual ethnic genealogies versus a larger "Hispanic" identity is apparent in the critical introductions to its publications. Most editions to emerge to date from the RUSHLH series claim their place in the "U.S. Hispanic heritage" on the basis of a more specific ethnic affiliation (e.g., the local *tejano* customs described by Jovita González, the Afro–Puerto Rican activism of Jesús Colón, or the complaints against the disenfranchisement of Mexican-American citizenship and property rights articulated by María Amparo Ruíz de Burton). However, none of these community-within-a-nation models adequately accounts for a text like *El laúd del desterrado* (The exile's lyre), a collection of patriotic poems by Cuban-born writers (including Heredia, but mainly comprising a younger generation) originally published in New York in 1858. The so-called *Laúd* Group plays an important role in Cuban literary history, but, as editor Matías Montes-Huidobro acknowledges, in no sense did the writers understand themselves as marginalized U.S. subjects at that time. *El laúd del desterrado* thus makes explicit an underlying tension that runs throughout this series: it requires a *transnational* critical frame in order to make its identity as a "pre-Latino" text meaningful.

2. In addition to a long tradition of Latin Americanists, a number of critical predecessors in the U.S. have questioned this imperial conflation; see especially Kutzinski (1987); Saldívar (1991, 1997); Porter (1994); and Kaplan (1998). Forceful arguments against the monolingual bias in U.S. literary study have recently been made by Lauter (1991) and Sollors (1998).

3. My approach thus echoes recent work in diasporic studies, but these links should be taken provisionally. Such critics as Arjun Appadurai and Néstor

García Canclini base their notion of a fluid diasporic identity on the material conditions of the media age: the near-spontaneity of communications and travel, as contrasted with "premodern" conditions in the developing world. Further historically grounded research into the conditions of reading and publication in the nineteenth and early twentieth centuries will, I believe, challenge Appadurai's claim that a *collective* transnational imagination, a "community of sentiment," is only made possible with the advent of the mass media in the later twentieth century (Appadurai 1996, 8).

4. An overview of borderlands periodicals can be found in Leal (1989); a complete bibliography is forthcoming from the RUSHLH project. The most detailed general reconstruction of the literary work of these organs has been done for the case of New Mexico; see Meyer (1996) and Meléndez (1997). More specifically, Luis Torres has written extensively about the genres of *californio* poetry (1994b). Some histories of Spanish-speaking communities in the border regions post–Guadalupe Hidalgo also discuss the role of the print community (Pitt 1971, 181–94).

5. Two highly informative, but relatively uncritical, studies from this period deserve mention as well: De Onís (1975) and Orjuela (1980). Comparative studies of the literature of the Americas that attend to common tropes with little or no attention to disparities of power include those of Alfred MacAdam (1987) and Earl Fitz (1991). The two groundbreaking collections edited by Gustavo Pérez-Firmat (1990), and Bell Chevigny and Gari Laguardia (1986) are uneven in this regard.

6. Many of the classic texts of American studies pivot around the three historical events I've just mentioned: R. W. B. Lewis's *American Adam,* Henry Nash Smith's *Virgin Land,* Leo Marx's *The Machine in the Garden,* and Alan Trachtenberg's *The Incorporation of America.*

REFERENCES

Amy, Francis J., ed. 1903. *Musa Bilingüe: Being a Collection of Translations, Principally from the Standard Anglo-American Poets, into Spanish; and Spanish, Cuban, and Porto Rican Poets, into English, with the Original Text Opposite, and Biographical Notes; Especially Intended for the Use of Students.* San Juan, Puerto Rico: El Boletín Mercantil.

Appadurai, Arjun. 1996. *Modernity at Large: Cultural Dimensions of Globalization.* Minneapolis: University of Minnesota Press.

Chevigny, Bell Gale, and Gari Laguardia. 1986. *Reinventing the Americas: Comparative Studies of Literature of the United States and Spanish America.* New York: Cambridge University Press.

De Onís, José. 1975. *The United States as Seen by Spanish American Writers, 1776–1890.* Cultural Relations between the United States and the Hispanic World, vol. 1. 2d ed. New York: Gordian Press.

Fitz, Earl E. 1991. *Rediscovering the New World: Inter-American Literature in a Comparative Context.* Iowa City: University of Iowa Press.

Haas, Lisbeth. 1995. *Conquests and Historical Identities in California, 1769–1936.* Berkeley: University of California Press.

Hanke, Lewis, ed. 1964. *Do the Americas Have a Common History? A Critique of the Bolton Theory.* New York: Alfred A. Knopf.

Johannsen, Robert Walter. 1985. *To the Halls of the Montezumas: The Mexican War in the American Imagination.* New York: Oxford University Press.

Kaplan, Amy. 1998. "Manifest Domesticity." *American Literature* 70, no. 3: 581–606.

Kaplan, Amy, and Donald E. Pease. 1993. *Cultures of United States Imperialism.* New Americanists. Durham, N.C.: Duke University Press.

Kutzinski, Vera M. 1987. *Against the American Grain: Myth and History in William Carlos Williams, Jay Wright, and Nicolás Guillén.* Baltimore: The Johns Hopkins University Press.

Lauter, Paul. 1991. *Canons and Contexts.* New York: Oxford University Press.

Leal, Luis. 1989. "The Spanish-Language Press: Function and Use." *Americas Review* 17, no. 3: 157–62.

MacAdam, Alfred J. 1987. *Textual Confrontations: Comparative Readings in Latin American Literature.* Chicago: University of Chicago Press.

Meléndez, A. Gabriel. 1997. *So All Is Not Lost: The Poetics of Print in Nuevomexicano Communities, 1834–1958.* Albuquerque: University of New Mexico Press.

Meyer, Doris. 1996. *Speaking for Themselves: Neomexicano Cultural Identity and the Spanish-Language Press, 1880–1920.* Pasó por aquí. Albuquerque: University of New Mexico Press.

O'Keeffe, Katherine O'Brien. 1990. *Visible Song: Transitional Literacy in Old English Verse.* Cambridge Studies in Anglo-Saxon England, vol. 4. Cambridge and New York: Cambridge University Press.

Ong, Walter J. 1991. *Orality and Literacy: The Technologizing of the Word.* London: Routledge.

Orjuela, Héctor H. 1980. *Imagen de los Estados Unidos en la poesía de Hispanoamérica.* 1st ed. Cuadernos del Instituto de Investigaciones Filológicas, vol. 4. Mexico: Universidad Nacional Autónoma de México Instituto de Investigaciones Filológicas.

Pérez-Firmat, Gustavo, ed. 1990. *Do the Americas Have a Common Literature?* Durham, N.C.: Duke University Press.

Pitt, Leonard. 1971. *The Decline of the Californios: A Social History of the Spanish-Speaking Californians, 1846–1890.* Berkeley: University of California Press.

Porter, Carolyn. 1994. "What We Know That We Don't Know: Remapping American Literary Studies." *American Literary History* 6 no. 3: 467–526.

Quijano, Aníbal, and Immanuel Wallerstein. 1992. "Americanity as a Concept, or The Americas in the Modern World-System." *International Social Science Journal* 44, no. 4: 549–57.

Saldívar, José David. 1991. *The Dialectics of Our America: Genealogy, Cultural Critique, and Literary History.* Post-contemporary Interventions. Durham, N.C.: Duke University Press.

———. 1997. *Border Matters: Remapping American Cultural Studies.* Berkeley: University of California Press.

Sánchez. Luis Alberto. 1973–76. *Historia comparada de las literaturas americanas.* 4 vols. Buenos Aires: Losada.

Sollors, Werner. 1998. *Multilingual America: Transnationalism, Ethnicity, and the Languages of American Literature.* New York: New York University Press.

Spillers, Hortense J. 1991. "Introduction: Who Cuts the Border? Some Readings on 'America.'" In *Comparative American Identities: Race, Sex, and Nationality in the Modern Text,* ed. Hortense J. Spillers. New York and London: Routledge.

Torres, Luis A. 1994a. "Bilingualism as Satire in Nineteenth Century Chicano Poetry." In *Another Tongue: Nation and Ethnicity in the Linguistic Borderlands,* ed. Alfred Arteaga. Durham, N.C.: Duke University Press. 247–62.

———. 1994b. *The World of Early Chicano Poetry: California Poetry, 1855–1881.* Encino, Calif.: Floricanto Press.

Williams, Stanley T. 1968. *The Spanish Background of American Literature.* 2 vols. New York: Archon Books.

Williams, William Appleman. 1980. *Empire as a Way of Life: An Essay on the Causes and Character of America's Present Predicament.* New York: Oxford University Press.

Zboray, Ronald J. 1993. *A Fictive People: Antebellum Economic Development and the American Reading Public.* New York: Oxford University Press.

Chapter 6

Indigenous Epistemologies in the Age of Globalization

Stefano Varese

Although Native American studies has gained a certain level of academic legitimacy in the United States and Canada, at least since the ethnic studies reform of the 1970s, in Latin America *los estudios indígenas* practically does not exist. I will focus my analysis on those themes that in Euramerican academic terms can be typified as epistemological. Epistemological inquiry, when exercised out of the dominant Euramerican cultural paradigm, must be concerned not only with the mode of knowledge but also with what could be called the ecology of knowledge: the interrelation between agency and culturally defined nature. Mode and ecology of knowledge require a diachronic and synchronic approach, therefore a historical-cultural as well as a sociopolitical contextualization.

Defining the multi/inter/cross or neodisciplinary attributes of Native American/indigenous studies is an issue of great academic importance and concern, but is also an opportunity for reasserting the epistemological and ethical uniqueness of the study (and praxis) of the indigenous peoples of the Americas. This claim of uniqueness and divergence from other humanities and social science fields is based not on scholarly arguments but on the long-standing trajectory and praxis of indigenous intelligentsia as critics and censurers of the lies of colonial and imperial academia that since the sixteenth century have constructed a distorted self-serving version of history, morality, and justice (Cook-Lynn 1999; Hernández-Avila and Varese 1999).[1] Native American studies/*estudios indígenas,* however, is more than revisionist history, subaltern studies, or a combination of ethnic studies, cultural studies, and postcolonial anthropology. It is the systematic attempt by millions of Indians of the hemisphere to reconfigure their nationhood, their sovereignty, their intellectual independence; their ethnic, cultural, social, and political projects.[2] Theory and practice, history and culture, as they intersect daily in the thousands of Indian rural and urban communities, become the nucleus of this enterprise that in the United States and Canada is called Native American studies and in Latin America is still condemned to alienation at the margins of anthropology. If the nuclei of indigenous studies are the issues of nationhood, sovereignty, independence, autonomy, and a contested, however larger and more inclusive, definition of citizenship, then two areas of discussion must be reintroduced vis-à-vis the current struggle of indigenous people of Latin America:

1. The issue of cultural and intellectual sovereignty of indigenous peoples and thus the related issue of their epistemological autonomy as peoples with their own grounded and spatial(ized) history.

2. The related question of territoriality, land, resources, and their rights to exercise political and cultural jurisdiction over them. Space, place, and memory are intertwined in indigenous societies that have not been totally uprooted by colonialism. They constitute what can be termed the inhabited culture, which is asserted always with the language of space even when the specific locality has been lost.

PROLOGUE AND PREMISE

This paper is based on the following eight principles:

1. Modernity is equivalent to and an integral part of Western Euramerican colonialism.

2. Modernity and colonialism are ontologically constituted by and express themselves through capitalism.

3. Contemporary science and knowledge (thus theory of knowledge and epistemology) are integral parts of the socio-ideological complex of modernity-colonialism-capitalism.

4. Ergo, modernity, colonialism, capitalism, and science express and practice themselves in Euramerican cultural and linguistic values (Indo-European) that are fundamentally Eurocentric.

5. Euramerican scientific and epistemological values are incapable (structurally disabled) of approaching, dealing, understanding, being sensitive to non-Western cosmologies *(weltanschauung)*, cultures, languages, and epistemic structures.

6. Commodification of nature, territory, land, and all the components of the world has been the permanent strategic threat against indigenous peoples. The socially constructed Indian spaces have been under the threat of commodification since the early sixteenth century.

7. Commodification and the logic of exchange value have pervaded every domain of social life, including tangible and intangible cultural configurations, knowledge, and science.

8. Internal opposition from Marxism, poststructuralism, colonial critique, subaltern studies, and postmodernist critiques in general are offshoots of Euramerican scientific methods that since their foundation have avoided any serious intellectual engagement with the "others," in this case, the indigenous peoples. Once established, such a dialogic engagement would induce the development of autonomous analytical tools, that is, decentered, non-Eurocentric epistemologies generated by indigenous organic intellectuals in dialogue with dissident Euramerican intellectuals.

First Vignette

J. S. Slotkin, who died in 1958, was an anthropologist who did his research among the Menominee Indians of Wisconsin. He was also a Peyotist, a member and officer of the Native American Church, the chief congregation of Peyotists. In his article "The Peyote Way," he tells the following story:

> During the (Peyote) rite each male participant in succession sings solo four songs at a time. Recently a Winnebago sitting next to me sang a song with what I heard as a Fox text (Fox is an Algonquian language closely related to Menomini, the language I used in the rite), sung so clearly and distinctly I understood every word.
>
> When he was through, I leaned over and asked, "How come you sang that song in Fox rather than Winnebago (a Siouan language unintelligible to me)?"

"I did sing it in Winnebago," he replied. The afternoon following the rite he sat down next to me and asked me to listen while he repeated the song; this time it was completely unintelligible to me because the effects of Peyote had worn off. (Tedlock and Tedlock 1975, 101–2)

Second Vignette

Marcos is a Triqui Indian from San Andrés Chicahuaxtla, Oaxaca, Mexico. He was selected to give the welcoming speech to Spain's royalty when they recently visited Oaxaca.

> We have been studied with the Western perception, in its different forms, but we have not been understood; it is still imposed on us with the Western form of development, its civilization, its way of seeing the world and relating to nature, thus denying all the knowledge generated by our different peoples. We have domesticated the corn, that sacred plant that gave us existence and we continue to improve it. But even so, whenever an agronomist comes to our towns, he tells us that the corn numbered and produced in his research center is better; if we build a house with our knowledge and materials, an architect comes to tell us that a dignified house can only be built with industrial products; if we invoke our old gods, someone comes to tell us that our faith is superstitious. (Esteva and Prakash 1998, 57)

Third Vignette

For millennia, the Wintu Indians occupied most of the valley of the Sacramento River in California. Today only a handful of Wintu people has survived the massacres and cultural genocide of the last one hundred years. Between the 1920s and the 1940s, philosopher and anthropologist Dorothy Lee, who studied their language, cosmology, and knowledge system, visited them. Here are some of Dorothy Lee's observations regarding Wintu language and consequently their epistemology:

> A basic tenet of the Wintu language, expressed both in nominal and verbal categories, is that reality—ultimate truth—exists irrespective of man. Man's experience actualized this reality, but does not otherwise affect its being. Outside man's experience, this reality is unbounded, undifferentiated, timeless. . . . To the Wintu, the given is not a series of particulars, to be classed into universals. The given is unpartitioned mass; a part of this the Wintu delimits into a particular individual. The particular then exists, not in nature, but in the consciousness of the speaker. What to

us is a class, a plurality of particulars, is to him a mass or a quality or an attribute. . . . For the Wintu, then, the essence or quality is generic and found in nature; it is permanent and remains unaffected by man. Form is imposed by man, through act of will. But the impression man makes is temporary. The deer stands out as an individual only at the moment of man's speech; as soon as he ceases speaking, the deer merges into deerness. . . . Recurring through all this—asserts Dorothy Lee—is the attitude of humility and respect toward reality, toward nature and society. I cannot find an adequate English term to apply to a habit of thought which is so alien to our culture. We are aggressive toward reality. . . . Our attitude toward nature is colored by a desire to control and exploit. The Wintu relationship with nature is one of intimacy and mutual courtesy. (Lee 1959, quoted in Tedlock and Tedlock 1975, 130–40)

A Short History

By the end of World War II, modernity and its travel companion colonialism had finally achieved the establishment of Eurocentrism as the hegemonic mode of thought and practice among the world's social minority, the elites of every single country of the globe. Neither Marxist socialist tradition nor the Third World nationalist movements were exempt from Eurocentric views, analyses, discourses, and praxis (Prakash 1994, 1475). By the mid-1960s George Gurvitch (1971) could write with total impunity his taxonomy of the sociology of knowledge in which, by using a social evolutionary scheme, he disqualified forms of knowledge linked to and based on the immediate apprehension, understanding, and organization of the locale, the concrete locus of cultural experience and reproduction. By then L. Lévy-Bruhl had produced *Primitive Mentality* (1935), in which he proposed, and imposed on non-Westerners, prelogical forms of primitive mentality associated with corresponding rudimentary levels of technological and social organization.

E. Durkheim and M. Mauss had formulated in 1903 their famous proposition that "the classification of things reproduces the classification of men" (Bloor 1984, 51) based on a Zuni Indian classificatory system, but their hypothesis was immediately challenged on the basis of its ethnographic value. What in fact was being challenged by Western science was the validity of so-called primitive societies' materials as empirical samples of human rationality. Western hegemonic thought could not even be moderated by heterodox views such as those expressed by Maurice Leenhardt (1947), who highlighted some of the most complex and sensitive traits of non-Western indigenous thought. Nor would any sense of revisionist moderation be achieved through the following revolution of C. Lévi-Strauss (1963, 1966), whose comparative and contrastive method of analysis of indigenous myths, rituals, kinship systems, and social practice allowed for a structural inquiry of non-Western worldviews and knowledge as highly complex and organized systems of meaning. Lévi-Strauss, in fact, may have followed the methodological road indicated by German philosopher Martin Heidegger (1966, cited in Tedlock and Tedlock 1975, 15–16), who had proposed the existence of *contemplative* thought, common among indigenous societies, as opposed to *calculative* thought, the dominant form in capitalist and late capitalist societies. The first oriented toward meaning, the latter toward results.

As the sociology of knowledge was approaching philosophy, and this, as epistemology, was increasingly becoming more sociological, it was clear that both disciplines were distancing themselves from the rich comparative materials gathered by ethnographers in indigenous regions and were especially incapable of accepting that there were other systems of knowledge, other epistemologies, and innumerable clandestine histories of non-Western, indigenous intellectuality (Bloor 1984; Luhmann 1984).

By the time ethnoscientists revisited, in the 1960s, the issue of indigenous knowledge systems, "discovering" the extreme rationality, analytical depth, and practicality of indigenous classificatory systems, it was too late. The hegemony of a superior Euramerican thought, "logos," and "scientific" system was well established and rooted in the minds and institutions of First as well as Third World hegemonic classes. Modernization theories proposed by analysts and policy makers of the empire, such as T. Parsons (1951) and W. Rostow (1960) and U.S. functionalist sociologists, were devastating any possibility of self-determination and intellectual sovereignty of the indigenous peoples and the peasants of the world. Nothing of what the indigenous local peoples knew had any value. Indian cultures, peripheral and marginalized, were considered to be empty vessels or rather obsolete urns of dead and heavy heritage that had to be substituted by Euramerican education, technology, forms of governance, and economic organization. The latter was obviously the most important point because Eurocentrism has placed the economy at the center of every social existence and Euramerican historicism has projected the West as history (Prakash 1994, 1475), moreover, as universal history. The main tenets of structural-functionalist modernization theory, particularly as it referred to indigenous peoples, were that "traditional society" is hindering economic development, that Third World countries need agents to help them break out of the jail of tradition, that such agents may be either recruited from within the society (modernizing elites, co-opted leadership) or imported from outside via educational models and capital injection, that dual economies may coexist in Third World countries, and finally that the desired outcome of modernization politics are societies similar to those in Western Europe and the United States.

It is well known that the criticism of modernization theory came principally from within the dominant Western sociological and economic theoretical models, albeit from its radical dissenting Marxist version (Frank 1967, 1969; Cardoso and Faletto 1979). During the 1960s and 1970s, dependency and underdevelopment theorists argued that modernization analysts had ignored the effects of colonialism and neo-colonialism on the structure of Third World societies, that traditionalism itself had been a colonial creation resulting from centuries of subordination to colonial metropolis, that dualism was a misrepresentation of Third World countries because the so-called traditional sector had been part of the national (and sometimes international) economy for centuries, and finally that the evolutionary model of development (or rather the social neo–Darwinism) imposed on every single society of the world was impeding and denying the possibility of novel forms of society emerging from postcolonial reconstruction. The political context of this criticism was obviously the demobilizing and counterrevolutionary objectives of U.S. ideological theorists and governmental advisors explicitly committed to curtailing the impact of the Cuban revolution of 1959 and the spread of socialist ideals in Latin America.

Significantly, the majority of U.S. and Latin American anthropologists stayed out of this polemic either for political reasons (most of their professional training was realized within the structural-functionalist sociology and neoclassical economics) and/or because even with Marxist analytical tools they were methodologically unprepared to represent claims of legitimate "scientific" knowledge and rationality on behalf of indigenous peoples and peasants. The drama of two generations of anthropologists who came to intellectual maturity in the 1960s and the 1980s was that the hegemony of scientific Eurocentrism had nullified their capacity to apply the new hermeneutics suggested by Thomas Kuhn in his *The Structure of Scientific Revolutions* (1962) to non-Western indigenous cultures and knowledge systems. They, as well as the indigenous peoples for whom or with whom they were supposed to be speaking, had been silenced on the central issue of the local, communal, ethnic indigenous intellectual sovereignty. That is to say, the intellectual and political task of identifying and establishing the enormous epistemological significance of alternative, non-Euramerican systems of knowledge of indigenous peoples for their own collective survival and future development and for the amendment of Western science was simply abdicated by one of the main disciplines of colonialism and postcolonialism.[3]

It is true, however, that a handful of Latin American anthropologists and Indian intellectuals were establishing fragile alliances and retrieving the autonomy of indigenous peoples as historical subjects and their cultural and political sovereignty. In 1971, during the tenuous socialist experiments of Chile with Salvador Allende and the progressive nationalist government of Juan Velasco in Peru, a group of Latin American social scientists challenged conventional anthropology by asserting the fundamental rights of the indigenous peoples to struggle for their self-determination and liberation in their own autonomous terms, using their own intellectual sovereignty freed of hegemonic compulsion from without and from the theoretical supremacy of Western academia (Barbados I, 1971). Again, in 1979 and 1993, the Group of Barbados (Grupo de Barbados 1979; Grünberg 1995), now enlarged to include indigenous intellectuals, activists, and militants, insisted on voicing the epistemological rights of the indigenous peoples to organize their liberation movements and their ethnic and social projects with independence from both Euramerican liberal and socialist models.

Indigenous Peoples Take the Initiative

What had been happening in Latin America, at least since the 1960s, was the emergence of a strong ethnopolitical Indian movement that was claiming self-determination and cultural sovereignty predicated on the long historical intellectual autonomy of each indigenous society. Although the indigenous peoples of the Americas had been struggling against colonial powers for five hundred years, it was mainly after World War II that they initiated political mobilization at the national and international scale in order to resist oppression and land expropriation. There were obviously hundreds of indigenous insurrections, messianic movements, and ethnonationalist independence rebellions that took place during the Iberian colonial administration and the following Republican period, as well as many other examples of early Indian political activism expressed in "modern" terms in the various national territories of Latin America. However, it is only during the last five decades that evidence of a substantial national and international Indian movement can be found in the massive proliferation of native organizations and supporting institutions of the civil society (NGOs).

The structural reasons for the rise of an international Indian movement can be traced in what has been called post–World War II Pax Americana, characterized by the massive expansion of the industrial base in the "core" countries, the dependent development efforts in Latin America with the connected expansion of the internal national frontier in search of energy resources, and the readjustment of nation-state structures in order to facilitate national integration and ethnic assimilation. Explorations and resource exploitation of peripheral regions by multinational corporations and their local national representatives suddenly became the single most threatening event for indigenous peoples and territories that had enjoyed relative isolation and autonomy. In the course of a few decades, indigenous peoples of the relatively marginal areas of the lowlands of Central and South America became "internal refugees of underdevelopment." The traditional strategy of retreating to isolated areas, zones of refuge, became less and less viable, forcing the Indians to go on the offensive while recognizing the changing characteristics of the antagonist forces now increasingly transnational and relatively out of the control of the regional elite.

STATE NATIONALISM AND TRANSNATIONALIZATION

A basic paradox appears in this process of transnationalization of the political economy of Latin American nation-states. On the one hand, the programs operated by transnational corporations in Latin America mitigate the burden on Latin American states of having to play the entrepreneurial role in substitution of the national oligarchies and bourgeoisie that have been traditionally passive. On the other hand, the multinational corporate projects create a problem of national security for the state by challenging precisely a weakly integrated and vulnerable national entity. Two antagonistic forces thus came into play in the Latin American scenario during the last few decades:

1. A strong trend toward national consolidation in which the state continues to act as the founding and generating principle of the nation, reshaping and attempting to give a sense of unity to heterogeneous territorial and ethnic spaces for the benefit of the ruling class.

2. The need of the same state, under pressure by the transnationalization of the political economy, to transform itself ideologically and objectively from a liberal nineteenth-century institution (centralized, authoritarian, homogeneous) into a more permeable, flexible, less nationalistic entity open to corporate penetration and transnational forces.

The expected result of this contradictory trend has increasingly been the movement of transnational capital to less controlled areas, to open regions: indigenous territories not yet totally exploited where environmental regulations, labor unions, and political organizations do not exist or are weak and controllable. Concurrent with this process of internationalization of capital, labor, and environment, the privatization of the state becomes a key requirement. Even basic state functions such as police control are increasingly posited in private terms, resulting during the 1980s in the proliferation of privatized police and paramilitary forces in charge of repression and control. The ideology and actual process of national integration and ethnic assimilation of the indigenous peoples therefore come under the ambiguous jurisdictions of a neo-dependent state formally in charge of defining the terms of citizenship for each member of the national community, and the informal, hidden, and powerful authority of transnational capital.

Indian Sovereignty, Territories, and Globalization

In this new, globalized, and complex political environment, however, the central struggle of the indigenous peoples is still the old one: *the defense of their lands and territories.* The renewed massive circular migration of indigenous peoples to *fincas*/haciendas/plantations, to industrial regions, to urban centers, and to transnational labor markets has not alleviated their objective need of land nor their political demands for territorial consolidation. It could be argued, in fact, that indigenous migration/deportation, even when practiced for many years, does not necessarily result in permanent immigration to the host region/city/country but rather in renovated efforts of the indigenous migrant to consolidate his/her communal citizenship by complying with ceremonial and civic demands and by expanding his/her access to communal lands and resources (see Stephen 1991). Circular migration, especially the transnational one with its relatively higher level of earnings, produces extra demands over the limited territorial and land resources of the community. It is interesting to note that six years after the enactment of the infamous modification of Article 27 of the Mexican Constitution, which allows *ejidos* and communities to rent or sell their lands, practically no transaction has taken place: peasants and indigenous people are tenaciously holding onto their lands (personal communication by anthropologist Carlos Moreno, director of the Procuraduría Agraria of the State of Oaxaca).

Economic deportation, migration, transnational diasporas, and the effects of globalization have not brought to an end the process of uprootedness, deterritorialization, and creation of a labor market of dispossessed Indians that was expected by the elites. The processes have rather linked and secured even more the indigenous people to their land and territory, producing an increase in number and a growth in intensity of communal rites of local identity and belonging (Stephen 1991).

Even a superficial look at the numerous indigenous organizations and movements that have emerged since the 1960s in Latin America shows that while the demographics of temporal territorial displacement are increasing, the politics of ethnicity and class are expressed in local and grounded terms, in the language of place, the language of spatially rooted time: a socially shared experience where a people's history can be read in the signs of land and space. The language of place, which is always ethnic, linked to concrete cultural and linguistic symbols of space and time, permeates the political discourse, platform, agenda, and strategy of most of the indigenous organizations. Even organizations like FIOB (Indigenous Bi-national Oaxacan Front), which rose out of Mixtec, Zapotec, Chinantec, and Trique Indian migrants to the United States and their experience of deterritorialization, diaspora, and the alleged hybridization process that would accompany these phenomena, are not producing political organizations and activism that are delinked from the issue of homeland. Preoccupations with land/territoriality and the autonomy of local government and management of the land and resources are still at the center of these transnational organizations. Oaxacan indigenous migrants to California are strong economic and political supporters of indigenous candidates at local municipal elections in their regions of origin, and similar commitment has been expressed for the Zapatista Mayan insurgents of Chiapas.

Until the Mayan rebellion of Chiapas in 1994, the issue of indigenous peoples' sovereignty was not spoken of in Latin America. The terms "sovereignty," "territorial autonomy," and "self-determination" in reference to Indian people could barely be whispered by anthropologists and indigenous intellectuals and could easily carry the accusation of subversive proclamations. Following a strict Napoleonic tradition, in Latin America the notion of sovereignty is applied exclusively to the nation-state. After more than four years of public debate in Mexico and in the world through the Internet, the concepts and possibilities of indigenous peoples' sovereignty and ethnic rights to self-determination and territorial autonomy have become part of the reluctantly accepted general political discourse. The specifics of what may constitute ethnosovereignty rights are still in the making and need to be addressed in each specific regional and national case. But first, there is the important question of the social and spatial definition of indigenous peoples and groups.

A Return to Local Epistemology

The socio-ideological complex of modernity-colonialism-capitalism has established the hegemony of a theory of knowledge that is deterritorialized, spaceless, without community, and thus with a limited, anonymous, moral, and social responsibility. In its pretense to be universal, the Western theory of knowledge claims one single epistemology that is centered on the exchange value and thus is "econocentric," monetized, and commodified. It is an epistemology whose main accountability lies finally in the marketplace. On the contrary, at the periphery, at the margins of the modernity complex in what is at the same time antimodern and postmodern, the indigenous systems of knowledge are deeply rooted in the land, in the community, in the culturally concrete and socially constructed places, places with ancient names and histories, landscapes of millenary dialogues between humans, animals, plants, soils, water, rocks, winds, and stars.

There was a purpose in my roundabout journey of the Latin American Indians' ethnopolitical movements: my intention was to show the fundamental importance of the politics of space for indigenous peoples, cultures, and knowledge systems. No other individual or collective relation has played historically, and still plays today, a more important role in indigenous life than the one they have, or they long to reestablish, with their space, their community, their land, their territory, their homeland. To be rooted to the land, even when exile is the temporary condition, means to be organically linked to the matrix of reference, the cultural (and linguistic) framework that sustains the whole interpretative system of life. Land means production, consumption, sacred celebration, mirror of divine creation, and what allows for the human creation of the mirror, too. To maintain social and cultural dominion over the territory means to exercise jurisdiction over the concrete, historical manifestation of one's own place of culture, one's own system of knowledge, one's own epistemic structure, and the mode of praxis that is linked to such belonging. To be linked epistemologically to the locale and to exercise its praxis does not mean to abdicate from the cosmopolitan and ecumenical worldview. It means to recognize that one's own universe is just a fragment of a "pluriverse" (not only a universe) with which each society and individual must learn to live. Communication between the diversity of systems is not only possible: it is a must. However, it requires mutuality and equity, a moral world system based on principles of symmetrical reciprocity at least at the level of intellectual and spiritual coexistence if not in the economic and political domains.

I am personally a strong advocate of the politicization (or *ethnopoliticization*) of indigenous peoples as the primary and fundamental tool for their liberation and autonomous development. I see this process of politicization (through local, regional, national, and transnational organizations) as the opportunity for indigenous peoples to make individual and collective choices and decisions that are based on the critical knowledge of their own cultures/politics and the culture/politics of the dominant national/global society. I believe that the critical (and comparative) recognition—consciousness of one's ethnic identity—presupposes the use of one's culture as a dynamic repository of resources that can then be mobilized for the achievement of a collectively defined covenant. It is in this sense that we should, as members of the global civil society, make a call for the definition of a "New Generation of Indigenous Human Rights" that would guarantee, in both the global biosphere and the global society, the existence, protection, and development of indigenous autonomous territories, cultural diversity, linguistic and epistemological specificity, and the right of indigenous peoples to dream their future in their own civilizational terms.

Notes

1. I think a clarification of my institutional affiliation and position regarding my formal academic disciplinary field is relevant. I am an anthropologist; actually, my degree shows a presumptuous title in ethnology, earned not so much in seminar classes at the Catholic University of Peru as under thatched roofs of Amazon indigenous *malocas* and in travels through rivers, forest, savannas, and *chacras*. After the 1960s, I tried to combine scholarly research and

pro-Indian activism, but I found it extremely difficult to strike an equilibrium between the two. I left academia in the early 1970s to involve myself with the struggle of the indigenous peoples of the Peruvian Amazon for the recuperation of their territories and cultural autonomy. During the following two decades I maintained my engagement with the indigenous peoples' struggles from my new residence in Southern Mexico and from different institutional settings that combined Mexican state-sponsored applied research and grassroots/NGOs initiatives. It is only since the early 1990s that I have been exclusively situated in an ethnopolitically engaged academic environment, the Department of Native American Studies at the University of California, Davis, which allows me the luxury of reaping the benefits of scholarly life while exercising my choice of activism in issues of indigenous peoples. I may have finally found a balance between scholarly and practical activities, academia and community activism, theory and practice. Even in a heterodox department such as Native American studies, there is a constant unresolved and creative tension between academia and activism. This is true especially in light of a career system that exclusively rewards conventional scholarly production while penalizing activities considered to be nonacademic and profane.

2. There are, in Latin America, an estimated 40 million indigenous peoples subdivided into four hundred major ethnolinguistic groups and possibly more than a thousand languages and dialect variations. When we say "Latin America," we expand this area-notion to a hemispheric, transborders, nationally independent conception and practice of occupation of the continent by peoples who come from the conventional delimitation of "Latin America." Hence, the few hundred thousand indigenous peoples from Mexico, Guatemala, Nicaragua, the rest of Central America, and most of the Andean countries of South America, together with millions of mestizos and criollos and people from countries south of the border who are currently living in the United States and Canada (with or without documents), constitute the "Latin America within" that is radically transforming both Anglo America and Latino America.

3. In 1995, Swiss-Canadian anthropologist Jeremy Narby published a revolutionary study on the Peruvian Amazon Campa-Ashaninka shamanistic knowledge that challenges conventional Western notions of science, theory of knowledge, nature, and especially biophysics and molecular biology (Narby 1995; Dubochet, Narby, and Kiefer 1997). Narby's study may be considered the first serious attempt by contemporary anthropology to analyze and validate alternative and radically different indigenous forms of knowledge. His study qualifies for what T. Kuhn called a revolutionary paradigm shift. In a public debate with microbiologist Jacques Dubochet held in Geneva in June 1997, Narby summarized his study: "At the beginning of my research I studied the botanical knowledge of these peoples [the Ashaninka]. It is an astounding knowledge, because the Amazon rain forest contains half of the plants of the world, and the Indians have an almost encyclopedic knowledge of them. I asked my consultants how

did they acquire their knowledge about the plants. They answered that nature has intelligence, that she is animated by identical essences in all forms of life, and that these essences are the origin of their knowledge. They told me that to communicate with nature the shamans drank a mixture of hallucinogens and spoke, in their visions, with the essences of life. . . . After years of reflection I noticed that there were astonishing similarities between these essences and the DNA. To begin with, the molecule of genetic information is found in each cell of every living entity. And shamans associate the animated essences with the form of the double helix, which is found in fact in the design of their visions. Now, the DNA has exactly this form, which is fundamental for its functioning. . . . Obviously the Amazon Indian do not speak of DNA, but I propose the hypothesis that there is a correspondence at various levels between the animated essences that the shamans perceive, and what we call DNA" (Dubochet, Narby, and Kiefer 1997, 13–14).

REFERENCES

Barbados I Declaration. 1971. IWGIA. Document no. 1, Copenhagen.

Bloor, D. 1984. "Durkheim and Mauss Revisited: Classification in the Sociology of Knowledge." In *Society and Knowledge: Contemporary Perspectives in the Sociology of Knowledge,* ed. N. Stehr and M. Volker. New Brunswick and London: Transaction Books. 51–75.

Cardoso, F., and E. Faletto. 1979. *Dependency and Development in Latin America.* Berkeley: University of California Press.

Cook-Lynn, Elizabeth. 1999. "American Indian Studies: An Overview." *Wicazo Sa Review* 14, no. 2: 14–24.

Dubochet, J., J. Narby, and B. Kiefer. 1997. *L'AND devant le souverain: Science, démocratie, et génie génétique.* Geneva: Terra Magna, Editions Georg.

Esteva, G., and M. S. Prakash. 1998. *Grassroots Post-Modernism.* London & New York: Zed Books.

Frank, A. 1967. *Capitalism and Underdevelopment in Latin America.* New York and London: Monthly Review Press.

———. 1969. *Latin America: Underdevelopment or Revolution.* Harmondsworth, England: Penguin.

Grünberg, G. 1995. *Articulación de la diversidad: Pluralidad etnica, autonomías, y democratización en América Latina.* Grupo de Barbados, no. 27. Quito, Ecuador: Ediciones AbyaYala.

Grupo de Barbados. 1979. *Indianidad y descolonización en América Latina.* Mexico: Editorial Nueva Imagen.

Gurvitch, G. 1971. *The Social Frameworks of Knowledge.* Oxford, England: Basil Blackwell.

Heidegger, M. 1966. *Discourse on Thinking.* Trans. John M. Anderson and E. Hans Freund. New York: Harper & Row.

Hernández-Avila, Inés, and Stefano Varese. 1999. "Indigenous Intellectual Sovereignties: A Hemispheric Convocation." *Wicazo Sa Review* 14, no. 2: 77–91.

Kuhn, T. 1962. *The Structure of Scientific Revolutions.* Chicago: Chicago University Press.

Lee, D. 1959. *Freedom and Culture.* Homewood, Ill.: Prentice Hall.

Leenhardt, M. 1947. *Do kamo: La personne et le mythe dans le monde mélanésien.* Paris: Galimard.

———. 1979. *Do Kamo: Person and Myth in the Melanesian World.* Trans. Basia Gulati. Chicago: University of Chicago Press.

Lévi-Strauss, C. 1963. *Structural Anthropology.* New York: Basic Books.

———. 1966. *The Savage Mind.* Chicago: University of Chicago Press.

Lévy-Bruhl, L. 1935. *Primitive Mentality.* Trans. L. A. Clare. Boston: Beacon Press.

Luhmann, N. 1984. "The Differentiation of Advances in Knowledge: The Genesis of Science." In *Society and Knowledge: Contemporary Perspectives in the Sociology of Knowledge,* ed. Nico Stehr and Volker Meja. New Brunswick and London: Transaction Books. 103–48.

Narby, J. 1995. *La serpent cosmique, l'AND et les origines du savoire.* Geneva: Editions Georg.

Parsons, T. 1951. *The Social System.* London: Routledge and Kegan Paul.

Prakash, G. 1994. "Subaltern Studies as Postcolonial Criticism." *American Historical Review* (December): 1475–90.

Rostow, W. 1960. *The Stages of Economic Growth: A Non-Communist Manifesto.* Cambridge: Cambridge University Press.

Stephen, L. 1991. *Zapotec Women.* Austin: University of Texas Press.

Tedlock, D., and B. Tedlock, eds. 1975. *Teaching from the American Earth: Indian Religion and Philosophy.* New York: Liveright.

Chapter 7

Deconstruction, Cultural Studies, and Global Capitalism: Implications for Latin America

Román de la Campa

Translated by Ivelise Faundez-Reitsma

For many intellectuals, cultural studies embraces a daring postdisciplinary desire, while for others it already configures a new and dignified field of study worthy of a global society. For still others, cultural studies contributes to a never-ending debate about the future of academia and its disciplinary objects. It is possible to intuit, however, that all of these views and approaches share a common challenge of considerable proportions: how to incorporate the legacy of Western culture into a New World Order being presently promoted by neoliberal capitalism. Those who oppose or question cultural studies, such as the renowned philosopher Richard Rorty (1991), observe in it a dangerous decimation of disciplinary rigors accumulated by humanistic discourses throughout the centuries, from Romanticism to deconstruction. Proponents of cultural studies, like Stuart Hall (1992) and other followers of the Birmingham School, on the other hand, find in it a special promise, a fertile register for an epistemology of turns, breaks, and interstices that gathers strength through poststructural praxis and postmodern experience.

There are, of course, many other views regarding cultural studies, yet it is important to note that the accrual of new and influential criticism on the matter has not necessarily lent itself to much dialogue or, for that matter, competition among differing approaches. It could be argued, instead, that cultural studies, as well as much of the theoretical work that informs it, increasingly responds to the forces of supply and demand, which may explain its capacity to generate and propel projects into an academic market in continous need of new packaging. In this growing market, there is no particular emphasis on clear-cut distinctions between cultural studies, feminism, Western Marxism, subalternity, postcolonialism, postmodernism, performativity, noncreative fiction, and other labels of interest to academic presses and journals in an increasingly privatized academic setting.

My main concern with the cultural studies turn, particularly in the American academy, is not just its marketing cycle but also an unsuspected theoretical problem behind it, that is, the contradictory ways in which deconstruction figures as the nondifferentiated common denominator in many of today's culturalist discourses. Regardless of the diverse and often opposing ways in which it is professed, deconstruction imbues modalities of reading, writing, and even thinking that inevitably turn toward designification of discourses that claim presence, logocentrism, in short, that it aims to problematize, complicate, and question how cultures and histories establish notions such as reality, identity, and worldviews. Thus understood, it is often said that deconstruction only aims to tear down critical paradigms once sacred to the humanities, yet one could argue it is equally capable of rebuilding or reconceptualizing them. After all, humanistic endeavors have gained considerable prominence through critiques that question the narratives of the modern period. They have welcomed an array of challenges posed by postmodernity in general, a term that generally includes certain strands of feminism, philosophy, writing as a philosophical praxis, film criticism, and various approaches to mass-mediatic culture. All of this has been done largely through the potent theoretical agency of deconstructive thinking.

There are, however, many questions and difficulties in this apparent dialectic of rupture and continuity. As the driving force behind the critique of modernity's legacy, deconstruction must now look in the mirror of a late capitalist market that has turned even more radical since 1989. Global capital also finds the modern constitution of reality—not only individual but also collective identities, including the nation—somewhat anachronistic to its ever-widening drive to create new and unobstructed markets. One could (should?) therefore wonder how far academic deconstruction can still distance itself from postcapitalism, that other force of designification. Equally important would be to ask if the critical distance needed by deconstruction would require a new attention to the social realm (or text), if it must now be understood, as Michael Hardt and Antonio Negri (2000, chapter 3) claim in *Empire,* as a pressing need for articulation and rearticulation rather than just as the object of incessant designification. The latter was the work of an academic praxis always predisposed to epistemic battles within the "lettered order," a type of work that remained mostly individualized and largely aloof from everyday life and experience. Postcapitalism, on the other hand, has found an unexpected immediacy between the culture of the library and the culture of the street through cable or satellite television, service industries, the Internet, and other mass media, all of it requiring a more collaborative approach to knowledge production and perhaps posing a considerable challenge to a theoretical activism caught in the calmness of negative epistemology.

Within these doubts, paradoxes, and questions, I would like to explore the need for a somewhat different framework in the production and discussion of discourses on Latin America. I am referring to a configuration that would recognize the comparative transnational condition of everything Latin American and its practitioners—Latin Americanists of multiple styles, methods, ideologies, and modes of subsistence. "Latin Americanism" here aims to include most particularly its contemporary practitioners as well as to question how they construct their object of study: Latin America. Such a new configuration of Latin American cultural studies—a discursive community of immanently different Latin American cultures and interlocutors—might possibly yield a resignification of novel interaction between social science disciplines bound by the rigors of empirical research and the new humanities geared to discursive critiques and epistemic designification. This project would require an inter- and multidisciplinarism, able to appropriate but also problematize deconstruction's important legacy and its impact on cultural studies. In such a case, it becomes imperative to clarify what Nelly Richard and Homi Bhabha have termed "verbal metaphors" when referring to the vast theoretical space that governs deconstruction.

I stress the need for clarification because "verbal metaphors" often invoke a vast array of deconstructive practices and applications, at times blind to each others' vastly different aims—if not internal contradictions—from Derridean critiques of Western metaphysics, for example, to de Manian approaches to literary history or to Latin American subalternity. The new cartography I am proposing would be a more heretical approach, beginning with an attentive ear to the contradictions inherent in the deconstructive paradigm, yet without negating its insights regarding metanarratives and epistemes embedded in our understanding of history and philosophy. I would further argue that cultural studies demands such a heretical focus even more than philosophy and literature because the field remains, after all, an unstable entity whose object of study has no limitations. In terms of a Latin American configuration of cultural studies, the problem is further magnified by the enormous diversity of a landscape that includes at least four historically distinct cultural constellations: Andean, Meso-American, Caribbean, and Southern Cone.

In a recent study on race in the United States, George Lipsitz (1995) finds that his object of study can only advance through a new conversation between the cutting edges of humanities and the social sciences, or at least by a narrowing of the gap between them. Lipsitz arrives at this conclusion through his work in ethnic studies, perhaps an analogous model for cultural studies in the United States. His own approach not only derives from the crosscurrents of various disciplines, it also seeks to recharge them with the specific consideration of racial issues demanded at this particular moment of history. The same concern appears in other key theoretical interventions of recent times, such as *The Politics of Culture in the Shadow of Capital,* edited by Lisa Lowe and David Lloyd (1997; see also Gugelberger 1996). It charts new paths through the openings so carefully diagnosed by deconstruction but with a very attentive ear to the exigencies of the social text—concrete nationalisms, emancipation movements, different types of feminist struggles—that may slip from writing as a self-enclosed deconstructive domain.

It could be said that cultural studies attempts to encompass two difficult issues of great importance at once: the immensity of cultural production and consumption on one hand, and the growing fusion of cultural forms on the other. Such an agenda constitutes a rather tall order for any discipline. The possibilities of establishing any internal rigor in such a field or, for that matter, of creating an object of study applicable to it largely depend on its capacity to amalgamate three basic elements faced by any conceptual framework that aims to intervene in the world of culture today.

1. *The split in disciplinary boundaries.* This speaks to the ongoing crisis in how we configure knowledge, a state of shifts and realignments that

impacts both the humanities and social sciences in different ways that remain by and large without serious debate or dialogue. Instead, each cluster has sought to accommodate disciplinary dispersion internally, either by negation or implosion. Numerology and discursivity thus acquire a new importance as both sets of disciplines attempt to account for the challenging displacement of cultural capital in the postmodern era. Economic production becomes increasingly cultural just as cultural production must show profitability. Products must go to the market endowed with artistry and self-conscious performativity at the same time that artistic and cultural products must assume market logic in order to survive. Even the academy and its practitioners respond to this logic.

In that context of disciplinary dispersals and retrievals, it seems crucial to note that in Latin America cultural studies remains largely confined to the realm of social sciences, while in the United States the field has mainly captured the attention of the humanities. The work of Néstor García Canclini, a Latin American anthropologist studying the cultural impact of globalization in Mexico in ways that are often conversant with philosophical and theoretical issues, could be the exception that proves the rule. His audience in the United States comes mainly, perhaps strictly, from literary critics currently concerned with cultural studies who only notice his occasional forays into humanistic issues. The silence among the paradigms thus multiplies across nations as does the absence of comparative frames within the disciplines portending to represent Latin Americanism. Once again, the radically different national contexts and distinct linguistic communities that make up Latin America remain overlooked, as the most influential groups of scholars continue to derive their samples from one nation or at most a region as well as their disciplinary purviews.

This (mis)reading is further complicated if one observes that thematic and even theoretical clusters pertaining to Latin American cultural studies are often very different in Latin America from those of the United States. The latter tend to privilege postmodern, postcolonial, subaltern, or feminist issues often derived from literature or history. In Latin America, on the other hand, the prevailing approaches to cultural studies have come from sociological, anthropological, and communication discourses such as the media studies of Jesus Martin Barbero or García Canclini's notion of cultural reconversion (González Stephan 1996). Possible exceptions to these trends are discussed later, but they remain largely bound to national or regional settings rather than to a broader Latin American approach from Latin America as a whole. It is not the same, obviously, to speak of subalternity, creolization, hybridity, and (post)modernity in the Andean region as it is to discuss these terms in the Caribbean, the Southern Cone, or, for that matter, in any U.S. university.

2. *Theoretical dissemination.* This second aspect, obviously an extension of the first one, points to the proliferation of theories within the last decade that focus primarily on metanarrative critiques, many of which often include the way in which "hard" social science and physical science discourses constitute themselves as objects of knowledge. It is important to note and clarify, however, the degree to which this practice brings about a new horizon partial to humanistic traditions over those in the social sciences. As a body of theory that looks upon writing as a self-referential domain, deconstruction remains closer to artistic practice, often distant from engaging how its critiques apply to the social, a disciplinary perspective that, in spite of its unquestionable possibilities as radical epistemology, basically retains the pattern of the humanist researcher engaging texts in isolation, banking on its pertinence in the postmodern lettered order or awaiting a call to action through distant connections to the social.

Deconstruction, largely understood as the designification of modern logocentric premises, taught us to engage polysemia, ambiguity, indeterminacy, and linguistic materiality—all integral crucial elements in the constitution of "the real." But what about research bound to empirical methods? One can argue that these disciplines tend to reify data at the expense of discursive embeddedness and that they are often privileged by the sheer applicability of their findings to instrumental reason. Yet, social science approaches to cultural studies continue nonetheless to address the entanglements of the lifeworld with a level of specificity largely dismissed by new humanistic approaches. Empirical scholarship can't help but engage the lifeworld, thereby occupying sites of applicability— what we might call the organization of the quotidian—that humanistic designification prefers to void or vacate. The extraordinary example of Pierre Bourdieu should suffice.

One of the greatest challenges for cultural studies will be to fathom links between the production of empirical and discursive knowledge, indeed, a reconfiguration of disciplines capable of articulating the richness of the living social text in its constructive as well as deconstructive realms. Without these reencounters, we attend to a postmodernity that only values economic data or epistemic speculation, a new order of knowledge anchored exclusively in the digital revolution, the stock market on one hand and epistemological indeterminism on the other. Perhaps the two mirror each other in ways totally unforeseen by the first waves of poststructuralist theory.

3. *The culturalist market of global capitalism.* By this I mean the transformation of consumerism into a subjective realm through postmodern mass-mediatic interactivity, a new terrain tightly bound, albeit in uncharted ways, to the energy of the arts. This link highlights one of the most contradictory aspects of globalization in academic production, to wit, that schools are becoming secondary agents of education as media and other corporate frameworks orchestrate the imaginary of citizens as consumers. There are no established channels to decipher or interpret the global society, and entry into middle-class status now demands a symbolic capital not always found in traditional schooling. Therein lies another challenge of great importance for cultural studies even if it has thus far been of little concern to deconstructive paradigms.

It is clear that studies about television, the Internet, and other mass media endeavors require a different relationship with academia. The space known hitherto as "the street" now bursts forth with new strength and legitimacy into knowledge production, a complex rearticulation that overturns the division between high and low culture. It now seems much more difficult to separate the realm of textual traditions from consumer sensibilities. Thanks to statistics that govern production, particularly by means of the Internet, cultural reception becomes instantly measurable. In short, the space of the researcher or intermediary is now unavoidably more public, which is to say more political, even if these unforeseen challenges evolve from capitalism's own culturalist strata and not from opposition to it as one may have expected.

These three aspects of cultural studies are obviously interrelated, yet each provides specific angles often taken for granted when they are discussed in unison. For instance, it has become commonplace to stumble on the notion that identity critiques, multitemporality, and multiculturalism have almost universal appeal. But such glances fail to get past the celebratory shores of postmodernity, which can either focus on popular or high culture, drawing a bit here and there from deconstructive practices inspired by the work of de Man, Derrida, Foucault, Lyotard, Kristeva, and other crucial theorists (Chanady 1994, introduction). Latin

American culture provides a telling register for such varied codification, since it often serves as a marker for postmodernity, postcoloniality, subalternity, or all of the above. The novelistic "boom" of the 1960s and 1970s imbued high cultural-style critiques until the 1980s, a form of literary postmodernism at first categorized as neo-Baroque. Other approaches closer to popular culture favored testimonial literature, first as a counter to the postmodern corpus, later as residues of postcolonial and subaltern perspectives. Ultimately, the latter took on the shape of a broader critique that went beyond literature to focus on indigenous popular uprisings and question the legitimacy of the Latin American modern state.

Yet, such theorizing often conflates Latin America's multiple cultures or, for that matter, state formations. The focus on failed modernities invokes a deconstruction of the twentieth century insufficiently distinguishable from a critique of nineteenth-century foundational errors or those from earlier periods. How do the citizens of various Latin American nations and regions make sense of everyday life where neither modernity nor postmodernity provides the means to chart a new cartography of possibilities, particularly after 1989, when the idea of a socialist path to modernization came to a sudden halt? Herein lies perhaps the greatest challenge to Latin American cultural studies. I am not suggesting that these issues find a natural solution in Latin America or that knowledge produced in the United States or Europe has nothing to contribute. Latin America's articulations also demand scrutiny, for a great deal of the work produced there remains caught in national boundaries as well. Having said that, however, one can't fail to acknowledge the increasing hegemonic quality of the Latin Americanism produced in the United States even if its practitioners are often diasporic Latin Americans now living there.

Projects engendered in the American academy betray certain propensities as one might expect. Generally they reveal a tendency toward historical sweep—proposals that seek to define the past, present, and future of Latin America—symptomatic of the quality of work possible under the auspices of an extraordinary research university system but also of the mounting production pressures faced by humanist intellectuals in this era of privatization. A key example may be found in Latin American postcolonial studies, fundamentally articulated by literary critics interested not just in the area's colonial constitution before independence, but also in how it has sustained itself afterward, up to our own time. The colonial gathers postcolonial importance as its lingering force becomes more evident. The act of repressing ongoing colonial and neocolonial order by the modernist hegemony during the twentieth century makes it particularly subject to deconstruction (Mignolo 1993; de la Campa 1996).

One should remember that as late as the 1960s colonial Latin American literature was still widely read as a secondary corpus of the Spanish golden age. The lines that define the postmodern characteristics of testimonial literature also deserve attention, as they help to see the links between postcolonial thinking and the work of scholars self-defined as the Latin American Subaltern Studies Group. In the work of John Beverley, often presented as spokesperson for this group, Latin American *testimonio* exemplifies a model of antiliterature or posthumanist literature, a type of writing no longer bound by the modernist or bourgeois sense of subjectivity. This entails an attempt to interject a left-oriented politics within postmodern critiques, a difficult fusion consisting of various moves and strategies; to argue that *testimonio* stands as the left-wing version of postmodern Latin American literature in contrast to the boom narrative, which would occupy, by simple deduction, a more conservative role; to designate the modern Latin American state project as a failed Creole utopia; to classify the subaltern classes in Latin America as models of resistance to modernity and thus as the subjects through which a postmodern society would be possible; and to mold a new role for the intellectuals who record this transmission of theoretical fusion from abroad.

Various aspects of this important undertaking deserve further discussion. The first would be to note that it contains a curious ambiguity regarding testimonial literature, since it both affirms and denies its literary nature. The main focus is to problematize the Latin American contemporary canon (above all, the boom) from the starting point of a new textuality that assigns *testimonio* the role of a new literary form (particularly those with indigenous content). One could say that the internal logic of this transference is equivalent to a transmission of postmodern influences from self-referential literary experimentation to narratives about the lives of subjects living in societies affected by both global capital and local elites pretending to establish modern states on top of the old colonial order. Within literature this reevaluation of *testimonio* seems like a shifting of the postmodern focus from Borges to Rigoberta Menchú, although it is more complicated than that.

One crucial question for subaltern studies and its reliance on *testimonio* would be the distinction between the academic debates in North American universities and Latin American societies. The modern Latin American corpus, largely integrated into the canon of world literature through Borges's influence, would thus find itself crisscrossed by the textual model that fueled multicultural debates in the United States where indigenous history continues to be fundamentally negated. In Latin America, obviously, both sides of this equation—textual models and indigenous influence—respond to different impulses and realities. In Latin America, postmodernism hasn't relied so heavily on boom literature, and multiculturalism, to the extent it exists as a program, works within the context of societies less bound to homogeneous racial narratives even if they retain their own social and racial hierarchies.

The Latin American subaltern project aims to transform the reception of testimonial literature that emerged in the 1960s with texts such as Miguel Barnet's *Autobiography of a Runaway Slave* (1968), a realist discourse bound to anthropological research and still fundamentally grounded on the problematic of the modern state. The new value of nonliterary literature awarded *testimonio* seems particularly explicable by the attempt to fuse, in the 1990s, two divergent approaches to deconstruction: the literary and the social. It is an ingenious undertaking in many respects, yet deeply contradictory in others because it also ratifies an already unquestionable fact: that *testimonio,* as a Latin American narrative subgenre, consists of a series of nuances shared between authors, editors, spokespersons, and informants that underscores a deep writerly condition not much different from that of literary works.

This literary second nature, however, does not justify the second-rate rank given to *testimonio* by critics who favor more self-referential boom texts, particularly those written in the 1960s and 1970s.[1] That very slight perhaps explains the move to redeploy *testimonio* as the other side of postmodernity on the part of the subaltern project, particularly after the setbacks of Central American revolutions—a political phenomenon that, in its early stages, inspired a considerable number of triumphant and utopic *testimonio* novels. This new-left, postmodern valorization implies separating *testimonio* from the nearness of defeat, restoring its value as an incomplete impulse of Latin American subalternity, and safeguarding a new role for those texts. It is, in many ways, a battle for recodifying and remarketing texts once viewed as narrating a possibility of revolutionary articulation. Their current redeployment of *testimonio* now imbued by designification rereads them as narratives of impossibility or ungovernability, in short, as the futility of all modern Creole state's projects regardless of whether they came about through a coup d'état, the ballot box, or a socialist revolution.[2] They all share the same postcolonial and subaltern symptoms.

The new life of testimonial literature also gathers strength from cultural wars and multicultural debates in the United States, a cultural studies agenda in the deepest sense (Gugelberger 1996). On the other hand, Beverley's proposal finds inspiration in the Gramscian aspects of British cultural studies, in this case anchored in a realist rather than a deconstructive reading of testimony, paying more attention to Menchú's own history as signifier of postnational conflicts than to the textual complexities of the text, which can only lead to a focus on literary lineaments or their absence. One can readily understand, as Beverley suggests, that restoring the paradigmatic value of Menchú's life story is crucial, not only for the benefit of academic debates in the United States but also for a broader sense of what Latin American postmodernity might mean. But it would also be helpful to research different receptions in various Latin American intellectual communities beyond the United States that may well understand these issues differently. How, for example, is Menchú read in Mexico and Argentina or Havana? Moreover, how would one account for multiple receptions within those communities? Would they provide an important contrast to the debates within the North American academy?

One may also note that the notion of *testimonio* as a posthumanistic literary model for Latin America demands clarification, since literature adheres to different historical, aesthetic, and epistemological domains. Collating indigenous life stories within postmodernity undoubtedly calls for political, economic, and textual considerations generally ignored by postmodern discourses and critiques. This also includes a greater focus on the ways in which *testimonio* contrasts with an elite, masculinist literature codified by the boom writers. But to establish a fundamental binary opposition between modern literature and postmodern subalternity can, on the other hand, turn somewhat reductionist, since it yields a one-dimensional view of Latin American cultural and state formation.

In an important book on the cultural politics of the Central American revolutions, Beverley and Zimmerman (1990) observed a few years ago that Rubén Darío's poetry acquired new value after Nicaragua's revolution. Could one expect the same fate in the case of García Márquez and other contemporary world-famous writers from Latin America? If so, why enclose their destiny to a subaltern hermeneutic that only understands Latin American modernity and its literature as the failed discourse of Creole neocolonialism? The symbolic realm of art and literature may be subject to stirring critiques, shake-ups, and counter-positions, but it doesn't quite extinguish itself any more than ideology or history. Indeed, the "end of symbolic order" proclamation may well constitute another symptom of globalization and as such be steeped in symbolism. Borges provides a particular illustration in this regard. During the first half of the twentieth century, his work ushered in the deepest challenge to traditional literary aesthetics, yet the latter managed to restore itself through his literature, ultimately assigning Borges a primary role within a new horizon of aesthetics largely bound to epistemological and deconstructive aesthetics.

Latin American subalternism, by and large, also attempts to take deconstruction beyond apolitical literary academics to a closer affinity with the political agendas of the left. But the move proved elusive because processes of designification are not prone to political engagements. The most important example is perhaps found in a much-rehearsed critique of Latin American literary modernity that underlines many subaltern and postcolonial proposals. Modernity here is understood as a broad historical period that covers everything from Latin American independence to the advent of the boom, including modernism, the avant-garde, and revolutionism. The resulting critique tends to reduce this long history of nations and cultures into one narrative of failure lacking any notable boundaries in the areas of literary, political, or historical entanglements. In the final analysis, this approach betrays a sense of political dismay over the failure of revolutionary insurgency more than a radicalized rereading of deconstruction. Moreover, such a reading looks at the difficult, untimely present of Latin America through a theoretical prism that barely allows us to imagine it differently from afar and in the abstract.

For a contrast, one could turn to Nelly Richard's critique of John Beverley's recodification of *testimonio*. Richard's (1996) own work involves a considerable investment in deconstructive discourses as they apply to the critique of the Chilean military dictatorship and its aftermath. Richard observes that the attempt to make *testimonio* the key manifestation of Latin American literary postmodernity betrays a metropolitan aesthetic model imposed from the United States. As Richard sees it, this assignation gives Latin American literature a use-value in the eyes of a postmodern hegemony in general and of specialists in the field of Latin American studies in particular. Although her critique appears to rehearse a return to the old center-periphery scheme, such is not its central purpose. Rather, Richard seeks to bring attention to the contradictions and hierarchies that pertain to the transnational discourse on postmodernity, a realm of order and privilege that remains active even within the codes of decentering Western epistemology.

Few Latin Americanists, regardless of national provenance or place of work, have written as incisively as Richard on the politics of deconstruction and its application to postmodern literary discourses. Yet, it could also be said that Richard's objection to Beverley's attempt to place *testimonio* at the center of the postmodern archive fails to acknowledge the implicit critique of the boom such a proposal carries. That, after all, may be Beverley's key concern, an attempt to counterweight the paradigm built around a corpus so readily appropriated by mainstream aesthetics. Moreover, Richard makes no mention of earlier attempts to codify the work of writers such as Borges and García Márquez as Latin American postmodernism, a paradigm in many ways much more metropolitan and hegemonic than *testimonio*.[3]

Richard's work provides a challenge to U.S. Latin Americanists from within deconstruction and from within Latin America. In that sense it is unique. She critiques how such a paradigm works in the United States, as we saw with the question of testimonial literature. On the other hand, her work, while deeply suggestive and generalizable in an abstract sense, remains strictly bound to Chile's dictatorial and post-dictatorial scene with few if any forays into the literature or culture of other Latin American nations. This confinement can best be observed in her first two books, *La estratificación de los márgenes* (1989) and *La insubordinación de los signos* (1994b). Both of these works were born out of an urgency to put together a deconstructive blueprint in the area of Chilean national culture, not only in regard to state politics but also in the institutional spheres of the academic Chilean left, most particularly in its reliance on social scientific projects. In that sense Richard takes deconstruction to a level of specificity hardly seen in the United States, that is, into institutional spaces of state culture, thus letting loose its potential to demystify proposals mired in leftist academic traditions as well as those of the right. With a rigorous performance and well-tuned analytic tools, Richard carefully examines the monumental nature of Chilean modernity, particularly as articulated by the regime after 1973.

As a potential blueprint for a Latin American mode of cultural critique, Richard's work seems quite suggestive. Deconstructing the links between Chile's academic culture and official state discourses, as performed by Richard, has unquestionable value for all of Latin America. Moreover, Richard's endeavor includes suggestive critiques of Latin Americanism in the United States. On the other hand, her primary, or perhaps exclusive, work on Chile, which happens to be both postdictatorial and postcapitalist at the same time, introduces a series of questions that remains unexplored. How, for example, would the critique of postdictatorial discourse in Chile apply to other Latin American nations, particularly those widely different from Southern Cone states and cultures? Moreover, Richard's deconstructive work retains an artistic-literary lens that turns the political back toward the aesthetic domain, leaving us with a process perennially committed to designifying the social text as its own reward without a hint as to its potential reconstruction.[4]

One must note at this point, however, the many schools, groupings, and tendencies dedicated to Latin Americanist work as a multiplicity of voices spoken in solitude. Not only is there a lack of debate but also a tendency to mass-produce critical-theoretical anthologies that include opposite voices with little or no editorial acknowledgment of these valuable differences. The consumer-reader thus faces an academic market world in which everything can be fitted into anything. Rather than a field of study or a community of specialists nurtured by difference, one observes a pattern of production aimed at promoting individuals and small groups whose constant production of symbolic capital remains analogous even if dissimilar. In that context I am inclined to reiterate that Latin American cultural studies requires a comparative framework capable of sustaining a diversity of views and allowing an intense debate on how the topic fits the widely different academic contexts of Latin America and the United States. It may also make room for a differentiated adaptation of postmodernity and the institutional frames that validate or bar deconstruction. Finally, it should attend the different political strategies behind wholesale critiques of literary and high culture as well as the whole gamut of readings suggested by *testimonio* and the power claimed by the metalanguage of criticism.

All of these possibilities may ultimately lead to a complex field of Latin American cultural studies through comparative frameworks. I ask myself, for example, if the Latin American *testimonio* debate in the United States, where it has now acquired national importance, should be more careful in noting the different readings of Menchú (the text as well as the political persona) in Latin America. Needless to say, that bit of research may well require some empirical work that lies beyond the interests of literary studies, traditional as well as deconstructive. Yet such data seem paramount for any serious attempt to do Latin American cultural studies. It may be that the social aspects of Menchú's text, just like the better-known boom corpus of postmodern literature, are integral parts of a Latin American culture that can only be studied in its contradictory simultaneity.

There is no doubt that the splitting of disciplinary boundaries shows itself through these voids and cracks to which one must add the demise of area studies, born out of the Cold War, as well as many new discourses on transnational and diasporic flows, including Latino discourses emitted in the United States. The promise of a comparative field encompassing all these discursive communities will require no less. The papal visit to Cuba in 1998, for example, showed the impact of repeated televised images from the United States to Latin America. Performed completely in Spanish, these transmissions evidenced the many ways in which the Latino factor has changed the North-South relationship in the 1990s, a U.S. cultural market beamed toward Latin America from the Spanish-speaking Latin diaspora in the United States. In this same context, although in the opposite direction, it becomes important to consider if the constant migration of Latin Americans has radically altered the self-definition of the Latino groups with a long historical presence in the United States. From "Chicano" and "Nuyorican," minority designators arising from literary manifestations of the 1960s and 1970s, mostly written in English, we witness now a Latino–North American transmission with an intensity only understandable as a hemispheric flow of peoples, economies, cultures, and languages in this era of global capitalism.

In any case, one should remember that all discourses on Latin America have their propensities, patterns, and hierarchies here as well as there, but their potential impact can be radically different depending on where one lives and works. One should not overlook the fact that the possibilities for producing and promoting research in the United States have become tremendously influential. It is pointless to pretend these spaces are not driving the field of studies from afar, which is why I much prefer to call them *loci of legitimation* rather than *loci of enunciation*. This differentiation considerably reduces the utopic notion that all Latin Americanists face a galaxy of enunciations of equal possibilities and values. If we were to make a comparative analysis of academic production and circulation, the question of deconstruction and Latin American cultural studies would acquire a totally new meaning.

NOTES

1. For example, according to Roberto González Echevarría (1990, 221), the postboom constitutes a return to the realist discourse of the telluric novel, although in a more naive form.

2. The strategy can be traced within John Beverley's books and writings of the 1990s. Beverley and Zimmerman (1990) and Beverley (1996) afford, in particular, a glimpse of the divergent articulated perspectives.

3. Regarding Borges's postsymbolic importance, see Alberto Moreiras (1994).

4. Richard's counterproposal of a different testimonial literature centers upon Diamela Eltit's (1989) testimony. Even though it does not take into consideration the limitations of its model as representative for Latin America, Richard's proposal is valuable in showing the deconstructive force inherent in the fiction of this important Chilean writer. There are obvious differences between Eltit's *El padre mio* (1989) and Menchú's text, but it is salutary to differentiate between Chile and Guatemala, and those aspects not governed by the type of cosmopolitan literary creation that Richard tends to privilege. In the final analysis, the debate needs a comparative frame that attends to the diversity of Latin American discourses and societies over one with a contrasting center-periphery outlook.

REFERENCES

Barnet, Miguel, ed. 1968. *The Autobiography of a Runaway Slave, Esteban Montejo.* Trans. Jocasta Innes. New York: Pantheon Books.

Beverley, John. 1996. "Our Rigoberta." In *The Real Thing: Testimonial Discourse and Latin America,* ed. George M. Gugelberger. Durham, N.C.: Duke University Press. 48–69.

Beverley, John, and Marc Zimmerman. 1990. *Literature and Politics in the Central American Revolutions.* Austin: University of Texas Press.

Chanady, Amaryll, ed. 1994. *Latin American Identity and Constructions of Difference.* Hispanic Issues, vol. 10. Minneapolis: University of Minnesota Press.

de la Campa, Román. 1996."Latinoamerica y sus nuevos cartógrafos: Discurso poscolonial, diásporas intelectuales y miradas fronterizas." *Revista Iberoamericana* 176–77: 34–59.

Eltit, Diamela. 1989. *El padre mio.* Santiago: Francisco Zegers.

González Echevarría, Roberto. 1990. *Myth and Archive.* Cambridge: Cambridge University Press.

González Stephan, Beatriz, ed. 1996. *Cultura y Tercer Mundo.* Caracas, Venezuela: Nueva Sociedad.

Gugelberger, George M., ed. 1996. *The Real Thing: Testimonial Discourse and Latin America.* Durham, N.C.: Duke University Press.

Hall, Stuart. 1992. "Cultural Studies and Its Theoretical Legacies." In *Cultural Studies,* ed. Lawrence Grossberg, Cary Nelson, and Paula A. Treichler. New York: Routledge. 277–94.

Hardt, Michael, and Antonio Negri. 2000. *Empire.* Cambridge: Harvard University Press.

Lipsitz, George. 1995. "'Swing Low, Sweet Cadillac': White Supremacy, Antiblack Racism, and the New Historicism." *American Literary History* 7, no. 4: 69–86.

Lowe, Lisa, and David Lloyd, eds. 1997. *The Politics of Culture in the Shadow of Capital.* Durham, N.C.: Duke University Press.

Mignolo, Walter. 1993. "Colonial and Postcolonial Discourse: Cultural Critique or Academic Colonialism?" *Latin American Research Review* 28, no. 3: 25–38.

Moreiras, Alberto. 1994. "Pastiche, Identity, and Allegory of Allegory." In *Latin American Identity and Constructions of Difference,* ed. Amaryll Chanady. Hispanic Issues, vol. 10. Minneapolis: University of Minnesota Press. 137–62.

Richard, Nelly. 1989. *La estratificación de los márgenes.* Santiago: F. Zegers.

———. 1994a. "Bordes, diseminación, posmodernismo: Una metáfora latinoamericana de fin de siglo." In *Las culturas de fin de siglo en América Latina,* ed. Josefina Ludmer. Buenos Aires: Beatriz Viterbo. 54–61.

———. 1994b. *La insubordinación de los signos: Cambio político, transformaciones culturales y poéticas de la crisis.* Santiago: Editorial Cuarto Propio.

———. 1996. "Signos culturales y mediaciones académicas." In *Cultura y Tercer Mundo,* ed. Beatríz González Stephan. Caracas, Venezuela: Nueva Sociedad. 82–98.

Rorty, Richard. 1991. *Objectivity, Relativism and Truth.* Cambridge: Cambridge University Press.

CHAPTER 8

Linguistic Constraints, Programmatic Fit, and Political Correctness: The Case of Spanish in the United States

Giorgio Perissinotto

HOUSING AND ADMINISTERING SPANISH LANGUAGE PROGRAMS

As recently as thirty years ago, Spanish language programs at the college and university level were invariably housed in language departments. Spanish was in most instances part of Romance, modern, or foreign language departments; only English departments had their own language labels and department. Though there were exceptions, all other languages were housed together, with Spanish often a poor citizen with fewer resources and less clout and enrollment than French, German, and Italian.[1] The current situation is very different and still evolving. Spanish is the language of the day, and most other languages, with the exception of Chinese, which is also enjoying a boom, are either barely holding on, experiencing serious enrollment decreases, or on the verge of programmatic oblivion. While the norm for smaller institutions is still a foreign language department, as the demand for Spanish grows so does the number of departments of Spanish, Hispanic languages and literatures, and so on.[2] In California, for example, every University of California campus has a department of Spanish, even though some have different nomenclatures or clusters; San Francisco, a predominately health sciences campus, does not have a language department. Almost all of them have thriving and nationally ranked graduate programs (indeed, most of them are in the top twenty in the nation), and in each of them Latino studies is carried out in a variety of fashions. There are joint appointments, shared courses, team-taught courses, release or bought faculty, and so on. How the departmental structure is responding to this unprecedented explosion is a subject of much debate, and Spanish departments, divisions, and colleges of humanities are struggling to manage—programmatically and financially—programs that are suddenly in high demand.

The eight general campuses of the University of California, though sharing the same general mission as mandated by the state, are nevertheless unique and largely free to set up their own colleges, divisions, and departments. At Santa Barbara there is a Center for Chicano Studies, a Department of Chicano Studies (undergraduate, soon graduate as well), a Center for Black Studies, a Department of Black Studies, a Department of Spanish and Portuguese (all the degrees), a Program in Latin American and Iberian Studies (undergraduate and graduate), and a Program in Comparative Literature (undergraduate and graduate); these last two are under the administrative responsibility of Spanish and Portuguese but each with its own director. UCLA has a Department of Spanish and Portuguese, a Program in Romance Linguistics and Literature, a Department of Comparative Literature, a César E. Chávez Instructional Center in Interdisciplinary Chicana and Chicano Studies, an Interdepartmental Program in Latin American Studies, and various other units that can house or administer Latino programs.

Where do these programs lie administratively? Though one would be hard pressed to find a department of Spanish and Portuguese that is not in a humanities division or college, the same is not true of Chicano/Latino studies. The Department of Chicano Studies at Santa Barbara is in the Division of Social Sciences and the chair reports to its dean; but the position of the chair of the Department of Chicano Studies is shared with Spanish and Portuguese, which is in the Division of Humanities and Fine Arts and thus has its own dean. Arrangements such as this one—and I can assure you that this is not unique—bring about problematic situations than can end in conflict. Teaching loads may be different in the two divisions; personnel actions need to be carried out in two departments and thus go to two deans and to committees with distinct guidelines for advancement; standards of excellence or competence may differ from division to division as can corresponding rewards. Though they are called joint appointments, these positions are better described by the now out-of-favor term "split appointment." Often this situation is not the result of a legitimate split of disciplinary expertise but rather a consequence of the lack of positions entirely dedicated to Latino/Chicano studies. When a university starts a program—as opposed to a full-fledged department—an FTE (a permanent position, a "line") needs a "home"; programs usually do not have permanent FTEs attached to them and therefore are built around adjacent, cognate departments. At UC Santa Barbara, as at several other campuses, there may be only one or two positions that are fully in an ethnic studies department. On the plus side, being in two or more intellectual homes provides flexibility and transferability. Cases of faculty who have asked to be moved out of an ethnic department to be entirely in a traditional one are by no means undocumented, nor are those wishing to be entirely in an ethnic program or department.

Another positive aspect of this somewhat complicated way of housing faculty is recruitment. Many Latino/Chicano studies faculty have multidisciplinary training or have developed cross-disciplinary leanings that cannot be addressed by one single department. With increased frequency we are seeing multidisciplinary job openings that cut across two or more departments. Closely related to this aspect is the programmatic need of a department. In the absence of a full program or department of Latino studies, a cognate department may be interested in the field but unwilling or unable to provide a full load of courses to one professor. This makes a shared appointment desirable in spite of the difficulties associated with it.

Programmatic Content

Traditional Spanish departments have the responsibility of teaching Spanish . . . in Spanish. Many have rigid guidelines regarding Spanish in the classroom, Spanish-only reading lists, research papers in Spanish, and so on. Even a cursory look at the MLA Job List would reveal that most positions in Spanish specify unequivocally "native-like fluency." Most Spanish departments allow majors to take only one or two upper-division courses in English translation. Yet the demand for courses in English translation is increasing. The issue here is not the notion "in translation" but rather courses that are not taught in Spanish or courses whose reading materials or texts are not in Spanish. As we all know, Latino/Chicano literature is written in Spanish, English, and both. Where this literature fits in a Spanish major is difficult to say and a matter of debate. One option would be to establish a track or emphasis in U.S. Latino literature within the Spanish major, though the issue of language would still remain. A Spanish literature major with a U.S. Latino emphasis would still take the regular Peninsular and Latin American survey courses but would also take an agreed-on number of electives in Latino literature. Though it sounds simple enough, this proposal would meet with fierce resistance or opposition from many faculty who would then call for tracks in Argentine, Mexican, or Peruvian literature. At the graduate level, on the other hand, a specialization in U.S. Latino literature is not a major problem, if at all, and perhaps there is something to be learned from it: many faculty are genuinely concerned about specializations and emphases that bypass the fundamentals. They are suspicious of students who insist on taking specialized courses to satisfy what they perceive as an individual—though legitimate—ethnic identity need at the expense of knowledge of the canon.

It is nevertheless beyond doubt that U.S. Latino literature is very much in demand and heavily subscribed. Which department should be the main deliverer, however, is another matter. Often the courses are cross-listed, but again, one course shared by two or more departments may serve two different masters with different standards. My impression is that cross-listed courses fare much better in interdisciplinary programs—as electives for nonmajors—and in a general education program than in a Spanish department. English departments, not surprisingly, have entered the arena and also offer courses in U.S. Latino literature. Many distinguished Chicano writers and critics are in English departments, which have more clout than Spanish departments.

Yet we all know that Spanish as a discipline is experiencing unprecedented success, if we consider high enrollments a measure of success. Nationally and locally, Spanish language courses are bursting at the seams, and some fear that they are dying of good health. Most institutions, however, are well past discussions of the legitimacy of Latino/Chicano studies. Centered more on content, extent, requirements, these discussions tend to be acrimonious and often confrontational, particularly when carried out in more traditional language and literature departments. Spanish, the language, is at the core of this discussion, particularly when it is the vehicle of Chicano literature, though it would not be hard to transfer these concerns to other disciplines.

What is the place, or for some, is there a place for Chicano literature in a Spanish major? Interestingly, the same question as it relates to the general education program has been answered with a resounding "yes." Chicano studies/literature is very much present in the general education curriculum, though at times in the non-Western areas, a notion that could be seriously questioned. In Spanish departments the issue is still hotly debated. Departments that require survey courses covering Peninsular and Latin American literature do not, on the whole, include Chicano literature in the syllabi. Chicano literature is available as an elective course or courses. But with Chicano literature quickly forming part of the canon, the pressure is on. There are more and more courses being proposed, and departments are asking themselves how many Chicano literature courses can be taken as electives, which in turn brings about the issue of prerequisites: should a Chicano literature course have a prerequisite, such as "Introduction to Literary Studies"? More difficult to answer is the question: should the prerequisite be "Introduction to Hispanic Literary Studies" or simply "Introduction to Literary Studies without Hispanic"? On an even higher level, some dispute the very notion that literary traditions informing Chicano literature are Hispanic at all.

A Matter of Standards: Which Spanish?

This welcome but sudden visibility of Spanish in national, educational, intellectual, and public arenas has rekindled the old discussion of which is the desirable variety of Spanish to be taught and used. While most linguists are not consumed by the notion of the superiority of one speech variety over another, in the past few years immigration from Mexico and Central and South America has brought together dialects of Spanish that are held as national languages by speakers who tend to be intolerant or dismissive of a language variety unfamiliar to them. Peninsular Castilian Spanish had been the academic norm for many decades in the United States and, for that matter, in all non-Hispanic countries. Language textbooks presented the Spanish language as a monolithic system where the only possible pronunciation of *casa* was with [s] and *caza* with [th]; *cayó* and *calló* were not homophones; *Lo vi hablando con José* was wrong, and *Le vi . . .* was the preferred form; *banqueta* and *vereda* were substandard forms to be substituted with *acera;* and *manzana* was better than *cuadra.* Neither hemispheric considerations nor demographics made any difference; the norm was set, and teachers and students alike made adjustments to their own dialects to conform to a perceived norm. More than a few non-Castilian native speakers had to actually learn this norm that, after all, was not general in Spain either. The 1960s and

1970s brought a new awareness of diversity that questioned the notion of linguistic homogeneity. In the language curriculum this meant more varied and therefore richer cultural content in textbooks and the presentation of alternate systems of pronunciation, syntax, and vocabulary. But it would not be until the 1980s and 1990s that the language spoken by millions of Hispanos, Hispanics, Latinos, Chicanos, Mexicans, Mexican Americans, and others would become both a matter of study and the subject of a possible emerging norm alongside the Pan-Hispanic one that was deeply rooted in the Spanish model. It can hardly be denied that the changing demographic reality of the United States in general and of the western states in particular have provided the pressure for a novel approach to Hispanic studies.

Though extracting reliable demographic information on the number of Latinos in the United States from the national census has been difficult, most researchers would agree that the 2000 census points to about 20 million Spanish speakers representing over 50 percent of the non-English-speaking population in the United States. This represents an increase of approximately 7 million since 1980 (Macías 1993). The impact on the educational system has been enormous, particularly in the limited English proficiency (LEP) population as it enters the school systems in the elementary grades. In what Latino minorities see as a clear case of racism and discrimination, and other sectors consider a push for full integration, various states and localities have passed legislation seriously limiting the use of Spanish both as a subject of study and as the language of instruction for the curriculum.[3] Colleges and universities face the same demographic pressure but a very different educational challenge.

THE EDUCATION OF SPANISH SPEAKERS IN AMERICAN SCHOOLS

Spanish language teaching—and all foreign language teaching for that matter—in the United States had to follow the model for native speakers of English and made no allowance for those individuals who had some type of proficiency in the language. The instructional program was designed for anglophone speakers who had to fulfill a university language requirement and for those who wished to go on to a major in the language. The few institutions that recognized a different type of student offered Spanish courses that were remedial—and frequently so labeled—and generally did not meet the institution's language requirement. This remedial approach to the teaching of Spanish to nontraditional students was in fact a tacit recognition that the best way to deal with the diversity problem was to homogenize the curriculum into one approach whose underlying tenet was that these students were speakers of a nonprestigious dialect of Spanish. This is, of course, more a generalization than a truth. The cohorts are more complex: from recent immigrants who speak prestigious dialects to speakers of rural and nonprestigious ones. To these one must add second- and third-generation speakers who have acquired a limited form of fluency—from receptive to productive—in Spanish through contact (Valdés 1997).

The labels to identify these groups of speakers are as varied as their language varieties: bilingual speakers, native speakers, residual speakers, heritage speakers, Spanish background speakers, Latino speakers. But given the dearth of instructional materials for such a diversified group of students, the academic departments face the daunting task of designing a curriculum to satisfy language proficiencies spanning the competency spectrum. These curricula were and are a far cry from a clearly stated or assumed framework of language teaching; more often than not the instructional material is a compilation that reflects the personal trajectory and experience of the instructor and is not grounded on firm theoretical grounds. But perhaps more important, the instruction was based on the perceived "weaknesses" of these speakers rather than on their knowledge. Standard orthography, for example, has always been one of the mainstays of basic language instruction and as such is present in all the basic texts. More important, it is taken as a sign of literacy in a language. Heritage speakers possess notoriously unconventional spelling characteristics that are topical in any language department: from the chronic *s, z, ce, ci* confusion (*confución, haser* or *aser, poyo* for *pollo,* for example) to egregious misspellings like *llo* for *yo.*

What is needed is a questioning of the notion of a linguistic norm for Spanish as used in the United States. Schools and universities clearly operate under a Pan-Hispanic linguistic norm that tries to, but cannot, be free of national or regional norms. This norm or norms are distillations of the Spanish Royal Academy (Real Academia Española de la Lengua), whose authoritative *Diccionario* and *Gramática* still constitute the canon for linguistic practice. There exists, to be sure, a North American Academy for the Spanish Language (Academia Norteamericana de la Lengua Española), whose aim is "la unidad y defensa del español en los Estados Unidos." Founded in 1973 and integrated into the Association of Academies in 1980, the North American Academy mirrors the activities of the Real Academia Española and keeps the membership informed of official changes in Spanish language usage. Its relative authority can perhaps be explained by the fact that in contrast to the Spanish model—where the Real Academia Española is indeed a source of language policy—in the United States there is no tradition of referring to a language academy to guide or resolve issues of language use or diversity. It is remarkable that English, as far as a national norm is concerned, is so linguistically homogeneous.

Spanish is currently sharing and trying to coexist in the same linguistic space occupied by English while attempting to unify its usage. It is still a long way removed from it. To use but one example, the national radio network in English is remarkably uniform in accents and grammatical usage. In the absence of a national Spanish-language network, it is quite easy to identify the national or regional origins of the radio announcers and with it the tolerance or intolerance of their sociolects. On the eastern seaboard the Caribbean dialectal norms are clearly recognizable even in the face of the often overemphasized attempts to restore the "s" in syllable final position. On the Pacific coast the Mexican variety of Spanish, itself homologated into a single "Mexican" norm, is again easily identified in its phonetics, grammar, and lexical choices. The situation is comparable in television, but the large Hispanic networks (such as Univisión and Televisa) are employing more and more anchorpersons whose accents are difficult to identify. I submit that this is a conscious effort that reflects the trend and practices of television in Europe and the United States where, with notable exceptions, newscasters show little or no regional accents. In the printed news media this has been happening for a number of years, probably because the written language is learned in an academic setting and tends to follow a uniform norm shared by most newswriters. Even the most local newswriter from Mexico City would write *tomate* rather than the standard Mexican *jitomate*[4] and would avoid the very precise Mexican use of *ahorita* and *ahorititita* in favor of *en un rato* and *ahora mismo*. The most *porteño* of reporters would likely avoid the ubiquitous *voseo* and attendant verb forms of Buenos Aires in favor of the standard *tú* and its regularized verb morphology when writing for audiences extending beyond Argentina.

SPANISH AND ENGLISH IN CONTACT:
DIGLOSSIA AND POLITICAL CORRECTNESS

I have left the issue of Spanish as a public language occupying or attempting to reach the language domains reserved for English as the last point, because it is divisive and even more difficult to handle and solve than the programmatic aspects. While most languages studied in American schools rarely share public and official space with English, Spanish is increasingly more visible—if not competing—in newspapers, commercial ads, television, governmental offices, social services, and workplaces. As such, considerable pressure has been placed on the language as a system and on its speakers to perform and act in a way that is parallel and consonant with English. English usage has changed substantially in the past quarter century in response to societal pressures and changes such as the civil rights and feminist movements. The generic *he* is often replaced by *she/he* or, increasingly, by *they,* even when the antecedent is singular. What was once considered a grammatical error is now acceptable and even desirable to avoid marking the grammatical gender and biological sex of the referent: *Everybody will bring their notebook to class.*[5] In a narrow interpretation of generic masculines, using *man, he,* or *his* would be exclusive of females and thus should be avoided in favor of *person,* the plural, or elegant and not so elegant syntactic and morphological gymnastics. The structure of English had the elasticity to do it and did it; editors now "clean" one's gender morphology without securing the author's permission. It is considered, in most cases, to be like a misspelling or a typographical error.[6]

Spanish, on the other hand, has a different morphological system. Every noun and adjective is always marked for grammatical gender, both in the singular and in the plural, thus committing the speaker and writer to an overtly marked form that can only be made generic *in spite of* its grammatical gender. If the English words *staff, personnel,* or *employees* are generic because they do not mark grammatical gender, Spanish *personal* is unequivocally marked as masculine and requires a masculine determiner and modifier, so that in order to say "the female staff" one would have to say *el personal femenino,* thus referring to females with masculine morphology.[7] Examples of this type of morphological one-way street are legion and on one level would seem to strengthen the argument that Spanish is a sexist language that needs intervention and structural changes similar to those that have affected English.

But Spanish has morphological constraints that, though seemingly constituting the paradigm for sexist language, do in fact make the case for a sex-free generic. The point is that in the absence of a neutral form, a language with gender markings must have a grammatical gender that is either masculine or feminine; the generic form encompassing the two genders must therefore be one of them. It is true, of course, that histori-cally the masculine has been favored and that the overwhelming cases of generics are indeed masculine in grammatical gender. It is also undeniable that this historical preference is the reflection of the favored roles of males in societal matters and, at the same time, the relegation of females to less visible roles. It is also true that a good portion of this unbalance is reflected in the harsh reality that most doctors, lawyers, kings, ministers, teachers, and soldiers have been men, thus creating a gender system that favored the masculine. As more women entered professions and circles where they were previously underrepresented or not represented at all, the language adjusted its morphology and either formed novel feminine forms like *ministra, jueza, médica* or relied on the generics, masculine or feminine.

Individual speakers and institutions react differently to a changing world that the language must, somehow, reflect and to which it must also conform. While an individual is free to maintain that there are no *ministras* or *juezas* in the Supreme Court even when there are sitting women justices and ministers, institutions must somehow codify this presence and adopt a formal rubric for it. English can do this very easily with nouns that are largely unmarked,[8] but Spanish must either choose a generic that is rarely accepted by all speakers as encompassing males and females, or adjust its noun morphology to accommodate cases such as *juez-a, estudiante-a, general-a,* and so on. This has resulted in an end-less variety—and discussions—over *médico-a, abogado/a, presidente/a, estudiante/a,* and the decisive choice of modifiers that can reveal a per-son's preference: *Ella es un excelente médico, abogado, presidente.*

While the discussions about the correctness or—more precisely—the acceptability of generic forms rage on in every Spanish-speaking coun-try, linguistic pulchritude and correctness acquire a special slant in the United States. It is unquestionably due, as I have stated before, to the lack of a common standard and to the proximity of English, which has its own agenda and solutions for linguistic correctness. Spanish, even with the morphological and syntactic idiosyncrasies noted above, is feel-ing the pressure and is therefore compelled to offer solutions similar and consonant with English, a language with which it shares a sociolinguistic space and of which it would like to be a peer.

CONCLUSIONS

In a linguistically leveled field, Spanish and English should share access to all the domains that a complex society can offer. There would not be di-

glossia, and there would exist a high percentage of individual bilingualism. But this is more of a desideratum than even a current possibility, as
there are ideological forces at work that may impede the attainment of
equal status for the Spanish language in the United States. It has been
poignantly stated that the far-reaching ideological principle of the superiority of the English language looms large not only in the United States
and in the Western world in general but has recently been recorded in
non-Western societies as well (Hidalgo 1997). This assumed superiority
is buttressed by—and likely based on—images of the United States as
heir to the linguistic imperialism of the British and as the outstanding
token of First World attainments, which in turn recall the Allies' victo-
ries in World War II. Because of this perceived superiority of English and
the almost total lack of a comparable major player in the international
arena,[9] linguistic norms, standards, and models do not offer major difficulties. English enjoys a high degree of standardization that can to a
large extent be attributed to the leveling role of the mass media.

The Spanish-speaking world, on the other hand, does not evoke, on
the whole, images of First World successes or of unity and certainly not
of linguistics unity or of common linguistic standards. Speaking Spanish
in the United States is, then, largely guided by one's own language and
ethnic background and tempered or mediated by the constant presence
of English, which acts as a resource and reminder of appropriate language conduct. The lack or slow development of a collective norm for
all the speakers of U.S. Spanish can thus be traced to the very notion
of normativity in language. Historically and in most if not all Western
traditions, the standard has been extracted from the literary language,
which supplies admired models and the linguistic structures to be imi-
tated, duplicated, and internalized to be then used in other registers.[10]
The mass media, as was just pointed out, acts as a mirror of standards in
that it collects and distributes language forms from a variety of sources
but ultimately legitimizes them by simply using them from a position of
accepted standard and norm.

But what is tacitly assumed for English is very much out of the
present reach of the Spanish speakers in the United States. There are,
to be sure, literary models aplenty, *national* models linked to the *national* literatures of the twenty-plus independent countries. Borges, Paz,
Asturias, Cela, among many others, are great writers whose works are
recognized as representing Hispanic letters rather than individual national literatures. But in the educational curriculum and in the minds of

Spanish speakers, they are icons of the literature of Argentina, Mexico, Guatemala, and Spain.[11] In terms of the language itself, the level of mutual intelligibility is high indeed. Readers on the whole have little difficulty understanding the language of any of the Spanish-writing countries; only very few lexical items would be unfamiliar or unknown to most readers.[12] But we do not know how these literatures inform, affect, and mold the Spanish in the United States.

Much has been said about the language diversity of the Hispanic world. The diversity is the result of multiple factors well known to linguists but not commonly cited as reasons for dialect differences. While this is not the place to review—however briefly—the reasons for the language variety of Spanish-speaking America, it may be useful to recall that the continent was not occupied and colonized in one quick swoop. The Carribbean islands were conquered at the end of the fifteenth century, but parts of the southern tip of America were not occupied permanently until the seventeenth century. Keeping in mind that a language evolves and changes considerably in a century, the Spanish language varieties that reached the regions colonized at different times were markedly different. Second, the indigenous substratum was culturally and linguistically heterogeneous. Though not generally accepted, the theory that the regional Spanish varieties of Latin America owe their characteristics to the Indian languages spoken at the time of the occupation and even today cannot be dismissed entirely. Third, the Spanish that was brought over by the conquerors, administrators, and settlers was itself far from respresenting one single variety; the first wave saw mainly people from Andalucía and Extremadura, while other regions, Castile in particular, were better represented in later periods.[13] A last factor to bear in mind is the nature of linguistic change: language is dynamic and therefore changes over time. When spread over such a large area, a language will not evolve uniformly but may follow localized trends. This is particularly noticeable in the lexicon, but also observable in the phonology and the grammar.

The independence of the Latin American countries from Spain during the first half of the nineteenth century contributed significantly to further linguistic differentiation among the various regions. Specific countries—Mexico is a prime example—sought to affirm political independence with consistent statements and policies of linguistic autonomy. Though surprising at first sight, this attempt at linguistic emancipation is—to put it simply—highly consonant with the distancing from Spain by the newly formed republics in political and economic terms. The categorical rejection of the Spanish colonial institutions and practices did not, however, include the rejection of Spanish as the language of the American nations. One would be hard-pressed to find a cogent proposal to substitute Spanish as the national language with languages such as French, English, or any Amerindian one. As one researcher noted, "The most distinguished American thinkers, from Andrés Bello to Rufino José Cuervo, clearly separated the Castilian language from the other cultural products inherited from Spain" (Torrejón 1991, 361).[14] This acceptance of the commonality of the Spanish language did not, however, include the dictates of the Spanish Royal Academy, which was considered "a decadent tool of Spanish absolutism, an institution alien to the new continent and therefore with no authority to regulate its linguistic practice" (362). By the end of the nineteenth century the fiery rhetoric of independence had given way to a tacit acceptance that indeed the American republics had drifted away from the Peninsular models and from each other, but that a supranational norm was still operating and somehow keeping the variants to a high degree of mutual understanding. This Pan-Hispanic norm is still in effect today, even though many would argue that the cultural and political fragmentation of the hemisphere has drawn very sharp and distinguishing lines between many countries that are now separated but not by language.

The United States as a Spanish-speaking region has not been, of course, a participant in the discussion and development of language policies and attitudes. The Spanish-speaking western territories that were annexed after 1848 very quickly lost the civic guarantees that seemed to be safeguarded by the Treaty of Guadalupe Hidalgo.[15] Spanish, formerly the institutional language of these vast territories, rapidly lost its position—linguistic space—to English, which became the language of all public life. Lacking the de jure status of an official language, Spanish retreated to the less prestigious domains of informal and familiar communication and relinquished its place to English.[16] The informal and familiar domains of language have been, however, greatly strengthened by the sustained immigration of Spanish speakers and the establishment of large communities where Spanish is the dominant language in all but the formal domains.

It is important to note that it is in these lower registers and domains that regional and often very localized usages are strongest, and educated and supraregional norms weakest or almost totally absent. There is, therefore, a much stronger dialectal identification among those speakers who do not transcend the lower registers than among those who venture beyond the familiar and into the more prestigious levels of usage.

Though in the United States there are Spanish-speaking communities that represent most if not all the dialect varieties of Spanish, linguists would agree that there are three large groups with long historical roots: Cuban Americans, Puerto Ricans, and Mexican Americans. These in turn can be grouped into two well-established dialect modalities, coastal and inland, corresponding to Caribbean (Cuba and Puerto Rico but also encompassing the Dominican Republic, coastal Venezuela, and Colombia) and most of Mexico and Central America.[17] One would surmise that it would be easy to develop a somewhat homogeneous or standard variety from two regional ones, however different these may be, but individual speakers, as users of a social dialect, have a strong affiliation and identification with an often very local variety, particularly when they are under-educated and living in a diglossic society. What is needed then is access to another prestigious dialect or variant that does not necessarily evoke nationalistic fervor or to a variety that has been stripped of national tags. This can only be a standard, educated norm that operates alongside the local and familiar. Currently, it seems that speakers do not have such a standard within their reach.

The challenge for the Spanish language in the United States is a multiple one. First and foremost is the maintenance of the language in whatever modality: informal, colloquial, familiar, or regional. Second is the expansion of the sphere of influence and use of Spanish both in space and in registers. But this objective cannot be achieved solely by the individual speakers or even the community. It needs the cooperation and support of the institutions—civic, educational, and cultural—where the prestigious varieties are in use. In order to claim and share these spaces, the Spanish speakers—through these institutions—must develop a Standard United States Spanish (SUSS) that supersedes any national norm, Peninsular or Latin American. Though this will be difficult to achieve, I think that already there are examples of this emerging norm. University departments of Spanish by and large use a supranational and supradialectal norm that in most cases does not point to any national norm. The same can be said about much academic writing that rarely betrays the regional origin of the author. The Spanish-language press is also moving toward a dialect-independent norm though at a somewhat slower pace. This relative slowness may be due to the fact that so many of the news items of interest to the readership are in fact national, regional, and zonal, but an increase in news coverage of the United States will bring about a dialectal leveling. Television programming is still heavily regional; reports of regional news are often marked by regional linguistic usage as are product ads and soap operas. But anchors are noticeably shedding dialect markings and becoming more and more difficult to categorize. Cyberspace, on the other hand, is arguably the most dialect-free, at least in the international spaces of multinational companies or services.

It would be nearsighted and naive, however, to claim that the survival and flourishing of Spanish as a conational language in the United States rest solely on the development of a regionalism-free and educated norm. Though linguistically this is certainly the path to follow, the move toward the establishment of an educated Spanish language norm for U.S. Spanish speakers must be accomplished with the explicit—not tacit—understanding and support of English speakers and their institutions.

NOTES

1. Classical and less commonly taught languages were at times housed in a variety of departments from classics to anthropology. It was not unusual to find foreign languages within an English department.

2. It would be cumbersome and idle to list all the variations in nomenclature for language departments. The yearly *Index* volume of the *PMLA (Publications of the Modern Language Association)* gives a flavor of the variety of rubrics used.

3. As of this writing the California courts have placed even stricter limitations on bilingual education by forbidding the school districts to issue waivers for bilingual instructions. Waivers can only be obtained, under this ruling, by individual parents on a case-by-case basis.

4. *Tomate* in Mexico City Spanish means "green tomato," which is called *tomatillo* in most of the country.

5. There is a hierarchy of acceptability being developed for English. The once generic *he* has been almost totally displaced by the plural *they,* which is not marked for grammatical gender. The same holds for a generic singular; *students* is preferred as subject over the singular *student* because the possessive *their* is unmarked for gender. *Every student will bring his notebook to class,* though once generic, is now considered marked and exclusive of female students. *Students will bring their notebooks to class* avoids this perceived sexism.

6. There are, to be sure, many writers who hold fast to their habits and continue to use—and believe in—the generic masculine.

7. It may not be superfluous to note, again, that two of the most often used Spanish generics are in fact grammatically feminine: *gente* and *persona.* So that

Él es bueno (He is good) and *Él es una buena persona* (He is a good person) are possible and may refer to the same male referent with the same—good—attribute, one in the masculine and the other in the feminine.

8. There are divergent opinions on whether English still retains a functional agentive suffix marked for the masculine. One could argue that in *widow-ER* the suffix is clearly intended to mark the sex of the referent to distinguish it from *widow*, which is feminine; in *driv-ER,* however, the situation is not so transparent, particularly in view of the form *woman driver.* There are, to be sure, remnants of overt gender and sex markings: *actor/actress, emperor/empress, god/goddess.*

9. French, to be sure, is still waging a gallant fight to retain and regain a measure of its former position of prestige. Chinese, although numerically on the rise, is still far from occupying a challenging position.

10. Shakespeare with "What's in a name?" *(Romeo and Juliet)* and the King James Bible with "clay feet" (Book of Daniel) are signal examples of the literary origins of now common phrases.

11. Readers of this essay will of course question the use of these names and will wonder why I omitted Carlos Fuentes, Juan Carlos Onetti, Isabel Allende, or any other.

12. One might recall that when Spanish American works were first introduced into the world reading market they often included glossaries to help the reader with regional usages. This is rarely done today.

13. The marked difference between coastal variety, as represented by the speech of Cuba, Caracas, and Veracruz, among others, and the highland Spanish of Mexico City, Bogotá, and Lima would be explained by these different cohorts of settlers. The first resembles closely the speech of Andalucía and Seville, while the second is closer to the language patterns of Castile.

14. [L]os más destacados pensadores americanos, desde Andrés Bello hasta Rufino José Cuervo, separaban nítidamente la lengua castellana de los demás productos culturales heredados de la península.

15. Though the treaty specifically guaranteed the civic rights of citizens of Mexico who overnight became U.S. citizens, the maintenance of the Spanish language was not overtly mentioned as part of those rights. Even though one could interpret this omission as an understood *inclusion* of language rights, the history of language policy in the United States reveals that the right to maintain one's language was not deemed inseparable from civic rights. See Perissinotto and Vázquez (1998).

16. It may not be superfluous to point out that one would be hard-pressed to prove that English is the official language of the United States. Though there are a few states that have ratified English as their official language, the founders of the nation saw more merit in omitting the issue of officialdom for English in the charter documents, a position we might want to see as tacit but wise recognition of the multilingualism and multiculturalism of the times.

17. This is, however, a very general dialectical tracing. For a recent treatment of the topic of dialect varieties, see Lipski (1994) and Moreno de Alba (1993).

References

Colombi, M. C., and F. X. Alarcón, eds. 1997. *La enseñanza del español a hispanohablantes.* Boston and New York: Houghton Mifflin.

Hernández, C., G. P. Granda, C. Hoyos, and V. Fernández, eds. 1991. *El español de América,* Valladolid: Junta de Castilla y León. 1: 361.

Hidalgo, M. 1997. "Citerios normativos e ideología lingüística: Aceptación y rechazo del español en los Estados Unidos." In *La enseñanza del español a hispanohablantes.* Ed. M. C. Colombi and F. X. Alarcón. Boston and New York: Houghton Mifflin. 109–20.

Lipski, J. M. 1994. *Latin American Spanish.* London and New York: Longman.

Macías, R. F. 1993. "Language and Ethnic Classification of Language Minorities: Chicano and Latino Students in the 1990s." *Hispanic Journal of the Behavioral Sciences* 15 (May 15): 230–57.

Moreno de Alba, J. G. 1993. *El español en América.* Mexico City: Fondo de Cultura Económica.

Perissinotto, Giorgio, and Guillermo Vázquez. 1998. "El Tratado de Guadalupe Hidalgo: Lengua española y derechos lingüísticos." *Ventana Abierta* 2, no. 5: 11–19.

Torreblanca, M. 1997. "El español hablado en el Suroeste de los Estados Unidos y las normas lingüísticas españolas." In *La enseñanza del español a hispanohablantes,* ed. M. C. Colombi and F. X. Alarcón. Boston and New York: Houghton Mifflin. 133–39.

Torrejón, Alfredo. 1991. "El castellano de América en el siglo XIX: Creación de una nueva identidad lingüística." In *El español de América,* vol. 1, ed. C. Hernández, G. P. Granda, C. Hoyos, and V. Fernández. Valladolid: Junta de Castilla y León. 361–69.

Valdés, Guadalupe. 1997. "The Teaching of Spanish to Bilingual Spanish-speaking Students: Outstanding Issues and Unanswered Questions." In *La enseñanza del español a hispanohablantes,* ed. M. C. Colombi and F. X. Alarcón. Boston and New York: Houghton Mifflin. 8–44.

PART III

The Critique of the Future and the Future of Critique

CHAPTER 9

Latino Studies: New Contexts, New Concepts

Juan Flores

Latino studies has been in the news. The most visible student protests of the mid-1990s on university campuses throughout the country have been directed at securing commitments from university administrations to establish programs in Latino and Asian American studies. The office takeovers, hunger strikes, and angry teach-ins represent a clamor for new programs, faculty, courses, and resources in these neglected areas of social knowledge. And it is making the news not because of any alarming tactics or massive participation, but because the demands are being lodged at the loftiest halls of postsecondary education in the country, the Ivy League schools. After a twenty-five-year history of such programs at public urban universities like the City University of New York (CUNY) and San Francisco State, the call for Latino studies and Asian American studies has been raised and can no longer be ignored at Columbia, Princeton, Cornell, Brown, the University of Pennsylvania, and most of the other Ivies.

There is, of course, always another face to such news, a more somber mobilization generally obscured from public view. While Latino and Asian students at the elite institutions were busy facing down deans and fasting in their tents, the iron hand of fiscal constraints and shifting ideological priorities is at work slashing, reducing, and consolidating those very programs and services at public colleges and universities that are often nearby. For example, in the spring of 1996, the president of CUNY's City College announced that the departments of Africana, Latin American and Hispanic Caribbean, Asian American, and Jewish studies were being downgraded into programs under the umbrella of ethnic studies. Though CUNY President Yolanda Moses claims that she only intends to "strengthen" instruction in those fields, the signal is clear from City College—a mere twenty Harlem blocks from the hunger tents at Columbia—that all such programs focusing on the experience of oppressed and historically excluded groups are under the gun as likely candidates for "consolidation." After all, President Moses was herself acting under strong fiscal and political pressures within CUNY, and her decisions were very much in tune with the tenor of the times set by Republican state and city administrations.[1]

The real news, then, is that Latino studies and the nascent (or re-nascent) movements to institutionalize the study of African American, Asian American, and other group experiences are caught in a cross fire. As interest in Latino studies grows at Harvard, Black and Puerto Rican studies are threatened at Hunter. The conjuncture is actually one of clashing priorities, a collision between the expressed educational needs of an increasingly nonwhite student population and the conservative inclinations of many social and educational power brokers. What would appear a threshold is at the same time a closing door; all attempts at curricular innovation are met with equally avid moves at intellectual retrenchment and wagon circling. This eminently contradictory cultural climate sets the immediate context for the struggle over Latino studies.

NEW CONTEXTS

An alert reading of prevailing and countervailing winds in the academy is a necessary starting point for an assessment of Latino studies and parallel movements for educational change. The calls for inclusion, focus, and self-determination, and the reluctance with which they are met by entrenched faculty and wary administrators reflect larger social contentions in which the issues at stake are not courses and professors but food, shelter, and citizenship. Like Asian American studies, Latino studies has its historical raison d'être in the unresolved historical struggles over immigration, racism, and colonialism. The proliferation of students of color, and the contestatory nature of their presence in higher education, attests to the salience of these issues to the attendant curricular challenges. The attacks on minority admissions, as manifested by Proposition 209 in California, are at the political crux over any claim for educational inclusion. As such, Latino studies needs to be understood as a social movement, as an extension within the academy of the movements against racism and on behalf of immigrant rights afoot in the wider society. Demographic, economic, and political changes, and the resolute efforts to stem their tide, thus undergird the widespread appeals for changes in educational institutions and their offerings. Only in such terms does the emergence of Latino studies harbor the legitimation enjoyed by the empowered gatekeepers of academic discourse.

Equally important is the need for historical memory. Today's Latino students, and much of the faculty, were very young or not yet born when coalitions of Black, Chicano, Puerto Rican, Asian, and Native American students first claimed their intellectual spaces at the university in the late 1960s and early 1970s. There is an awareness, of course, that all this happened before, and that many of the present demands closely echo those that inaugurated the varied ethnic studies programs still in place, however precariously, in the 1990s. But that sense of continuity, and an understanding of the disjunctures, has been blurred with the passing of an entire generation and the dramatic geopolitical changes of the intervening years.

One of the most obvious differences between previous and more recent university movements is that the earlier initiatives did not go by the name of Latino studies. By and large they were called Chicano studies or Puerto Rican studies, the university movements corresponding directly to the vocal, spirited, and politically grounded struggles of the Chicano and Puerto Rican communities for justice and liberation. There were exceptions, such as Raza studies at San Francisco State, where the Latino student constituency was largely non-Chicano, or Chicano-Boricua studies at Wayne State, where comparable numbers of students from both groups joined forces. However, for the most part, the forebears of the present-day Latino studies efforts tended to be focused on specific national groups, and the communities to which they were invariably accountable were nearer at hand, both geographically and culturally.

Much of this difference in nomenclature, and in relative distance from the communities, may be attributed to the ebb and flow of historical movements for change. The previous generation of Latino students and faculty activism coincided with a time of radical challenges to persistent colonial oppression on a global, national, and local scale. Militant opposition to the Vietnam War, support for the Cuban revolution, and the Black and Brown Power movements informed the rhetoric and strategic vision of Chicano and Puerto Rican studies at their inception. That charged revolutionary aura does not surround the Latino studies agenda in our time, though further ebbs and flows may eventually reconnect the unversity-based struggle to such systemic types of social confrontation.

The point of this historical view of Latino studies is neither to romanticize nor to reject the past, but to help save us from reinventing the wheel. Drawing lessons from the past must not blind us to new insights and approaches, or to the possibility that conditions today may in some ways be even more propitious for the establishment of Latino studies than they were a generation ago.

The main shift marking off the present context of Latino studies from its previous manifestation twenty-five years ago is perhaps best summed up in the words "global" and "globalization," with all due caution of what has aptly been called "globaloney."[2] The economic restructuring of world capitalism that took off in the mid-1970s along with the further revolutionizing of telecommunications have made for radically new levels of interaction and interconnectedness among populations at a regional level. The growing mass migrations generated by these changes are also affected by them, and in their circular and transnational character differ markedly from the migratory experiences of the early 1970s.

The diversification and geographic dispersal of the Latino population is the most visible evidence of these changes in the present-day Latino studies context. In addition to the largest groups, Mexican Americans and Puerto Ricans, there are now sizable immigrant communities in the United States from most Latin American countries. As many of these diasporas, notably the Mexican and the Puerto Rican, have fanned out across the country, the demographic landscape, as well as the political and cultural setting, has been further altered for U.S. Latinos.

This "globalizing" of the Latino presence is, of course, clearly evident at U.S. colleges and universities. On most campuses the Latino student body is diverse, often a mix between one large group—Mexican American, Puerto Rican, Cuban, or Dominican—and Latinos from a variety of other backgrounds. In some areas where there is a preponderance of one national group, it remains necessary, and feasible, to mount and sustain programs focusing on that group—such as departments, programs, and research centers in Mexican American, Puerto Rican, or

Cuban studies. But at most sites—including those in which students are calling for programs—Latino studies makes sense, not only bureaucratically but also because of the increasingly transnational nature of the student population and of their communities, as well as the geopolitical relations in which they find themselves.

It is not only the panethnic demography that explains—and perhaps justifies—the shift from a Chicano or Puerto Rican to a Latino studies framework. The global reach that so willfully moves people to and from determined places does so by adjusting and altering the historical relations among societies and their fragments relocated by impelled migratory movement. Not only has the student constituency and subject matter of Latino studies become more multigroup in the sense of numerical diversity; but also, because of global and hemispheric restructuring, exemplified recently by such moves as NAFTA and the Caribbean Basin Initiative, the Latino communities in the United States are far more intricately tied to economic and political realities in their countries and regions of origin than ever before. Pan-Latino necessarily implies "trans-Latino," a more rigorously transnational unit of Latino studies analysis than even the staunch Third World and anti-imperialist perspective of Latino studies in its foundation.

NEW CONCEPTS

This sociohistorical context thus generates new concepts and conceptual approaches for what remains essentially the same object/subject of study: the experience of Latin American and Caribbean peoples in the United States. With all the caveats, and fully recognizing that the very terms "Latino" and "Hispanic" are first of all imposed labels, ideological hoodwinks aimed at tightening hegemony and capturing markets, the Latino concept is still useful, if not indispensable, for charting out an area of contemporary intellectual inquiry and political advocacy.[3] It builds on and complements the perspectives, curricular orientations, and programmatic structures of established Chicano and Puerto Rican studies programs. The concept of Latino studies allows for some space to mediate issues of inclusion and solidarity sometimes strained in nationality-specific situations; for example, what to do about Central Americans, Dominicans, Colombians, and "other" Latinos who do not feel they fit into, say, a Chicano-exclusive notion of "La Raza." Such strains persist, of course, and it is still often difficult in many settings to get Puerto Ricans,

Chicanos, and Ecuadorians, for instance, to come to the same Latino meetings or to the same Latino dances.

In addition to the global economic and political shifts and their impact, the period since the first wave of Latino studies has also witnessed significant new developments in social theory and methodology, or at least new emphases in thinking about issues of race, ethnicity, coloniality, nationality, gender, sexuality, and class. The altered historical field has made for a changed discursive field, much of it occupied by questions of cultural and group identity. If the early 1970s articulation of Latino studies was guided by a rallying cry of cultural nationalism—boisterous and contestatory but also parochial and unreflexive—a current understanding of Latino experience is necessarily informed by insights and approaches developed by feminist, postcolonial, and race theory, as well as lesbian and gay studies. The presumed seamlessness and discreteness of group identities characteristic of earlier Latino perspectives have given way to more complex, interactive, and transgressive notions of hybrid and multiple positionalities.

Theorizing about gender and sexuality has done the most to dissolve the sexist and heterosexist conception of Latino group unity and inclusion and to complicate the meanings of Latino claims and affirmation. Latina, Chicana, and Puertorriqueña areas of political activism and intellectual work have involved changes in prevailing ideas of Latino history and culture and have helped bring into the foreground testimonial and ethnographic methods of social research. Revamping the canonical—straight male—notion of Latino identity with a view toward contemporary theories of sexuality leads not only to new political stances and possibilities, but beyond that to new kinds of knowledge about cultural history and even a new, more variegated relation to theoretical practice. A striking account of this interface of Latino and sexual identities and its intellectual consequences was voiced cogently by Oscar Montero, a Cuban American professor from CUNY, at the 1996 conference of the East of California Network of the Association of Asian American Studies. "It goes without saying," Montero states, "that 'Latino' and 'homosexual' signal different histories and different stories, unevenly deployed. Bringing the two together creates a lopsided image, but perhaps a useful one. The experiences of the body justify the mask, and this mask wants to question the received metaphors for defining identity: Latino by birth, queer by choice. Latino by choice, queer by birth. What matters is that having taken a stance, linking with this mask the two identities, a reader, a critic, a student, can turn to the salient works of his or her tradition and read them anew, availing herself of whatever theories might do the job."[4]

The contemporary Latino construct, and the intellectual project of Latino studies, is laced with this open, multidimensional disposition toward theory, and must also incorporate critical understandings of processes of racialization and translocality. In addition to differentiation along lines of gender and sexuality, the specific identity positions of Black Latinos and of those of mixed Latino backgrounds—Puerto Rican and Dominican, Mexican and Salvadoran—have drawn increasing attention and have done much to sunder the more or less monolithic and essentialist tenets of inherited conceptualizations. Angie Chabram-Dernersesian, the noted Chicana feminist and cultural studies theorist, has staked out new grounds for a critique of traditional Chicano (and even Chicana) perspectives by reading the new-found significance of her other, "repressed" Puerto Rican half. In her essay "'Chicana! Rican? No, Chicana-Riqueña!' Refashioning the Transnational Connection," Chabram-Dernersesian writes forcefully of the residual identity traces left by her absent Boricua father, as filtered through her rooted Chicana mother, and their jarring repercussions on her Chicanismo: "It does not cease to amaze me that it was *she* who nurtured a sense of Puerto Ricanness in me—she who had all the right to be a nationalist following the purist dictates associated with this politics, for she was a Chicana, she was not mixed in my way with the Riqueña. In retrospect, it occurs to me that what she presented me with throughout one of the trajectories of our lives as mother and daughter was a pedagogy of Chicanas/os, a mode of knowing Puerto Rico from inside of Chicana/o, a way of speaking across fractured ethnicities, a way of initiating a dialogue among and between different ethnic groups."[5] Chabram-Dernersesian draws from these lessons a way of "countering our presumed singularity with our historically verifiable pluralities, the ones that are intersected, and . . . engage positions from diverse fields of contestation"; she builds on her personal experience to summon "a strategic location from which to refashion a transnational connection to ourselves and one another, and to contribute to a widening of imagined communities and spheres of contestation."[6]

Opinions will vary as to the utility and relevance of an explicitly postmodern frame and vocabulary for these new lines of theoretical inquiry, and particular reluctance is surely due any too hasty applications of postcolonial models to situations, like those of Chicanos and Puerto Ricans, that would still seem to be emphatically colonial in both historical trajectory and present condition.[7] The term "multicultural" is another coinage of the last decades that Latino studies should treat with caution, since in its most prevalent usage it clearly echoes the grave inadequacies of its ideological predecessor, cultural pluralism. Yet while Marxist and other anti-imperialist intellectual and political traditions remain pertinent to a liberatory analysis of Latino reality, these new insights from multicultural and postcolonial theory are by now invaluable for purposes of spanning the full range of Latino positionalities under the complex transnational conditions of our time. Whatever we may think of the vocabulary, reflections on questions of "hybridity," "liminality," "transgressivity," and the like, and the new intellectual horizons they signal, are clearly germane to any contemporary work in Latino studies. They complement, and add philosophical range to, what has been the guiding metaphor of Latino studies: "la frontera," the border.

It is the idea of the nation, and of national culture and identity, that has entailed the recent rethinking perhaps most pertinent to a new discursive field for Latino studies. Both Chicano and Puerto Rican studies have relied, for their foundational narratives, on the national concept, whether that term referred to historical home countries or newly formed internal colonies in U.S. barrios. Latino social experience was conditioned and defined by the hierarchized interaction of nations, and cultural identities were first and above all national identities. The boundedness and relative uniformity of their original territories went largely unquestioned, particularly in demarcating each Latino group from an "American" nationality, mainstream or otherwise. The guiding theoretical premises were adopted directly from thinkers like Frantz Fanon, Amilcar Cabral, and of course Lenin, with Black nationalism, Pedro Albizu Campos, and even José Vasconcelos and Octavio Paz being more immediate intellectual sources.

Nationality is still no doubt the main binding principle and sensibility for each of the Latino groups, as evidenced at the annual Puerto Rican Day Parade, Cinco de Mayo, and other celebrations. Indeed, it is important to insist on this persistence of specifically national affiliation in countering the tendency of U.S. social science and public policy to reduce Latinos to an ethnic group experience, with its implicit analogy to the prototypical story of immigrant incorporation. Yet despite the non-assimilationist thrust of most Latino discourse, the idea of the nation

as the ontological locus of difference and opposition to the hegemonic
Anglo "Other" has been seriously revised from many theoretical angles
and Latina/o subject positions.

Here again, the varied feminist and queer critiques have been most
incisive in their exposure of the "brotherhoods" of nations and their
foundational narratives. For contemporary Latino studies, this under-
mining of the nation as heteromasculinist mask extends to the diasporic
communities spun off of the "home" nations in the course of global
and regional reconfigurations. The nation also continues to be dissected
and deconstructed along lines of race and class, dimensions that were
already strongly etched in the earlier stage of Latino studies. Yet even the
strident Third World, anti-imperialist stance of the early 1970s did con-
tain some serious gaps, which subsequent theoretical work, especially
on race, does much to fill. Updating the class critique of the nation is
less visible within Latino studies since the Marxist analyses of around
1980 (such as the Center for Puerto Rican Studies' *Labor Migration under
Capitalism* and Mario Barrera's *Race and Class in the Southwest*), though
some fruitful lines of thinking have emerged from an application of "subaltern studies."[8] It is as though, with the abruptly changing economic
geography of the past decade, historical reality has lunged far ahead of
the reach of social theory: no new sociological terminology has surfaced
that can account for the class relations resulting from the radical changes
in the socialist world and the intricate transnational alignments and restructurings of present-day capitalism.

None of these critical assaults on the nation, nor even a broadside of
all combined, has spelled the final demise of the concept, which continues to be central as a social category to the intellectual agenda of Latino
studies and to the struggle of Latino national groups in the United States.
But these critiques have generated a radical rethinking of the meaning
of nationality, and a recognition that the concept of nation is reliable as
a political principle and rallying point only in its interaction with these
other forms of social differentiation and liberatory movements.

The reinterpretation of the nation that informs today's Latino studies hovers around the idea of "imagined communities" as formulated
by Benedict Anderson in his frequently cited book of that title. The nation as a fixed and primordial territory of inclusion/exclusion becomes
a malleable, fluid, permeable construct, a group given form by shared
imaginaries. The idea of imagined communities lends itself well to
the conceptual terminology of Latino studies today because it helps to

describe the "national" experience of Latino diasporas in all its ambiguity. The sense of belonging and not belonging to the nation—driven home to Nuyoricans and Chicanos when they "return" to their "native" lands—confirms that nationality can be not only imagined, but actually created as a social reality by the force of the imagination. The paradox of being nationals in a thoroughly transnationalized economic geography—Latinos as "transnations" or translocal nationalities—is captured well with a loose, dynamic, and relational concept like imagined communities. Such a concept is certainly more adequate than the essentialist and mechanical categories of the "national question" that had informed much of Latino studies in its earlier stage.

Some theorists used to refer to this problematic of nationality and nationhood, true to Marxist-Leninist vocabulary, as the national-colonial question. Indeed, the renovation of the concept of nation and national culture begs the question of coloniality and, for Latino studies, the pertinence of postcolonial theory. When Latino studies programs were founded, nobody spoke of a postcolonial condition or era; on the contrary, colonialism and anticolonial struggle were precisely the terms around which that and other movements of the same time were defined. In the United States, at least, the postcolonial discourse is definitely a child of the intervening years, gaining ground in theoretical debates only in the past decade or so. Imperialism—which became a buzzword during that same period—is surely one of the subtexts. But the pressing questions from the perspective of Latino studies are whether Puerto Rico and the Southwest at some point ceased occupying a colonial position, and if so, when and how. More particularly, can the experience of diasporic migrants from former colonial nations serve as a model, or analogue, for that of transnational communities like those of U.S. Latinos? The insights of theorists like Homi Bhabha and Gayatri Spivak are no doubt of great explanatory value, as is the critique of Anderson's imagined communities by Partha Chatterjee and others.[9] However, for the purpose of identifying the conditions faced by Puerto Rican, Mexican American, Dominican, and other Latino peoples in the United States, and the economic and political domination of their home countries, the term "postcolonial" seems to be jumping the gun at best. Even those most bent on minimizing the collision and incompatibility between Latino and U.S. nationalities cannot fail to detect the signs of some kind of systemic social subordination, call it colonial or otherwise, and independent of any proposed remedy.

PROSPECTS AND PREMISES

While the activist relationship of Latino studies programs to their social contexts and communities is weaker than in its founding years, the
theoretical field of Latino studies is now wider and more complex. The
implementation of this rich intellectual agenda is also more complex
and certainly as challenging as in the years when Latino and other ethnic studies programs were first set in place. Current ideological and fiscal obstacles are the most obvious challenges in this regard and must be
faced without the momentum of the civil rights movement to build on.
But even more pragmatic questions of institutional location and leverage present problems that were not faced when building ethnic studies
was still a matter of filling a vacuum.

By our time there are already ethnic and minority studies programs
long in place on many campuses, including, of course, Chicano, Puerto
Rican, and more recently Cuban and Dominican studies. There are professional associations, academic research centers and networks, policy
institutes, journals—scholarly and otherwise, and a proliferation of Web
sites all devoted to ethnic and minority studies. Within the academy
there are emergent disciplines and areas (such as ethnic, cultural, and
multicultural studies) and groundswells of change in already established interdisciplines and area studies (communications, comparative
literature, and American, Latin American, and Caribbean studies), all
of which run parallel with or border closely on Latino studies. It is also
important to constantly rethink the relation of a reemergent area like
Latino studies to the traditional disciplines, where some of the best work
about Latinos is being produced and most of which are also in flux or in
a state of crisis.

What the best fit for Latino studies may be in the present and shifting structure of the U.S. academy is clearly an enigma, especially as
none of these umbrellas or potential federations is guaranteed to feel
like home in a suspicious, reluctant, and sometimes dog-eat-dog institutional environment. Like Latino studies itself, all of these abstractions
from the specific historical experiences of the composite groups tend to
dilute and distort those experiences and to set up new exclusions and
reductions. Furthermore, each of these transdisciplinary rubrics has its
own trajectory and baggage that is often at odds with guiding tenets
of Latino studies. Think of Latin American area studies, for instance,
or even American studies, which in their founding intentions were so

consonant with the interests of U.S. and Anglo hegemony.[10] Special caution should be observed in dealing with concoctions that sometimes go under the name of Hispanic studies but that are often no more than opportune creations of Spanish departments desperate to shore up their ever-waning student appeal while retaining their doggedly Hispanophile ideological conservatism. It would seem that nothing short of an autonomous, free-standing university Department of Latino Studies could promise a location conducive to the confidence needed to carry forward an adequate instructional and research project.

While departmental status may stand as a goal or desideratum for Latino studies, a pragmatic and flexible approach is probably advisable under the present political conditions. Whether and how Latino studies may be folded or built into some larger configuration would seem to be a case-by-case kind of decision, depending on the relative strength and compatibility of existing programs and alliances. Ethnic studies, for example, might be right, provided there is a strong accent on questions of race and social oppression, and insofar as it is moving from a focus on strictly domestic issues of group difference and rights into the international arena. Some affiliation within American studies could also work, as scholars and students in that area deepen their critical analysis of the field's reactionary and chauvinist origins and expand its horizons toward something like "Americas studies" or "New American studies." With certain intellectual and political provisos, Latino studies could also find a hospitable and productive place in relation to Latin American or cultural studies. An issue of central importance, though, and often obscured in this quest for a larger floor plan, is the relation of Latino studies to African-American studies on the one hand, and to women's studies on the other. The circumscription of the Latino concept in terms of ethnicity, geography, and language culture tends to cordon off Latino studies from full engagement with issues of gender, sexuality, and "racial" identity.

If certain key theoretical principles of methodology and research practice are clear, the main immediate goal at some institutions may be getting a foot in the door, in others standing firm in defense of the spaces that have already been created, however flawed. For in the longer view, the objective is not limited to securing those spaces and opportunities but extends to advancing new knowledge and new ways of understanding what knowledge is for and about. Latino studies will become ghettoized and easy prey for closure or consolidation if it is divorced from this wider intellectual and social project, both at the university and in the larger community.

In this respect, and with all the contextual and conceptual changes, contemporary Latino studies has much to learn from, and to reaffirm in, its own history. In its founding meetings and declarations, Chicano studies and Puerto Rican studies set forth certain principles of research and educational practice that continue to underlie the Latino studies project today.[11] To extrapolate from the many goals and methods proclaimed, these founding plans called for knowledge production that was to be interdisciplinary in its methodological range, collective in its practice, and tied to the community. The primary methodological aims of bridging the divide between humanities and the social sciences remains the order of the day, with areas like ethnic and cultural studies and communications moving the discourse from "inter" in the direction of "trans-," "post-," and even "antidisciplinary." Collective research practice is still an obvious necessity, if only for the volume and scope of this supposedly narrow and particularist object of study. We are now more aware that collective work means more than coauthorship or tight-knit study groups; rather, coordinations and collaborations at many levels, from anthology readers and conference panels to on-line co-thinking, are indispensable to cover the ground and live up to the multiple challenges posed by recent theorizing. For one instance, the close attention to multiple positionalities in the analysis of sociocultural experience reinforces the need for the coordination of diverse research and teaching perspectives.

As for the ties of Latino studies to community, that tenet would seem to hold more strongly than ever, partly because of the relative distance of much academic work—Latino and other—from the extramural "Other," but also because there is an immense ideological stake in keeping Latino higher education and Latino communities apart, and even at odds. The notion of community, of course, has also been subjected to critical deconstruction and demystification. Though the concept of imagined communities is useful in displacing "nation" in its traditional sense, the very vagueness and mantra-like resonance of "community" can render it as meaningless as the oft-stated sanctities of the "national family."

Still, an affiliation, reference, and accountability to Latino people and social realities remains a sine qua non of Latino studies, as it does for any emergent area focusing on an oppressed group in our society. It is not a matter of studying the community/communities as something outside of and separate from ourselves. Socially, many of us are part of and from these communities, and it is in this sense of intellectual work that the political is also personal. With all due caution with regard to fallacies of authenticity and a politics of experience, Latino studies does affirm the need for (for lack of a better word) indigenous perspectives on the reality under study, perspectives that are generally ignored, or colonized, in much academic and journalistic coverage of Latino life.

For all its sensitivity to differences within the Latino community, and its critical rejection of imposed group labels, Latino studies also needs to reflect continually on the real or constitutive unities within and among the Latino population as a whole. The history of Latinos is already in midnarrative, and even if we don't propose to imagine the Hispanic community as a nation in formation—a recent book on the subject is actually entitled *Hispanic Nation*[12]—some form of pan-group amalgam is always at least potentially on the horizon. Though it is important to view *lo Latino* (Latino-ness) from the optic of the particular national groups, the social and cultural perspective of each group also harbors and evokes some relation to a Latino ethnoscape of transnational dimensions.[13]

But even to consider such prospects, to trace historical congruences and study practical interactions, requires not only new curricula but also new attitudes about mounting curricular strategies adequate to the task. It also requires a space very different from that provided by many universities in the present climate. Oscar Montero, cited earlier, summons this broader discursive and institutional agenda in his closing remarks. "New curricula cannot succeed," he says, "by mere inclusion of emergent discourses, after the fashion of eighteenth-century encyclopedists. It must incorporate a point of view, or a series of points of view, a different dialectic, and in the long haul, perhaps a different kind of university."[14]

Notes

1. The events at City College are reported in the *New York Times,* March 19, 1996, B4; and in the *Chronicle of Higher Education,* March 29, 1996, 18. A report on the strike at Columbia University appears in the *New York Times,* April 15, 1996, B1, B3.

2. The use of the term "globaloney" to refer to obfuscation of local, national, and regional realities and contradictions by imposing a global or transnational framework occurs in Robert Fitch, *The Assassination of New York* (London: Verso, 1993).

3. See *The Latino Studies Reader: Culture, Economy, and Society,* ed. Antonia Darder and Rodolfo D. Torres (Malden, Mass.: Blackwell, 1998).

4. Montero, "Coalitions/Collisions: Notes from a Latino Queer," in *Common Grounds: Charting Asian American Studies East of California,* ed. Robert Ji-Song Ku (New York: Hunter College/Columbia University, 1994), 45.

5. Chabram, in *Multiculturalism: A Critical Reader,* ed. David Theo Goldberg (Oxford: Blackwell, 1994), 284.

6. Ibid., 290, 292.

7. It is interesting that the editors of *The Latino Studies Reader* (note 3) assume a strong stand against postmodernist orientations, while at the same time adopting much of the vocabulary and many of the theoretical concerns of postmodernist discourse (see especially page 5).

8. Mario Barrera, *Race and Class in the Southwest: A Theory of Racial Inequality* (Notre Dame, Ind.: University of Notre Dame Press, 1979); Center for Puerto Rican Studies, City University of New York, *Labor Migration under Capitalism: The Puerto Rican Experience* (New York: Monthly Review Press, 1979). See also, for example, Kelvin Santiago, *"Subject People" and Colonial Discourses: Economic Transformation and Social Disorder in Puerto Rico, 1898–1947* (Albany: State University of New York Press, 1994).

9. See, for example, Partha Chatterjee, *The Nation and Its Fragments: Colonial and Postcolonial Histories* (Princeton, N.J.: Princeton University Press, 1993), especially pages 1–13. See also Patrick Williams and Laura Chrisman, eds. *Colonial Discourse and Postcolonial Theory* (New York: Columbia University Press, 1994).

10. See Bertell Ollman and Edward Vernoff, eds., *The Left Academy: Marxist Scholarship on American Campuses* (New York: Praeger, 1986); Noam Chomsky et al., eds., *The Cold War and the University: Toward an Intellectual History of the Cold War* (New York: New Press, 1997); and Mark T. Berger, *Under Northern Eyes: Latin American Studies and U.S. Hegemony in the Americas, 1898–1990* (Bloomington: Indiana University Press, 1995).

11. An account of the struggle for Chicano studies, including the original "Plan de Santa Barbara," may be found in Carlos Muñoz, *Youth, Identity, Power: The Chicano Movement* (London: Verso, 1989). On Puerto Rican studies, see María E. Sánchez and Antonio M. Stevens-Arroyo, eds., *Toward a Renaissance of Puerto Rican Studies: Ethnic and Area Studies in University Education* (Boulder, Colo.: Social Science Monographs, 1987). See also Frank Bonilla, Ricardo Campos, and Juan Flores, "Puerto Rican Studies: Promptings for the Academy and the Left," in *The Left Academy,* ed. Ollman and Vernoff, 3: 67–102.

12. Geoffrey Fox, *Hispanic Nation: Culture, Politics, and the Construction of Identity* (Secaucus, N.J.: Carol, 1996).

13. On the term "ethnoscape" and other pertinent concepts of transnational cultural studies, see Arjun Appadurai, *Modernity at Large: Cultural Dimensions of Globalization* (Minneapolis: University of Minnesota Press, 1996).

14. Montero, "Coalitions/Collisions," 46.

CHAPTER 10

At the Crossroads of Race: Latino/a Studies and Race Making in the United States

Tomás Almaguer

We have been challenged to rethink the relationship between ethnic and area studies in a period in which terms like "globalization" and "transnationalism" are bridging these previously discrete areas of scholarly inquiry. I am less concerned with proposing a more felicitous concept or elegant trope specifically linking area and ethnic studies than exploring the utility of the concept of racialization, which could potentially be overshadowed or obscured in this ambitious remapping of these fields.

I want to argue that race and race making are absolutely central to our understanding of the Latino/a condition and that our multiraciality is the single most unique feature of the Latino/a experience in the United States today. I also want to propose ways in which this mapping of the Latino/a experience opens up interesting programmatic and curricular challenges for both Latino/a studies programs and related area studies. By complicating and recentering the unstable meaning of race in Latino/a studies, we are forced to move beyond the ethnic experience of one particular group (e.g., Chicano or Puerto Rican studies) to a panethnic framing in which Latino/a multiraciality provides the central problematic for a more comparative reframing of Latino/a studies in the United States. This, in turn, provides the central lens through which other lines of difference among Latinos/as (such as nationality, class, generation, gender, or sexuality) are more productively understood and critically interrogated.

The unique meaning of race for Latinos/as in the United States, as well as in their countries of origin, raises the central historical process that binds these discrete areas of scholarly inquiry. The historical legacy and contemporary reworking of systems of white supremacy, both in the United States and the Latin American/Caribbean contexts, provide the common thread knitting together these historical relationships and contemporary migration processes. While other linkages and historical processes are also clearly at play, we should not lose sight of the way in which racialization has been absolutely central in systematically structuring the cultural and material conditions of individual life chances in these particular contexts.

LATINOS AND THE CLASHING CULTURES OF RACE

In their influential book *Racial Formation in the United States,* Omi and Winant (1986, 64) define racialization as "the extension of racial meaning to a previously racially unclassified relationship or group." Reviewing U.S. history through this conceptual lens, one can chart a continually unfolding process of racialization as American Indians, Africans, and later Mexicans, Chinese, Japanese, and so on have successively come into prolonged contact with whites and consequently been racially classified.[1] But it is misleading to suggest that "the extension of racial meaning" is a unilateral process that simply imposes racial categories onto preracial peoples. Indeed, with the exception of the earliest encounters between Europeans and Indians and between Europeans and Africans, there have been few if any encounters between the dominant white group and subsequent ethnic groups in the United States that can be characterized in such unilateral terms.

Mexicans, Chinese, Japanese, Koreans, Asian Indians, Filipinos, and others of the nineteenth and early twentieth centuries were scarcely preracial peoples lacking their own preformed racial worldviews. And certainly the post-1965 immigrants from Latin America and Asia bring with them racial schemas and cultures of race that are quite different from those that prevail in the United States. What then transpires is an encounter between different cultures of race from which new syntheses may emerge. Although, admittedly, the encounter is between groups that do not have equal power to enact their racial schemas, it does not follow that the definitions of the dominant culture will prevail absolutely. As Nader Sohrabi (1999) writes about the clash of two cultures of the state in Iran at the turn of the current century, the "new emergent culture" of race is not "the result of a linear, one-way diffusion" of the dominant culture "but a synthesis that emerge[s] out of the clash of two cultures of" race.

We have seen that despite their multiple ethnic origins, the state now defines Chinese, Japanese, Korean, Indian, Filipino, Guamanian, Vietnamese, and similar peoples as belonging to the same race. Similarly, "black" includes not only descendants from the original African slave population (regardless of gradations in pigmentation) but also more recent immigrants from Africa or the Caribbean. In the case of the equally multiethnic category of "Hispanic," however, the state, rather than designating this category as a "race," refracts it along those categories the state officially recognizes as races: white, black, and, to a lesser extent, Native American and Asian.

Faced with this official classificatory scheme, significantly high percentages of Latinos/as have, in census questionnaires, simply opted out of what they consider an irrelevant schema by reporting their racial status as "Other" (Toro 1998). The uniquely multiracial nature of the Latino/a population is principally due to the clash of cultures of race, which draw racial lines differently. As the aforementioned large-scale opting out signals, the clash has yet to result in a coherent synthesis, but, as discussed below, the state's dominant racial classification scheme has not been and is not likely to operate unchallenged or unchanged.

The varied ways Latinos/as make sense of the state's racial categories are quite palpable and, for example, strikingly apparent in my former workplace. The academic department in which I previously held an academic appointment had three Latino faculty members: a Cuban American, a Puerto Rican, and a Chicano. Despite our common ethnic identification, we placed ourselves in three different racial categories on the recent federal census: the Puerto Rican as "Black," the Cuban American as "White," and the Chicano as "mestizo." The same likely held true for the other Latino faculty on campus that were ethnically Cuban, Dominican, Mexican, Puerto Rican, or South American. Although most comfortably self-identified as Latino or Latina, when this category was not a choice, the majority likely self-identified as "White," at least one (a Dominican) as "Black," probably none as Native American or Asian, while more than a few as the "Other" racial category or a mixed racial category like "mestizo."

There are profound historical factors that account for this unique mapping of race among Latinos/as in the United States. Their multiracial composition has its roots in Spanish colonialism during which the colonial states imposed racial hierarchies that were more gradational and fluid in nature than in their northern counterparts. More so than in the English colonies, Spanish colonization in Cuba, Mexico, Puerto Rico, and elsewhere in Latin America entailed widespread miscegenation among the Spanish, Indian, and African populations. The racial order in Mexico, for example, where the colonized Indians composed the most subordinate racial group and principal labor force, was organized primarily around Spanish/Indian miscegenation. The racial order in the Caribbean, on the other hand, where African slaves assumed the most subordinate position, was organized in Spanish/African terms. These historical patterns, in addition to the differences in the timing of the subsequent colonization by the United States in the mid- and late nineteenth century, have factored centrally in the complex reracialization of the Latino/a population in the contemporary United States. These patterns, in turn, have important implications for the life chances of Latinos/as within the racial hierarchy and in varied social locations due to other lines of group difference.

At the point of their respective colonization by the United States, Mexican, Puerto Rican, and Cuban (and Filipino) populations had already experienced centuries of Spanish colonial rule. In these earlier colonial contexts, local hierarchical racial orders had emerged that were far more fluid than the U.S. white/black distinction based on hypo-descent. In Mexico, it is estimated that by 1900 mestizos (individuals of Spanish/Indian ancestry) composed 85 to 90 percent of the population. In the Spanish Caribbean during the eighteenth century, the Spanish (free) and black (slave) populations were fairly even in number (Williams 1970, 109). By 1898, when Puerto Rico and Cuba passed into U.S. hands as a result of the Spanish-American War, the largest racial category in the islands was *blanco* (white); an intermediate stratum (variously defined as *mulatto* or *trigueno*) was the next largest; and the smallest, but discernible, category was *negro* (black). In 1910, for example, 65.5 percent of Puerto Ricans were identified in the Puerto Rican census as *blanco* (as opposed to *mulatto* or *negro*), a figure that continued to rise throughout the century. Indicating that the *blanco* category could include "mixed," unlike the white category in the United States, anthropologist Virginia Dominguez explains, "When given the choice to identify themselves as either white or black, most Spanish-speaking people from the Caribbean identify themselves as white" (1986, 273).

The way that the racial lines were drawn during the Spanish colonial period and then later remapped under U.S. rule is central to the racial dilemmas Latinos/as have confronted historically as well as in the present day. For example, in the American Southwest prior to its annexation by the United States at the conclusion of the Mexico-U.S. War of 1846–48, there existed a racial order that was similar to those established elsewhere in the Spanish colonial world. Historian Ramon Gutiérrez's highly acclaimed *When Jesus Came, the Corn Mothers Went Away* insightfully explores its initial construction and transformation in colonial New Mexico from the sixteenth to the mid-nineteenth century. According to Gutiérrez:

> Throughout colonial Spanish America, race functioned as a metalanguage: with few exceptions, a person's occupation and status was often quickly deduced by simple appearance. For such visual evaluations of race to be correct, a close correlation had to exist between all constituting elements of racial definition: legal color, actual physical color, and phenotype. When such a correspondence existed, it meant that in the daily life of face-to-face community, race was a visual metonymic sign of a person's position in the social division of labor, symbolic of a propinquity to the infidel, or in the case of slaves, dishonor and social death. Racial and religious lines in New Mexico revolved along a relational axis that privileged the conquering Spaniards (who were Christian, "civilized," and White) at one end and the vanquished Amerindians (who were deemed heathen, "uncivilized," and dark) at the other. (1992, 202–3)

The above racial order in what is now the American Southwest had important consequences for the way that the Mexican population was reracialized under U.S. colonial rule in the mid-nineteenth century. Those living in the territory ceded by Mexico, for instance, were initially defined as "honorary" whites through the Treaty of Guadalupe Hidalgo that officially ended the Mexico-U.S. War. The treaty formally extended to them access to U.S. citizenship, a privileged status that was reserved only for "free white persons" at the time (Almaguer 1994; Martinez 1998). While the mixed Spanish/Indian background of most Mexicans was the basis of derision, antipathy, and ambiguity, the fact that they were not of African ancestry factored centrally in their attaining an honorary white status at this time. (The late antebellum period was a time of drawing a stark distinction between white and black through the ever stricter enforcement of the hypo-descent rule.)[2] Hence, we can see that even at this initial point the U.S. state was trying to symbolically capture Mexicans with its classification system centered on whites and blacks.

At the same time, however, the newly conquered Mexicans—especially the elites—were attempting to assert their own culture of race. For example, in making the case that Mexicans were white during the California State Constitutional Convention in 1849, a prominent Mexican *ranchero* from Santa Barbara passionately argued that the term was a reference to European ancestry and social standing, as it was understood under Spanish and Mexican rule, not merely to skin color. Don Pablo de la Guerra, a delegate to the convention, maintained:

> It should be perfectly understood in the first place, what is the true significance of the word "white." Many citizens of California have received by nature a very dark skin; nevertheless, there are among them men who have heretofore been allowed to vote, and not only that, but to fill the highest public offices. It would be very unjust to deprive them of the privileges of citizenship merely because nature had not made them white. (Almaguer 1994, 55–56)

In drawing attention to the Californio elite's European ancestry, de la Guerra strategically downplayed the predominantly mestizo backgrounds of most Mexican Californians, closing his eyes to the Indian and perhaps African blood flowing in their veins. Moreover, he apparently allayed Anglo concerns over Mexicans attaining an honorary white status by reassuring them that if they used the word "white" as a term intended to "exclude the African race" from the franchise, de la Guerra was in full agreement with this usage (55–56).

The synthesis resulting from the clash of the two cultures of race was a racial order that recognized the "whiteness," and hence the citizenship rights, of some Mexicans but denied them to others. The latter was particularly true in the case of working-class and/or darker Mexicans who were often denied their legal rights by being categorized summarily as Indians (as the Chinese were at one point) despite the Mexicans' own racial antipathy toward Indians. A notable example involved Manuel Dominguez, a dark-skinned mestizo, who served as an elected delegate to the California State Constitutional Convention of 1849 and as a member of the Los Angeles County Board of Supervisors. In 1857, he traveled to northern California to enter testimony in a San Francisco courtroom. Before Dominguez could testify, however, the Anglo lawyer for the plaintiff objected to his taking the witness stand. The lawyer argued that

Dominguez was an Indian and, therefore, ineligible to enter testimony in the state. Despite Dominguez's high social standing among Mexican Californians, the judge upheld the objection, and Dominguez was dismissed (57).

But the above synthesis was not permanent. With continual immigration of large numbers of Mexicans of working-class origins to the Southwest, and the heated politics around it, a new synthesis has yet to fully emerge. Examining the census categories applied to people of Mexican origin throughout the twentieth century reveals the state's ambivalence toward the racial status of Mexicans. After classifying Mexicans as white, at least in theory, for a lengthy period of time, the 1930 federal census listed "Mexican" as a racial category for the first time. Then the category was absent once again just ten years later. In 1950 and 1960, Latinos/as appeared as an ethnic category with the designation "Persons of Spanish Mother Tongue." In 1970, the appellation for the category changed to "Persons of Both Spanish Surname and Spanish Mother Tongue." And in the 1980s and 1990s, the "Hispanic" category emerged (Omi and Winant 1994, 82). But from 1950 to the present day, this ethnic category was to be marked in conjunction with one of the state's recognized racial categories.

As the state imposed these changes in racial/ethnic categorization vis-à-vis Mexicans (and other Latinos/as), people of Mexican origin tried to make sense of the changes in their own cultural terms by either declaring themselves to be white (whereas neither the state nor the society may share this view) or opting out of the categories altogether. For example, more than 40 percent of people of Mexican origin in 1980 and nearly 50 percent in 1990 opted out of the state's predetermined racial categories (see Tables 1 and 2).[3]

Table 1. Percentage of Latinos by Ethnicity and Race in the 1980 Federal Census

Race	Mexican	Puerto Rican	Cuban	Other Hispanic	Total
White	55.4	48.3	83.8	63.4	57.7
Black	1.9	3.5	2.9	4.5	2.7
American Indian	0.7	0.2	0.1	1.1	0.7
Asian/Pacific Islanders	0.3	0.6	0.2	4.7	1.2
Other	41.7	47.5	13.1	26.4	37.7

Source: Ruggles et al., Integrated Public Use Microdata Series (IPUMS) (1997).

Table 2. Percentage of Latinos by Ethnicity and Race in the
1990 Federal Census

Race	Mexican	Puerto Rican	Cuban	Other Hispanic	Total
White	50.4	45.8	83.6	50.9	51.6
Black	0.9	5.9	3.8	7.3	2.9
American Indian	0.8	0.2	0.1	0.7	0.7
Asian/Pacific Islanders	0.5	1	0.3	2.5	1
Other	47.4	47.2	12.2	38.5	43.9

Source: Steven Ruggles et al., *Integrated Public Use Microdata Series* (IPUMS), (1997).

The situation reflects a clash between two cultures of race, as a Latino/a population, racialized according to one racial regime, is reracialized in the United States according to a different racial logic. Similar ambiguities of race within the Latino population are also vividly captured in the way that these lines are configured among Puerto Rican migrants in the United States. According to sociologist Clara Rodriguez (1994), Puerto Ricans bring with them a more complex understanding of racial categories than the state categories of the United States. Her interesting review of the scholarly literature on this issue suggests that there exists among Puerto Ricans a variegated continuum of racial types. These include individuals who are defined "as *blanco* (white), *indio* (dark skinned and straight haired), *moreno* (dark skinned but with a variety of Negroid or Caucasian features and hair forms), *negro* (black or African-American in appearance), and *trigueno* (brown or wheat-colored), a term that can be applied broadly to each of the foregoing types except for the very blond *blancos*" (133; see also Rodriguez-Morazzani 1996). Eduardo Bonilla-Silva suggests a less differentiated racial classification scheme among Puerto Ricans, one that contains three principal categories—white, *trigueno,* and black—with the first two being the major categories and the latter a smaller, subordinate one (personal communication, 1998).

Either way, C. Rodriguez and Bonilla-Silva agree that, as in the rest of Latin America, one can be racially reclassified through class mobility and other mitigating factors and that persons within the same family may identify and be identified as belonging to different races based on color, hair texture, and other somatic features. Unlike racial classification in the United States, which depends above all on descent and hence is perceived as immutable, racial classification in Latin America is more fluid and variegated. Hence, Rodriguez concludes about Puerto Ricans' racial practices, "[M]embers of the same kin groups can be identified with varying racial terms, and an individual might change racial status with changes in class or education" (1994, 134).

One plausible reading of the U.S. census vis-à-vis Puerto Ricans is that while the state recognizes their distinctness or "Latino-ness" with the "Hispanic" category, it nonetheless attempts to impose a choice between the black and white racial categories, which have their roots in the historical enforcement of the hypo-descent rule. But, like their Mexican counterparts, Puerto Ricans in the United States assert their own understandings of race, their culture of race, within the strictures of the state-sanctioned categories. Hence, we see that although a large majority of Puerto Ricans may be perceived by the state and the society at large as "Black," only 3.5 percent of Puerto Ricans identified as being "Black" in the 1980 federal census, whereas 48.3 percent and 47.5 percent identified as being "White" and "Other," respectively. Similarly, ten years later, 45.8 percent, 5.9 percent, and 47.2 percent of Puerto Ricans identified as being "White," "Black," and "Other," respectively (see Tables 1 and 2).

In this regard, racialization is not simply a unilateral process imposed by the state but also reflects the Latino population's active engagement with its own culturally determined understandings of race. But to paraphrase Marx, they do not choose their racial status as they please but inherit it as a product of the particular histories that have shaped their individual life chances. While money may whiten in this context, it does so within certain limits that circumscribe the Latino/a population's active engagement with both their own culturally determined racializations (in their countries of origin) and that codified by the U.S. government. These complicated and often contradictory processes, in turn, have direct consequences for the hierarchical and often problematic racial identities that they generate among Latinos/as in the United States.

For example, the racial classification scheme in Cuba is similar to that of Puerto Rico, as it recognizes three racial categories (black, white, and mulatto [*trigueno* in Puerto Rico]) and also takes phenotype and social class into consideration (Pedraza 1996, 274). The similarity between the two, however, is not replicated among the Cuban and Puerto Rican populations in the United States. The intervening variables are the open borders between the United States and Puerto Rico, a U.S. commonwealth, and the relatively closed borders between the United States and Cuba, a U.S. political foe. Immigration from Cuba has been in distinct waves and has been less racially (and politically) reflective of Cuba than the migration from Puerto Rico. Hence, the relatively recent arrival of the Marielitos in the 1980s was the first major wave of Cuban immigrants with a sizable number of blacks. According to Pedraza, "Over 91 percent of the refugees who came over in the first wave, Cuba's elite, were white. But the proportion of whites declined quite markedly during the second wave. From 14 to 19 percent of those who immigrated from 1965 to 1979 considered themselves as 'other.' The Marielitos had the lowest proportion white of any wave (77 percent) while 16 percent considered themselves 'other' and 6 percent considered themselves Black" (1996, 274–75). As with the Puerto Ricans' usage of the census categories, the numbers of "Whites," "Blacks," and "Others" are probably reflective of the Cubans' understandings of these racial categories, not the state's.[4]

IMPLICATIONS FOR LATINO/A STUDIES CURRICULUM

For almost the entirety of U.S. history, the (re)production of racial categories, in general, and the state's formative role in it, in particular, have been inextricably tied to the structuring of white supremacist systems of racial domination. However, in the past several decades, this link has become somewhat ambiguous. The racial social movements of the 1960s and 1970s transformed the nonwhite racial categories into meaningful political identities, and the state responded, in part, by instituting race-conscious programs to redress past and present discrimination. As a result, the racial distinctions, which had been used to subjugate, are now partially the tools with which to resist subjugation: evil has become necessary evil. So, what are the implications of this paradoxical shift for social scientific research and a revisioning of Latino/a studies curriculum in the contemporary period?

Paralleling antiracist politics of race, social scientific study of race cannot simply abandon "race" on the grounds that it is biologically groundless or "merely" an ideology. Both in politics and scholarship, "color blindness" does not present us with a compelling choice, which would only leave us blind to the vast racial inequalities that remain with us. On the other hand, social scientists also cannot merely ratify and reify the state's official racial categories and become complicit in their naturalization. This analytic route only leads us back to treating race *as if* it were biologically tenable. Because "one of the major powers of the state is to produce and impose . . . categories of thought that we spontaneously apply to all things of the social world," Pierre Bourdieu (1994) writes, "when it comes to the state, one never doubts enough" (1).

As social scientists, we should vigilantly doubt the racial categories we employ in our scholarly research. Historical analyses must always be mindful of the historical specificity and mutability of the boundaries and meanings of racial categories. Likewise, contemporary analyses must contextualize race and theoretically justify the racial categories they use. In the process, the important project of studying the powerful effects of the "color line" can and must be closely tied to the study of the construction of the "color line" itself.

The implications of this reframing of racialization as a central thematic in Latino/a studies suggests that while race is an inherently unstable social category, it does profoundly shape the complex way in which the life chances of Latinos/as are structured in the contemporary United States. Moreover, it also carries with it an important basis on which other "existential categories" of group life and hierarchies of difference intersect and are experienced at the individual level. One need only recall two well-known personal narratives of Latino/a immigrant children that have received widespread currency in Latino/a studies programs in recent years to fully appreciate how this process is personally experienced.

Consider for the moment the following plaintive lamentations of Richard Rodriguez in his autobiographical work *Hunger of Memory* (1982) and those by Piri Thomas in his classic work *Down These Mean Streets* (1997). Although rooted in different times and places, both Rodriguez's and Thomas's narratives capture well differences in the meaning of race among Mexican and Puerto Rican immigrant families. Each was born into immigrant families that brought with them an understanding of race that was fundamentally rooted in the complex colonial experiences in their countries of origin. As noted earlier, the cultures of race in these contexts refracted around the different relationships that Spanish colonizers had with the Indian and African populations that were subjugated. In these colonial settings being designated as "Indio" (Indian in Mexico) or "Negro" (black in Puerto Rico) marked and relegated one for placement at the very bottom of the racial order. Consequently, Rodriguez being seen as Indian and Thomas as black became painful aspects of their childhood experiences in Sacramento, California, and New York City, respectively.

In the chapter titled "Complexion" in *Hunger of Memory*, author Richard Rodriguez soberly reflects on the historical reasons for the varying skin tones and racial features of his family of origin. He writes:

Regarding my family, I see faces that do not closely resemble my own. Like some other Mexican families, my family suggests Mexico's confused colonial past. Gathered around a table, we appear to be from separate continents. My father's face recalls faces I have seen in France. His complexion is white—he does not tan; he does not burn. Over the years, his dark wavy hair has grayed handsomely. But with time his face has sagged to a perpetual sigh. My mother, whose surname is inexplicably Irish—Moran—has an olive complexion. People have frequently wondered if, perhaps, she is Italian or Portuguese. And, in fact, she looks as though she could be from southern Europe. My brother has inherited her good looks. . . . I envied him his skin that burned red and peeled like the skin of the *gringos*. His complexion never darkened like mine. My youngest sister is exotically pale, almost ashen. She is delicately featured, Near Eastern, people have said. Only my older sister has a complexion as dark as mine, though her facial features are much less harshly defined than my own. (114–15)

In the process of discussing his own skin color, Rodriguez painfully reflects on the fact that his somatic features are unmistakably Indian in appearance. This fact carried with it profound cultural and symbolic meaning within his Mexican immigrant family:

I am the only one in the family whose face is severely cut to the line of ancient Indian ancestors. My face is mournfully long, the classical Indian manner; my profile suggests one of the beak-nosed Mayan sculptures—eaglelike face upturned, open-mouthed, against the deserted, primitive sky.

"We are Mexicans," my mother and father would say, and taught their four children to say whenever we (often) were asked about our ancestry. My mother and father scorned those "white" Mexican-Americans who tried to pass themselves off as Spanish. My parents would never have thought of denying their ancestry. I never denied it: My ancestry is Mexican, I told strangers mechanically. But I never forgot that only my sister's complexion was as dark as mine. . . .

As a boy, I'd stay in the kitchen (never seeming to attract any notice), listening while my aunts spoke of their pleasure at having light children. (The men, some of whom were dark-skinned from years of working out of doors, would be in another part of the house). It was the woman's spoken concern: the fear of having a dark-skinned son or daughter. Remedies were exchanged. One aunt prescribed to her sisters the elixir of large doses of castor oil during the last weeks of pregnancy. (The remedy risked an abortion.) Children born dark grew up to have their faces treated regularly with a mixture of egg white and lemon juice concentrate. (In my case, the solution never would take.) (115–16)

As a result of this culture of race, Rodriguez's childhood was punctu-ated with an undeniable feeling of "shame and sexual inferiority I was to feel in later years because of my dark complexion. I was to grow up an ugly child. Or one who thought himself ugly" (124).

If the template of being dark, ugly, and, in a word, Indian served as the central feature of Rodriguez's childhood in Sacramento in the 1950s and 1960s, the specter of being black played a similar role in Piri Thomas's childhood years in Spanish Harlem in the 1940s and 1950s. Thomas baldly poses this issue in the chapter titled "Brothers under the Skin" in his autobiographical work, *Down These Mean Streets*. In the course of a pointed exchange with his brother Jose about the varying skin tones in his family—and whether or not the Thomas family is seen as black—Piri reflects on the different way in which blackness is defined in Puerto Rico and the United States. He incredulously points out that:

> "[T]here's stone-white Puerto Ricans, like from pure Spanish way back— but it ain't us. Poppa's a Negro, and, even if Momma's blanca, Poppa's blood carries more weight with Mr. Charlie," I said.
>
> "I'm not black, no matter what you say, Piri."
>
> ". . . Maybe not outside, Jose," I said. "But you're sure that way inside."
>
> "I ain't black, damn you! Look at my hair. It's almost blond. My eyes are blue, my nose is straight. My motherfuckin' lips are not like a baboon's ass. My skin is white. White, goddamit! White! Maybe Poppa's a little dark, but that's the Indian blood in him. He's got white blood in him and . . . Yeah, you're my brother, and James an' Sis, and we all came out of Momma an' Poppa—but we ain't Negros. We're Puerto Ricans, an' we're white."
>
> "Boy, you, Poppa and James sure are sold on that white kick. Poppa thinks that marrying a white woman made him white. He's wrong. It's just another nigger marrying a white woman and making her as black as him. That's the way the paddy looks at it. The Negro just stays black. Period. Dig it?"
>
> ". . . Say, Jose, didn't you know the Negro made the scene in Puerto Rico way back? And when the Spanish spics ran outta Indian coolies, they brought them big blacks from you know where. Poppa's got *moyeto*

blood. I got it. Sis got it. James got it. And, mah deah brudder, you-all got it! Dig it! It's with us till game time. Like I said, man, this shit-ass poison I've been living with is on its way out. It's a played-out lie about me—us—being white. There ain't nobody in this fucking house can lay any claim to bein' paddy exceptin' Momma, and she's never made it a mountain of fever like we have. You and James are like houses—painted white outside, and blacker'n a mother inside. An' I'm close to being like Poppa—trying to be white on both sides." (144–45)

This well-known narrative of Latino immigrant life captures well the cultural and symbolic meanings that Mexicans and Puerto Ricans attach to racial designations in their countries of origin. Moreover, it underscores how immigrants from these countries are reracialized upon arrival in the United States. There is clearly much complexity and nuance captured in both Rodriguez's and Thomas's autobiographies; the cultures of race in these cultural contexts are hierarchical (with whiteness being privileged), but there exists a great deal of fluidity in how racial lines are drawn in this gradational scheme. This is not the case in the United States where an overarching black-white binary shapes both the construction of racial categories and the placement of individuals and families therein.

While the life chances of both Richard Rodriguez and Piri Thomas were also certainly shaped by their class backgrounds, gender, and generational cohort, all of these lines of difference were circumscribed and filtered by their ascribed racial status. Being white, black, or Indian—the principle protagonists in the Spanish colonial regimes in the Americas—weighed heavily on them because it was the first thing that people noticed. Making sense of the individual meaning and consequences of their particular location within the racial hierarchy profoundly shaped both Rodriguez's and Thomas's racial self-perceptions and senses of the social costs of this racialization.

It is perhaps fitting to close this discussion with the observation that Richard Rodriguez's mother made about the importance of race and skin color in *Hunger of Memory.* Mrs. Rodriguez often reminded Richard as a child to cover his body so that Sacramento's blistering summer weather did not darken him too much:

"You look like a *negrito*," she'd say, angry, sorry to be angry, frustrated almost to laughing, scorn. "You know how important looks are in this country. With los gringos looks are all that they judge on. But you! Look at you! You're so careless!" Then she'd start in all over again. "You won't be satisfied till you end up looking like *los pobres* [the poor] who work in the fields, *los braceros*" [Mexican contracted laborers]. (114)

Given these maternal words of advice, it is little wonder that Rodriguez was so preoccupied with the color of his skin as a child. It was, after all, the women in the family who took responsibility for socializing the young into the prevailing norms of the new country in which they had settled. While the Rodriguez family often joked about this among themselves—as a way of relieving the stressful burdens of color consciousness placed on them—young Richard never forgot what "the women had said, with unsmiling voices, concerning dark skin. Nothing I heard outside the house regarding my skin," he reflected in later life, "was so impressive to me" (117). One can only regret that this same type of socialization continues into the present day and that we continue to live under the specter of the dehumanizing racial categorization and alchemy of race that has been the central organizing principle of group relations in this country.

NOTES

1. Of course "white" itself is not a natural racial identity. In anglophone North America, the English and other Europeans initially imaged this new identity into being in the late seventeenth century in the course of their interactions with Africans and American Indians (Jordan 1968).

2. The notion of hypo-descent, or the one-drop rule, has a unique meaning in the U.S. context. According to Marvin Harris (1964): "In the United States, the mechanism [of racial categorization] employed is the rule of hypo-descent. This descent rule requires Americans to believe that anyone who is known to have had a Negro ancestor is a Negro. . . . We admit nothing in between. . . . 'Hypo-descent' means affiliation with the subordinate rather than the super ordinate group in order to avoid the ambiguity of intermediate identity. . . . That a half-white should be a Negro rather than a white cannot be explained by rational argument. . . . The rule of hypo-descent is, therefore, an invention which we in the United States have made in order to keep biological facts from intruding into our collective racist fantasies" (56).

3. I want to gratefully acknowledge the valuable research assistance of Sylvia Ordinal of the Department of Sociology at the University of Michigan in compiling the census data used in this article. The data are drawn from the 1980 and 1990 *Integrated Public Use Microdata Series* (IPUMS) (Ruggles et al., 1997), a 5 percent weighted sample. Professor Reynolds Farley also provided invaluable advice and guidance in answering various questions that arose about the data set.

4. The distorting impact of the Cubans' more selective immigration to the United States is reflected in the federal census as Cuban Americans are far more likely than Puerto Ricans (or Mexicans) to identity themselves as white. For example, according to the 1980 and 1990 censuses, 83.8 percent and 83.6 percent of the Cuban Americans identified themselves as white, respectively. The comparable figure for Puerto Ricans was 48.3 percent and 45.8 percent (see Tables 1 and 2).

REFERENCES

Almaguer, Tomás. 1994. *Racial Fault Lines: The Historical Origins of White Supremacy in California.* Berkeley: University of California Press.

Bourdieu, Pierre. 1994. "Rethinking the State: Genesis and Structure of the Bureaucratic Field." *Sociological Theory* 12: 1–18.

Dominguez, Virginia R. 1986. *White by Definition: Social Classification in Creole Louisiana.* New Brunswick, N.J.: Rutgers University Press.

Gutiérrez, Ramon A. 1992. *When Jesus Came, the Corn Mothers Went Away: Marriage, Sexuality, and Power in Colonial New Mexico, 1500–1846.* Stanford, Calif.: Stanford University Press.

Harris, Marvin. 1964. *Patterns of Race in the Americas.* New York: W. W. Norton.

Jordan, Winthrop D. 1968. *White over Black: American Attitudes toward the Negro, 1550–1812.* Chapel Hill: University of North Carolina Press.

Martinez, George A. 1998. "Mexican Americans and Whiteness." In *The Latino/a Condition: A Critical Reader,* ed. Richard Delgado and Jean Stefancic. New York: New York University Press. 175–79.

Omi, Michael, and Howard Winant. 1986 (1st ed.); 1994 (2d ed.). *Racial Formation in the United States: From the 1960s to the 1990s,* New York: Routledge.

Pedraza, Silvia. 1996. "Cuba's Refugees: Manifold Migrations." In *Origins and Destinies,* ed. Silvia Pedraza and Ruben Rumbault. Belmont, Calif.: Wadsworth. 263–79.

Rodriguez, Clara. 1994. "Challenging Racial Hegemony: Puerto Ricans in the United States." In *Race,* ed. Steven Gregory and Roger Sanjek. New Brunswick, N.J.: Rutgers University Press. 131–45.

Rodriguez, Richard. 1982. *Hunger of Memory: The Education of Richard Rodriguez.* New York: Bantam Books.

Rodriguez-Morazanni, Roberto P. 1996. "Beyond the Rainbow: Mapping the Discourse on Puerto Ricans and 'Race.'" *CENTRO* 8, no. 1–2: 151–69.

Ruggles, Steven, Matthew Sobek, et al. 1997. *Integrated Public Use Microdata Series: Version 2.0.* Minneapolis: Historical Census Projects, University of Minnesota. At http://www.ipums.org.

Sohrabi, Nader. 1999. "Revolution and State Culture: The Circle of Justice and Constitutionalism in 1906 Iran." In *State/Culture: State-formation after the Cultural Turn,* ed. George Steinmetz. Ithaca, N.Y.: Cornell University Press.

Thomas, Piri. 1997. *Down These Mean Streets.* New York: Vintage Books.

Toro, Luis Angel. 1998. "Race, Identity, and 'Box Checking': The Hispanic Classification in OMB Directive No. 15." In *The Latino/a Condition: A Critical Reader,* ed. Richard Delgado and Jean Stefancic. New York: New York University Press. 52–59.

Williams, Eric. 1970. *From Columbus to Castro: The History of the Caribbean, 1492–1969.* New York: Vintage Books.

CHAPTER 11

Multiculturalism and Hegemony

John Beverley

Many of you will be aware of the by now familiar argument that multicultural identity politics has become the graveyard of the American left. In statements over the last several years by Todd Gitlin, Richard Rorty, William Julius Wilson, Ruy Texiera, Slavoj Žižek, Russell Jacoby, and Phillip Roth, among many other prominent left-liberal public intellectuals, the claim is made in various, not always commensurate, ways, that by heeding the siren song of Foucault, feminism, black nationalism, gay liberation, and the like, the left has lost its ability to speak for the majority of the American middle and working classes. The very logic of identity politics—depending as it does on a segmentation of subject positions—has come to prohibit the formation of a hegemonic political position from the left and has led to the dead end of academic "political correctness." I would like to try to counter this claim, which my friend Paul Bové has characterized as "left conservativism," and to argue instead that the future of the left in the United States—assuming it is still meaningful to speak of the left at all—is bound up with multiculturalism.

Let me start with a well-known passage from Judith Butler's *Gender Trouble:*

223

What new shape of politics emerges when identity as a common ground no longer constrains the discourse on feminist politics? And to what extent does the effort to locate a common identity as the foundation for a feminist politics preclude a radical inquiry into the political construction and regulation of identity itself? (1990, xi)

What Gramsci understood as hegemonic articulation might be a way of suturing or, in a more American idiom, "finessing" the gap between identity politics and a political project such as the one Butler imagines based on the deconstruction of identities. That is because in a process of hegemonic articulation it is not clear in advance what the identities of the individuals, parties, groups, or classes involved will be because they modify their identities in the process itself, since the possibility of attaining hegemony by definition modifies or inverts the structural relation of subalternity that constituted those identities in the first place.[1] But if to win hegemony subaltern classes and groups have to become essentially like that which is *already* hegemonic, then in a sense the old ruling class or classes and the dominant culture will continue to win even in defeat.

Is the concept and desire for hegemony itself simply a screen onto which already privileged groups—and intellectuals above all—project their anxiety about being displaced by a heterogeneous, multiform popular subject, what the Italian political theorist Paolo Virno (1996) calls the "multitude"? Can we imagine hegemony apart from the cultural forms of that which is already hegemonic?

Gramsci's own thought founders on this question, which carries today the additional implication that the passage from Butler expresses: any attempt to stabilize a positional identity—of nationality, class, gender, sexual orientation, race, or ethnicity—feeds into the logic of globalization itself. At the same time, we are all aware of the epistemological and political problem that Gayatri Spivak's concept of "strategic essentialism" is meant to address (1988). Deconstruction does not have a politics specific to it; that is, it is not *in itself* a politics. Politics necessarily involves representation in the double sense Spivak invokes of speaking about and speaking for, and it is on the field of culture broadly speaking, seen as the space of disaggregation and construction of ideologies, that such representations happen. The culture wars are not between ideology and "truth" or science but rather between contesting ideologies, which, *pace* Alan Sokal, may or may not invoke an idea of truth or science in their self-legitimization but do always involve what Spivak calls the metalepsis of positing a subject as sovereign cause.

We might rephrase the question of hegemony as follows. For Gramsci, the form of territoriality that corresponds to hegemony was the nation-state (vice versa, the nation was in some sense an effect of hegemony). Does the postcolonial critique of the nation-form and nationalism, which is based on an awareness of the incommensurability of what Dipesh Chakrabarty (1997) calls the "radical heterogeneity" of the subaltern and the nation-state, necessarily preclude that critique from contributing to a redefinition of the nation? And if one were able in fact to achieve hegemony at the level of the state apparatus, as, for example, some movements of national liberation were able to do in the sixties, what would this mean, given the subnational and transnational parameters that govern the nation-state today as a consequence of economic and communicative globalization? If the territoriality of the nation-state has become a *limited* one in a radically new way, then the notion of hegemony has likewise become limited.

Probably the closest thing in the United States in our lifetime to a potentially hegemonic formation of the left (though some would contest this characterization) was the Rainbow Coalition in the late 1980s. It is with regard to the Rainbow that I want to recall the distinction Ernesto Laclau and Chantal Mouffe (1985) draw in *Hegemony and Socialist Strategy* between what they call popular subject position and democratic subject position.

What Laclau and Mouffe mean by "democratic subject position" is, in essence, identity politics; "popular subject position," by contrast, refers to the kind of politics that seeks to produce a division of the political space into two broad antagonistic camps: the bloc of "the people" and the bloc of the elite or the "power bloc." Laclau and Mouffe see the Rainbow Coalition as governed essentially by an additive logic of the first or democratic subject position type: that is, women plus African Americans plus Latinos plus gays plus labor plus family farmers plus working poor plus unemployed equal the general constituency and appeal of the Rainbow, but each of these groups or categories retains its specific identity and demands. They remain heterogeneous to each other. There is no overarching interpellation or instance that constitutes all of these groups into the people except the figure of Jesse Jackson as such. That is why the Rainbow Coalition essentially collapses with the collapse of Jackson's presidential campaign. But is there a way to imagine the possibility of the Rainbow in terms of Laclau and Mouffe's second political logic: the logic of the people/power bloc contradiction?

There is no question that the kind of politics represented by the social movements the Rainbow sought to incorporate—that is, politics based in civil society around forms of public voluntary association based on identities or interests—are effective in drawing people into action. On the other hand, whatever their strong points in actually mobilizing people, the social movements remain essentially in the position of "petitioning" the state and power structures from a position of subordination (Young 1990). That is, they are not hegemonic, they involve limited territorialities, they do not address the possibility of changing structural relations of power and control over resources. They depend on the additive logic of *and . . . and . . . and* that Laclau and Mouffe saw in the Rainbow, where the identity and value claims of the one can only be made in distinction with the many, even where solidarity and membership in a larger group are present in principle.

It is no secret in this respect that multiculturalism and the corresponding practices of identity politics and the new social movements can appear not only as coincident with, but also as requiring neoliberal hegemony—that is a key theme in the critique of identity politics from the left I began with. Perhaps the greatest challenge neoliberalism poses to the left is the fact that, in principle, it does not presuppose any hierarchy of value apart from that expressed in the rationality underlying market choice. If, in turn, market choice is seen as formally free—that is, not subject to external normative constraints—then in a sense Habermas's communicative rationality is already implicit in globalization, and with the extension of the principle of the market and parliamentary democracy to all social spaces we are for all practical purposes indeed at the end of history.

The problem is compounded by the theoretical representation of multiculturalism in cultural studies and new social movement theory. In both, global/national or (to use Néstor García Canclini's term) "glocal" civil society is seen as the place where multicultural heterogeneity or hybridity appears, as against the supposedly monological and homogenizing discourses of the nation-state. Paradoxically, however, in making this identification between cultural heterogeneity and civil society—an identification that seeks to displace hermeneutic authority from bourgeois high culture to mass culture and popular reception—cultural studies and new social movement theory end up legitimizing the market and globalization in some ways. The very logic of heterogeneity and hybridity they seek to represent points in the direction of assuming that hegemony is no longer a possibility, because there no longer exists a common cultural basis for forming the collective national-popular subject required to exercise hegemony. There are only deterritorialized identities or identities in the process of becoming deterritorialized. In the manner of Foucault, power is seen as disseminated in all social spaces, instead of being concentrated in the state and the state ideological apparatus.

Even though it sometimes claims to embrace postmodernism, the project of cultural studies in particular tends to simply transfer the dynamic of modernization and transculturation from the sphere of high culture to mass culture, now seen as more capable of producing new forms of cultural citizenship. In this sense, cultural studies and the new theories of social agency do not break with the values of capitalist modernity and do not, in themselves, point beyond the limits of neoliberal hegemony.

Given that what is expressed in the various forms of identity politics are material relations of subordination and marginalization produced by the historically specific forms of capitalist modernity, would it be possible to derive from multiculturalism more radical consequences?

If multiculturalism is essentially a demand for equality of opportunity—in accord with the legal category of the subject and the principle of individual rights—then it not only presumes but also requires the market and the institutions of liberal democracy to constitute itself as such (that is, as interest group politics centered on rights demands). But if the demand is not so much for formal equality as for *actual* epistemological, cultural, economic, and civic-political equality, then the logic of multiculturalism will necessarily have to come up against neoliberal hegemony and the governing institutions of American and global society and government. Multiculturalism conforms to liberal pluralism because the identities in play in multiculturalism find in themselves the principle of their validity and rationality rather than in a transcendental social principle or goal. On the other hand, to the extent that the auto-constitution of multicultural identities is tied to forms of subalternity produced by both capitalist and precapitalist forms of inequality and exploitation untransformed or reinforced by capitalism, then identity claims all share tacitly or explicitly a common "egalitarian imaginary"— as Laclau and Mouffe call it. What fuels identity politics, in other words, is a negation of social inequality and discrimination as such. This makes it possible to produce from identity politics not only segmented interest-group politics but also Laclau and Mouffe's popular subject position, dividing the political space into the bloc of the people—defined by an essentially egalitarian logic of equivalence—and the bloc of the elite or ruling class—defined, as neoliberal theory makes explicit, by a requirement of social inequality (since the motivation for market rationality is securing relative advantage over others).

The idea inherent here is that one can derive the possibility of a new form of hegemony in American life from the principle of multiculturalism. Laclau and Mouffe's argument suggests that it is wrong to simply dissolve the identity claim of this or that social movement into the identity of "the people" or the working class because the social movement depends on that claim for its articulation and force. That is why the argument that the left must abandon identity politics as antithetical to what Todd Gitlin calls "building bridges" is ultimately a kind of neo-Fabian middle-class fantasy, which, given the race, gender, and class divisions in the United States itself and U.S. domination of the world, amounts to a kind of social imperialism. (In this sense, Rorty is perhaps a more farseeing ideologue of U.S. global hegemony than the neoliberals.)

If the egalitarian imaginary is a necessary rather than a contingent aspect of multicultural identity, this means, in turn, that "the people" is correspondingly multicultural: that is, multiculturalism is a necessary rather than a contingent aspect of its identity as such. That is, the possibility of heterogeneity is *internal* to the bloc of the people, which has to be articulated against that which it is not, what Laclau and Mouffe call its "constitutive outside." That outside would have to be the logic of acculturation or transculturation of capitalist modernity, seen in the last instance as incompatible with the character of the recognition/redistribution claims of both class and multicultural identity politics.

To put this in other words, the unity and mutual reciprocity of the elements of "the people" depends (as the idea of the Rainbow Coalition was intended to symbolize) on a recognition of sociocultural difference and incommensurability and of the inevitability and desirability of "contradictions among the people"—without the need to resolve difference and incommensurability into a transcendent or unitary cultural or political logic. A potentially hegemonic articulation of multiculturalism would be something like a postmodernist version of the Popular Front. Such a formation would seek to interpellate "the people" as a unified historical *bloc* but not as a unitary, homogeneously modern *subject,* rather as internally fissured, heterogeneous, multiple, like Paolo Virno's idea of "multitude." The people-multitude, as opposed to the people-as-one of facist or populist modernity, would be the political-cultural expression of the egalitarian imaginary inherent in multicultural heterogeneity.

Would, however, such a political-cultural formation still articulate, like its historical ancestor, the Popular Front, the various identities as *national*—that is, in a common relation to the idea and interests of the nation? Would not their interpellation as such risk erasing their specificity, which consists in part in being under or at the margin of the nation? Virno himself (1996) and Michael Hardt and Antonio Negri in their influential manifesto *Empire* (2000) explicitly disconnect the "multitude" from "nation." Here the question of the *adequacy* of the nation-state as a form of territoriality under conditions of globalization reappears. The loss of faith in and/or antagonism toward the nation-state is a real enough feature of contemporary life (in one way or another we all share it). But it needs to be reframed in the context of the relation of the state to the requirements of capitalist political economy. To keep accumulation going in the post-Fordist context of the last quarter century has required a spectacular reduction of the distributive and regulatory functions of the state. The consequence is that the state at all levels—never in the first place exactly coincident with the people—is perceived as inefficient, ineffective, unrepresentative, hostile: a "cold monster." But this perception is itself an overdetermined effect of a central contradiction of capitalist hegemony, whose "economic" requirements now include trashing the state, at the same time that neoliberal ideology celebrates the mechanisms of the market and civil society over those of state planning. But the attack on the state is not only ideologically determined—that is, impelled by the hegemony of neoliberal political economy; the hegemony of neoliberalism itself expresses a new reality principle of capitalism in its present stage.

The problem of a counterhegemony, it seems to me, is how to generate first the idea and then the institutional form of a different kind of nation-state, one that would be driven by the democratic, egalitarian, multinational, multiethnic, and multicultural character of the people: that is, a people-state.

It is of course true that the economic limits of what any government in power can accomplish are extremely narrow (this has made *all* socialist or social democratic governments currently or recently in power essentially accomplices of neoliberal economic policies). In this sense, transnational projects to resist or limit the power of capital can broaden the space for maneuvers at the national or local level. But these projects cannot become themselves hegemonic unless they articulate themselves to a national context (that context could be a national community rather than a nation in the formal sense or a perception of the need or desire to create a new nation or national community). Failing that, they remain movements of "resistance"—or items on an ethical wish list of middle-class or elite political correctness in the metropolitan centers of power and accumulation.

To move beyond the nation-state as a point of reference for hegemony, therefore, seems premature. Unless it is possible to imagine a new form of hegemony that no longer depends on the territoriality of the nation-state, hegemony is still to be won, or lost, at the level of the nation-state and/or the local state. To put this another way: hegemony still has to *pass through* the nation-state at some point or another.

Let me return in closing to Gramsci's point about the relation of the nation-state as a legal-territorial entity and political-cultural hegemony. Familiarly, the articulation of the people/power bloc antagonism positions the people *against* the state, which is seen as the instrument of an oligarchy, dominant class, foreign interests, the "Man," or the like. To construct the people/power bloc antagonism today, under the conditions of globalization and in the face of the neoliberal critique and privatization of state functions, may require, by contrast, a *relegitimization* of the state.

What constitutes the unity of the national-popular for Gramsci is the putative identity between the interests of the people and the nation (which is why he sometimes used the expression "people-nation" in place of "national-popular"). The relation between the terms "national" and "popular" is one of a moving equilibrium that can shift ideologically one way or another depending on who controls their representation. In the case of Italian history, Gramsci claimed, the nation had been more a legal and rhetorical concept elaborated by intellectual and economic elites than a genuine cultural experience at the level of popular life: "people" and "nation" were disarticulated, in other words. But the disarticulation of the national and the popular can also take the form of a disarticulation of the nation and the state.

As Laclau (1977) showed in a seminal essay based on Gramsci's idea of the national-popular, populist interpellation involves picturing the integrity of the nation or national community as undermined in some way or another by the interests represented by the power bloc that controls (usually by an alleged act of usurpation) the state. What concretely the power bloc is in class or social identity terms—mandarinate, feudal aristocracy, oligarchy, colonial administration, capitalist class, comprador bourgeoisie, foreign interests, multinational finance capital and corporations, and so on—depends on the class-ideological character of the interpellation, which can range from religious fundamentalism, to fascism and various kinds of right-wing nationalism, to the New Deal Democratic party in the United States, to social-democratic formations like British Labor, to Maoism or Sandinism.

In the case of Popular Front antifascist politics in the late thirties and forties, the people-nation as such is interpellated as threatened in both its collective and individual identities by the interests of certain (not all) capitalist or elite groups, both within the nation (finance capital, reactionaries) and outside it (foreign interests, military invasion, colonialism, or imperialism). The problem, of course, is that this sort of interpellation risks creating or reinforcing a narrative of national unity and identity that excludes or may exclude significant sectors of the population (and by "excludes" is implied, for all practical purposes, "makes them subaltern or resubalternizes them").

If, however, the "people-nation" is understood as heterogeneous in character, then multiculturalism—seen as one of the constitutive features of the people as such—can be detached from its subsumption as a form of liberal pluralism and made into a signifier for the unity of a popular subject position.[2] Positing "the people" as heterogeneous and multicultural dispels the anxiety about uncontrolled immigration, since there is no identity that is specifically and exclusively national. Moreover, a national identity need not be necessarily an accultured or transcultured one: that is, it need not imply a modernizing teleology, nor a narrative of immigrant assimilation, which ends up affirming a hegemonic liberal conception of the state. As Xavier Albó remarks apropos indigenous and peasant organizations in Latin America today, what prevails in them is "the desire to continue being themselves . . . and that is what they call a *nation*" (1995, 25).[3]

This is a crucial point, because what makes multiculturalism a potentially *radical* force in the world today—perhaps even something like what an earlier Marxism would have called "the main contradiction"—is that the principle of procedural equality of rights and obligations for all citizens, which is both the ideological and legal basis of the liberal capitalist state, is ultimately incommensurable with demands for differential rights, territorialities, and forms of cultural autonomy or self-determination that emerge from "the desire to continue being themselves" of identity-based social movements. The result of this incommensurability in the existing order of things is that identity demands either become unduly particularized and exacerbated, because by definition "minorities" can never become hegemonic in a given nation-state (this is a problem shared by both U.S.-style "political correctness" and ethnic cleansing), or disappear as those minorities are eventually assimilated to the dominant national culture in a process of acculturation/transculturation imposed by both the state ideological apparatus (above all, the educational system and the media) and market forces.

Can the nation-state be a salad bowl instead of a melting pot? Can a nation exist across the frontiers of existing states (for example, the Basque nation in France-Spain, or the Aymara in Peru-Bolivia)? In a way, these questions are moot, because the nation (any nation) is always already multicultural and multinational. The identification of the nation-state with a dominant nationality within its territoriality (Anglos in the United States, Catholic speakers of Castilian in Spain after 1492, Jews in Israel today), is an effect of a historically specific form of hegemony or domination, not the "truth" of the national community (the United States, like Spain, was from its inception a polyglot nation; one out of five citizens of Israel today is a Palestinian Arab). The problem, then, is how to make the state and the state ideological apparatuses more like the (real) nation/s. This is a problem, ultimately, of hegemony, because, in Gramsci's phrase, hegemony is the "ethical content" of the state.

I have been trying to outline the elements of a possible hegemonic political-cultural project founded on multiculturalism as its articulating principle within, or *between,* the territorialities of existing nation-states. My concern has been, above all, to ask whether it might be possible, as the Rainbow Coalition attempted in a tentative, although ultimately unsuccessful way in this country, to create a "politics of the people" out of a cultural "politics of difference." This is not to ignore or criticize political, social, and intellectual projects that seek to move "beyond the nation" or that are "post-hegemonic," such as those envisioned in Bonnie Honig's idea of a "democratic cosmopolitanism" (1998) or Hardt and Negri's *Empire* (2000), mentioned earlier. I do think, however, that in the current climate of left discourse, founded above all on highly visible international anticorporate mobilizations such as Seattle, there is a danger of polarizing such projects with those that still seek to articulate themselves within or from the nation-state (the Seattle-type protests invariably have had both transnational and "national" dimensions). Vice versa, the tendency to polarization of options can appear from the other side as well, for example, in Western Europe today where the defense of the "national economy" by sectors of the left is used to suppress or side-line multicultural demands and to appeal electorally to national chauvinism and anti-immigrant sentiments. The politics of the left today should not be a zero-sum game of either transnational social movements of the "multitude," on the one hand, or "defense of the nation," on the other. The idea of a multicultural/multinational nation-state is not a question of "socialism in one country" (or, perhaps more pertinently today, of social democracy in one country), but of imagining in new ways what it would mean for a country, many countries, to be socialist.

Four points in closing:

1. As we have seen, Laclau and Mouffe show that identity politics can point either in the direction of a proliferation of "democratic subject positions" within the rules of the game of the liberal state or in the direction of the "popular subject position" of a new historical bloc that seeks to redefine the identity of the state as such. But it should be immediately evident that what is operative in both of these alternatives is essentially the *same* sociocultural logic of marginality and subalternity. This argues for a convergence between certain forms of advanced liberalism (and I consider philosophical deconstruction one of these) and the project of reimagining the left from multiculturalism, a convergence that would, of necessity, pass beyond the consensus expressed in both social democratic and New Democrat politics. That is, a new form of the left would also require or entail new forms of liberalism (this would be another point of coincidence with the historical Popular Front).

2. If one of the defining characteristics of the poststructualist intervention has been the emphasis on the overdetermination of class identity by other identities, by the same token it would be necessary to insist in return on the overdetermination of those other identities by class identity (this is a truism, but in the current climate of premature post-Marxism it perhaps bears repeating). But this is also to ask how class itself functions politically as an "identity," which is not exactly the same thing as asking how it is articulated as a relation of production.

3. Classical Marxism and non-Marxist socialism was either hostile to nationalism (like Marx himself or Rosa Luxemburg) or (like Lenin) prioritized national liberation struggle, but conceived of the nation essentially as a "unity" of language, cultural tradition, territory, and market,

as in Stalin's infamous 1923 essay on the "national question." It may be worth reconsidering an alternative tradition in socialist thought represented in the work of Otto Bauer ([1907] 2000) and Austro-Marxism— a tradition anathematized by both the Bolsheviks (Stalin's tract was commissioned by Lenin as a response to Bauer) and the dominant tendencies in European social democracy—which conceives the nation as multicultural/multinational and tries to work out some of the political and legal implications of this for the construction of a socialist polity.

4. One of the characteristics of global postmodernity is the breakdown of what José Joaquín Brunner (1995) has usefully called "the 'cultural' conception of culture"—the concept that identifies culture essentially with the academic humanities and the Sunday supplement of the newspaper. The new centrality of culture in globalization that the culture wars marks also imposes a new challenge on our own role and responsibility as intellectuals. It means that the task of reimagining the project of the left will require not only a radically new political imaginary but also, at the same time, a critique of the forms of academic knowledge as we practice them, that is, of our own complicity in producing and reproducing relations of social and cultural inequality.

Postscript

I am aware that the times are not propitious for such a project. I write these words in the wake of the September 11, 2001, terrorist attacks on the World Trade Center and the Pentagon, attacks that seem to legitimize, as many neoconservative commentators have hastened to note, Samuel Huntington's idea of a "clash of civilizations" (the West versus the rest). The first casualty of September 11, then, is perhaps the future of the multicultural left. The European representatives of the Third Way, notably Tony Blair, have hastened to join the coalition formed by the United States to wage war on Afghanistan and the Taliban, and now perhaps Iraq. But both this coalition and the enmity represented by Bin Laden testify more to a political impasse that favors the perpetuation of reactionary positions on both sides of the conflict. Meanwhile, real people and real conflicts of class, gender, race, sexual orientation, cultural authority, exploitation, inequality, and identity continue to escape any attempt to subsume them under what are essentially monological (and monotheistic) discourses. In that sense, however unpromising the structure of the present, the possibility of a politics of difference is also the possibility of a different future.

NOTES

1. Laclau and Mouffe (1985) put it this way: "[W]hereas political leadership can be grounded upon a conjunctural coincidence of interests in which the participating sectors retain their separate identity, moral and intellectual leadership [hegemony] requires that an ensemble of 'ideas' and 'values' be shared by a number of sectors—or, to use our own terminology, that certain subject positions traverse a number of class sectors. Intellectual and moral leadership constitutes, according to Gramsci, in a higher synthesis, a 'collective will,' which, through ideology, becomes the organic concept unifying a historic bloc." Thus, "a class does not *take State power*, it *becomes* the State, transforming its own identity by articulating to itself a plurality of struggles and democratic demands" (66–67, 70).

2. In its initial formulations at least, the idea of multiculturalism incorporated explicitly an emphasis on social inequality. For example, "Multiculturalism is not a tourist's eye view of 'ethnicity,' nor is it a paean to the American mythology defining the nation as a collection of diverse and plural groups living happily together and united by their knowledge of, and proper respect for, something called 'Western Culture.' Multiculturalism, as an organizing principle to which universities are increasingly paying at least lip service, is understood at its most simplistic to mean exposure to different cultures. Simple exposure, however, is absolutely meaningless without a reconsideration and restructuring of the ways in which knowledge is organized, disseminated, and used to support inequitable power differentials" (Gordon and Lubianao 1992, 249–50).

3. It is worth reproducing more extensively the argument by Albó in which this phrase occurs: "For our purposes here, the principal point of friction is probably the force with which the modern state wants to monopolize for itself the concept of *nation*. In its permanent dialectic to consolidate its power with the repressive and ideological apparatuses, the state considers it fundamental that all citizens feel themselves to be, more than anything else, members of that *nation* whose limits coincide with those of its borders, laws, government, currency, and flag. But in the sense that this same state is in the hands of a particular group, which does not necessarily represent, or even understand, the interests of others, the marginalized sectors will not always accept this proposal. . . . Concretely, this principle of the union of the state and the nation, which has been [in Latin America] the apple of the eye of those who, in fact, control our states, certainly produces the corset effect, especially with regard to our continental identity and future. Let me suggest here two possible alternatives: the nation-under-the-state (or multinational state), and the nation-over-the-state (or transstate nation). . . . I want to draw attention to some aspects of the indigenous organizations that differentiate them from European substate *national* proposals. In the first place, they do not take into account teleological historical models, typical of Marxist-Stalinist analysis, according to which there is a necessary historical evolution of the sort: tribe > ethnicity > nationality >

nation > state. In this narrative scheme, nation, characterized by the creation of its own internal market system, would be the waiting room for the possibility of forming an independent state. None of this interests our indigenous and peasant organizations. In their proposals, the desire to continue being themselves prevails, more than anything else, whatever their size and degree of economic development, and that is what they call a *nation*. While they posit the requirement that the state in which they live should be truly pluri*national,* they do not propose the formation of their own independent states but rather only the recognition of their territory and of certain margins of autonomy. Perhaps for this reason, they have not made their proposals more specific in the face of the very current circumstances of finding themselves divided as *nations* by the borders of two or more states, when these were drawn without their consultation" (Albó 1995, 23–25).

References

Albó, Xavier. 1995. "Our Identity Starting from Pluralism in the Base." In *The Postmodernism Debate in Latin America,* ed. John Beverley et al. Durham, N.C.: Duke University Press. 18–33.

Bauer, Otto. [1907] 2000. *The Question of Nationalities and Social Democracy.* Minneapolis: University of Minnesota Press.

Beverley, John. 1999. *Subalternity and Representation: Arguments in Cultural Theory.* Durham, N.C.: Duke University Press.

Beverley, John, José Oviedo, and Michael Aronna, eds. 1995. *The Postmodernism Debate in Latin America,* Durham, N.C.: Duke University Press.

Brunner, José Joaquín. 1995. "Notes on Modernity and Postmodernity in Latin American Culture." In *The Postmodernism Debate in Latin America,* ed. Beverley et al. Durham, N.C.: Duke University Press. 34–54.

Butler, Judith. 1990. *Gender Trouble: Feminism and the Subversion of Identity.* New York: Routledge.

Chakrabarty, Dipesh. 1997. "Postcoloniality and the Artifice of History." In *A Subaltern Studies Reader, 1986–1995,* ed. Ranajit Guha. Minneapolis: University of Minnesota Press. 263–94.

Gordon, Ted, and Wahneema Lubianao. 1992. "The Statement of the Black Faculty Caucus." In *Debating P.C.: The Controversy over Political Correctness on College Campuses,* ed. Paul Berman. New York: Dell-Laurel. 249–50.

Hardt, Michael, and Antonio Negri. 2000. *Empire.* Cambridge: Harvard University Press.

Honig, Bonnie. 1998. "Ruth, the Model Émigré: Mourning and the Symbolic Politics of Immigration." In *Cosmopolitics,* ed. Pheng Cheah and Bruce Robbins. Minneapolis: University of Minnesota Press. 192–215.

Laclau, Ernesto. 1977. *Politics and Ideology in Marxist Theory.* London: New Left Books.

Laclau, Ernesto, and Chantal Mouffe. 1985. *Hegemony and Socialist Strategy: Towards a Radical Democratic Politics.* London: Verso.

Rorty, Richard. 1998. *Achieving Our Country: Leftist Thought in Twentieth-Century America.* Cambridge: Harvard University Press.

Spivak, Gayatri. 1988. "Deconstructing Historiography." In *Selected Subaltern Studies,* ed. R. Guha and G. Spivak. New York: Oxford University Press. 3–32.

Virno, Paolo. 1996. "Virtuosity and Revolution: The Political Theory of Exodus." In *Radical Thought in Italy: A Potential Politics,* ed. Paolo Virno and Michael Hardt. Minneapolis: University of Minnesota Press. 189–210.

Young, Iris Marion. 1990. *Justice and the Politics of Difference.* Princeton, N.J.: Princeton University Press.

Contributors

Juan Zevallos Aguilar recently completed postdoctoral studies at the Humanities Institute at Dartmouth College. His latest research concerns the cultural identity of Andean migrants in the United States. He is the author of *Indigenismo y nación: Desafíos a la representación de la subalternidad quechua y aymara (Puno, 1926–1930)* and *MK (1982–1984): Cultura urbana juvenil de la postmodernidad periférica peruana.* He is the U.S. executive secretary of both Jornadas Andinas de Literatura Latinoamericana and the International Association of Peruvianists.

Tomás Almaguer is dean of the College of Ethnic Studies, as well as professor of ethnic studies and raza studies and interim director of the César E. Chávez Institute for Public Policy, at San Francisco State University. He is the author of *Racial Fault Lines: The Historical Origins of White Supremacy in California.*

Frances R. Aparicio is professor and director of the Latin American and Latino Studies Program at the University of Illinois at Chicago. She is author of *Listening to Salsa* and coeditor of *Tropicalizations.* She has published widely on Latino/a cultural studies.

John Beverley teaches in the Department of Hispanic Languages and Literatures and the Program in Cultural Studies at the University of Pittsburgh. He was a member of the Latin American Subaltern Studies Group, and his most recent book, *Subalternity and Representation,* comes out of that experience.

Angie Chabram-Dernersesian teaches at the University of California, Davis. She is the editor of the forthcoming *The Chicana/o Cultural Studies Reader* and has published several essays on Chicana/o culture, identity, feminism, cultural studies, and criticism.

Román de la Campa is professor of Latin American and comparative literature at Stony Brook University. His recent books include *Cuba on My Mind: Journeys to a Severed Nation, Late Imperial Culture,* and *Latin Americanism* (Minnesota, 1999).

Juan Flores is professor of Black and Puerto Rican studies at Hunter College and professor of sociology at the CUNY Graduate Center. He has written and lectured widely on Puerto Rican and Latino culture, and his publications include *From Bomba to Hip-Hop: Puerto Rican Culture and Latino Identity* and *Divided Borders: Essays on Puerto Rican Culture.*

Walter D. Mignolo is William H. Wannemaker Professor and director of the Center of Global Studies and the Humanities at Duke University. He is coeditor of *Nepantla: Views from South,* author of *The Darker Side of the Renaissance* and *Local Histories/Global Designs,* and editor of *Capitalismo y geopolítica del conocimiento.*

Giorgio Perissinotto is professor of Hispanic linguistics at the University of California, Santa Barbara. He has published in the fields of medieval literature, phonology, dialectology, and language variation. His most recent book is *Documenting Everyday Life in Early Spanish California,* and he is working on a glossary of material culture in the colonial Southwest and on a database of California place-names.

Juan Poblete is assistant professor of Latin American literature at the University of California, Santa Cruz. He is the author of *Literatura chilena del siglo XIX: Entre públicos lectores y figuras autoriales,* and has written on literature and literary pedagogy as institutions, transnational literatures, Latin(o) American cultural studies, and the history of reading practices. He is working on projects about the Chilean feminist station Radio Tierra and the work of Pedro Lemebel.

Kirsten Silva Gruesz is associate professor of literature at the University of California, Santa Cruz. She is the author of *Ambassadors of Culture: The Transamerican Origins of Latino Writing* and several articles on nineteenth-century poetry in the Americas. Her current project is a historical study of representations of bilingualism in the United States.

Stefano Varese is an anthropologist, professor of Native American studies, and director of the Indigenous Research Center of the Americas at the University of California, Davis. He is the author of *La sal de los cerros* and its translation *Salt of the Mountains: Campa Asháninka History and Resistance in the Peruvian Jungle*. He has also written *Las minorias étnicas y la sociedad nacional* and *Proyectos étnicos y proyectos nacionales*.

George Yúdice teaches in the American studies program and in the Spanish and Portuguese department at New York University, where he is also director of the Center for Latin American and Caribbean Studies. He is author of *The Expediency of Culture*.